Commerce

Richard Barrett and Marion Gow

Senior Lecturer,
North Manchester Community College

Lecturer,
North Manchester Community College

Stanley Thornes (Publishers) Ltd

First published in 1988 by:
Stanley Thornes (Publishers) Ltd
Old Station Drive
Leckhampton
CHELTENHAM GL53 0DN
England

British Library Cataloguing in Publication Data

Barrett, Richard
    Commerce skills
    1. Commerce
    I. Title   II. Gow, Marion, 1932-
    380.1

    ISBN 0-85950-129-9

Typeset by Tech-Set, Gateshead, Tyne & Wear
in 10½/13 Plantin
Printed and bound at Butler and Tanner Ltd, Frome

Contents

Preface   v

Acknowledgements   vi

1   An introduction to commerce   1

2   The retailer   13

3   The wholesaler   32

4   Business documents   43

5   Business ownership   56

6   Share transactions   78

7   Advertising   89

8   Banking   104

9   Transport   128

10   Insurance   151

11   The Post Office   176

12   Telecommunications   192

13   Building societies   206

14   Consumer protection   219

15   Foreign trade   234

Appendix – Understanding data   257

Index   263

This book is dedicated to Mohammed Ashraf, former head of Commerce at Harpurhey High School and Head of Business Studies at Margaret Ashton VIth Form College, Manchester.
In tribute to a respected colleague and friend.

Can those who have the knowledge and those who haven't the knowledge ever be equal?

Only men of understanding do accept admonition

     39 : 9
(Surah) (Ayyah)

Preface

An examination syllabus invariably determines *what* is to be learned. Now, with the introduction of GCSE, it also attempts to determine the *skills* young people need to acquire. The essence of good teaching is the exercise of professional judgement about the appropriate learning strategies to be used to help young people to achieve their full potential, in both academic and personal terms. The purpose of this textbook is to provide a basis of choice on which that professional judgement can be exercised.

This basis of choice takes various forms. For example, all GCSE Commerce syllabuses are covered. This means that teachers who may want to revise their original choice of examination can use this text knowing that a new choice will not be hindered by the lack of an appropriate textbook. Furthermore, specimen examination questions from the GCSE boards have been included. Exercises and activities within the book are representative of the techniques being used by each of the GCSE courses. Each chapter contains ideas for projects and assignments which are intended to stimulate students' choice of course work for assessment, while giving experience and help with the investigatory skills necessary for successful course work. In addition, a range of stepped essays, stimulus response, short answer and multiple choice questions is provided at the end of each chapter. The various group and class activities are designed to enable the development of interpersonal skills while, at the same time, providing opportunities to exercise knowledge in a way which is amusing and different from the more traditional forms of learning. The 'check this out' sections within each chapter give students an opportunity to consolidate previous learning in small easily-absorbed segments, thus enhancing the understanding of subsequent reading. A greater emphasis on numerical techniques has led us to provide an elementary explanation of some basic procedures in an appendix which can be used for reference.

In order that this text can be as helpful as possible to students and teachers alike, we invite comments from readers who feel that more could have been done to meet their particular requirements.

In conclusion we would like to thank our publishers for their continued support and to acknowledge the time spent by John Loveridge in providing a thought-provoking appraisal of our manuscript. We accept responsibility for any errors or omissions the reader may discover.

Richard Barratt
Marion Gow
May 1988

Acknowledgements

The authors and publishers are grateful to the following examination boards for permission to reproduce questions from specimen papers:
   The London and East Anglian Group
   Northern Examining Association
   Southern Regional Examinations Board
   Welsh Joint Education Committee

We are also grateful to the following who provided illustrative material and/or permission to reproduce:

Asda PLC
Association of British Travel Agents
David Barrett
Boots PLC
British Aerospace
British Insurance Association
British Rail
British Standards Institution
British Telecom
British Transport Films
Co-operative Bank
D.K. Edwards/Sharpe Electronics (UK) Ltd
Gloucestershire Echo
Guildhall Library, London
Harris/3M Document Products Ltd
Kendals, Manchester
Lloyd's of London
Midland Bank PLC
National Girobank
National Savings
National Westminster Bank PLC
Park Cake Bakeries, Oldham
Pictor International
Photo Library International
Post Office Counters Ltd
Ken Pyne/*Private Eye*
Smith, Anderson & Co.
The Stock Photobank
Waste Management Ltd

Every effort has been made to trace copyright owners, but we apologise if any have been overlooked.

CHAPTER 1

AN INTRODUCTION TO COMMERCE

Production

In the United Kingdom today about 23 million people are available for full-time work, although not all of them are employed at any one time. Why do people want to work? Usually the main reason is that they want to earn money. They need this money to buy goods and services of various kinds. One reason people buy these goods and services is because they need them to stay alive. Basic human needs have not changed through the centuries and can be summed up in three words: *food, clothes, shelter*. Everyone needs food to eat, somewhere to shelter from the weather – be it a cave or mansion – and clothes to protect their bodies from extremes of heat and cold.

As society developed, people had more choice about these three essential needs. Improvements in farming and the discovery of new plants and animals – particularly from overseas – provided a greater choice of food. Improved skills in weaving and spinning, and the introduction of new inventions in clothes-making, also meant a wider choice of styles, colours and materials in the clothes. The types of shelter developed from caves and covered holes in the ground to huts, and to bigger, better and more comfortable houses. In these ways, people had more choice in how they satisfied their basic needs.

However, people will obviously want different things. For instance, the house you live in or the clothes you wear may not appeal to your friends. Even if your house is not the choice you would make, given enough money to spend on it, you accept that it gives you adequate shelter. Most of us have, at some time in our lives, been made to wear (usually by our parents) dresses or trousers which we didn't like and didn't want to wear. Even if they were not our choice, they still satisfied one of the basic human needs, the need for clothes.

We can all think of things we *want* but don't really need. Minced beef and mashed potatoes will satisfy our *need* for food, even though we might *want* steak and chips. Modern society gives us a choice of goods which satisfy our basic human needs and also gives us a chance to get the things we want. These may be more attractive, more fashionable or more comfortable, but they are not absolutely essential to our needs.

Things may change – but human needs don't!

In addition to our needs and wants in the form of goods, we also require services. Again, some of these are needs, such as medical services, while others are less important wants such as entertainment.

All of our working activities which result in goods and services becoming available to satisfy our needs and wants are called 'production'. There are in fact many thousands of types of work through which people are involved in such production. Here are a few of them:

- assembling a car;
- working out a firm's accounts;
- cleaning windows;
- typing in a government office;
- building a house;
- serving in the Army;
- designing books;
- catching fish;
- growing wheat;
- mining for coal.

There are also unemployed people, for example those made redundant and seeking new employment or school leavers who cannot yet find a job.

All of our working activities can be divided into three broad types: primary, secondary and tertiary.

1   Primary production

This is the first stage in any productive activity, sometimes known as the *extractive* stage, and it involves people such as miners, farmers, fishermen and forestry workers. Anyone who is concerned with taking natural resources from the earth is an extractive worker. The product of these workers is generally in a raw, unusable state. For example, wood has to be made into planks, and fish have to be cleaned and gutted, which leads to secondary production outlined below.

2   Secondary production

The *manufacturing and construction industries*, as secondary production is sometimes known, transform raw materials into the various goods we use. Manufacturing includes activities such as making bread, refining oil and moulding plastic, while construction includes building roads, laying pipelines and erecting houses. In practice, many raw materials will not go in at one end of the factory and come out as finished products at the other. They may be turned into semi-manufactured goods in one factory and then sent to another factory to be finished or added to another product. An example of this is car production, where car parts are made in many different factories and then sent to another factory to be assembled into a car.

Primary and secondary production together are referred to as *industry*.

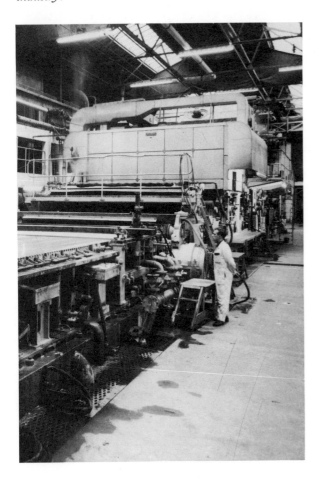

3   Tertiary production

This third type of production has two main parts and provides the services which help primary and secondary production to work efficiently:

COMMERCE   By commerce we mean 'that branch of human activity involved in the distribution and exchange of goods and services'. It is commerce which gets the goods to where they are needed at the time when they are needed – by storing, transporting, advertising, providing the finance, selling and in many other ways. In commercial occupations we include, for example, dockers, drivers, bank clerks, insurance agents and shopkeepers.

DIRECT SERVICES   People like doctors, nurses, pop stars, footballers and actors who do not produce goods which we can hold and pass on, but who give us services which are important to us as people, are part of the tertiary sector. They help to keep people healthy, happy and amused and indirectly help them to work more productively.

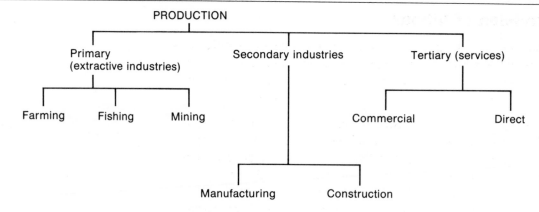

The diagram above shows that commerce (commercial services) is one type of production, coming within the tertiary category. Commerce itself can be divided into many different branches which are shown in the diagram below, and each of these is considered in later chapters of this book. These services can be divided broadly into two: *trade* and the *aids to trade* (ancillary services). Trade is concerned directly with the buying and selling of goods, while the aids to trade help this buying and selling to take place. For example, retailing is one branch of buying and selling, and banking is an aid to retailing by providing cheques and other payment methods in retail transactions.

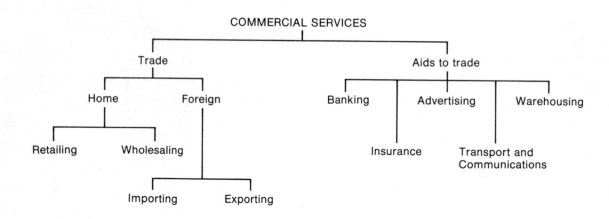

CHECK THIS OUT

Write out the following sentences, filling in the missing words:

1 Basic human needs consist of _____ , _____ and _____ .

2 The extractive industries come under the heading of _____ production.

3 The industries which transform raw materials into goods we use are known as the _____ and construction industries.

4 Tertiary production includes both _____ services and _____ services.

5 An example of a person who provides a direct service is _____ .

The division of labour

The earlier section on production gave some examples of different working activities which bring goods and services into existence. In our modern economic system, a person in work usually concentrates only on one of these activities. We say that the person *specialises*.

This system has not always existed. In early times each family had to satisfy its own needs by building its own home, making its own clothes, and providing heating and food. As families depended only on themselves to satisfy their needs, they were 'self-sufficient'. Even today, families still provide directly for some of their requirements, for example by home decorating, servicing the car or growing fruit and vegetables in a garden.

However, we generally earn our living by specialising in a particular line of work for which we receive an income. This can be a wage if we work for a business, or profit if we have our own business. With this income we are able to buy the goods and services which we require, and which themselves have been produced by other people specialising in other types of work.

In today's world, individuals not only specialise, but to a certain extent so do regions of countries and countries themselves. For instance, although the Midlands of the United Kingdom produces many different goods, it specialises in motor vehicle production. Canada is well-known for producing and exporting wheat, among many other activities. We can see, therefore, that not only are individuals dependent on one another for their livelihood, but all countries of the world are interdependent.

Specialisation has come about by dividing our productive work into many different occupations and processes. We say that there is a *division of labour*. Some activities have been broken down into broad occupations, such as teaching, retailing and nursing. This kind of division of labour is referred to as 'division of labour by *occupation*'. People specialise even within these, for example a teacher may specialise in business studies, while a retailer may sell only clothing. Beyond this, many activities have been divided into even smaller parts or processes. For instance, no one worker makes a complete car, but carries out only one small part of the work. Someone installs the engine, another person puts on the windscreen wipers, while a third fits the wheels, and so on. We refer to this sort of division of labour as 'division of labour by *process*'.

Advantages of division of labour

The advantages of the division of labour are many. If workers specialise in particular tasks production can be greatly increased. Most jobs in a modern factory can be mastered quickly. This means that training periods become shorter because each task is simple. The tasks, as well as being easy, are repetitive, so that workers soon become confident and more competent at their work. Because the tasks are so simple, it is often possible to employ people who do not

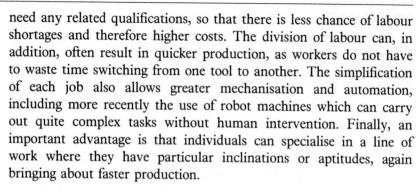

need any related qualifications, so that there is less chance of labour shortages and therefore higher costs. The division of labour can, in addition, often result in quicker production, as workers do not have to waste time switching from one tool to another. The simplification of each job also allows greater mechanisation and automation, including more recently the use of robot machines which can carry out quite complex tasks without human intervention. Finally, an important advantage is that individuals can specialise in a line of work where they have particular inclinations or aptitudes, again bringing about faster production.

Since dividing up the work makes it possible to produce more goods more cheaply than if one person produced the whole unit, consumers can buy more goods, and their standard of living rises.

Disadvantages of division of labour

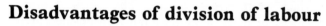

Although division of labour does have many economic advantages, we should always compare them with the many disadvantages. The work is often so repetitive that it can become very boring, possibly causing loss of quality and lower output. To overcome this and increase production, workers are often switched from one job to another. With the division of labour, craft knowledge and therefore quality are often lost and with them any skill which may have gone into the production of an item.

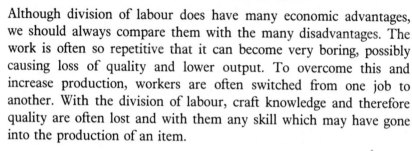

Workers can sometimes find themselves in a very difficult position if they become redundant or need to leave a firm for some other reason. After having trained to do one very limited task, it may become difficult to find similar employment in another firm. Their particular skill may be too specialised to be of any use to another employer. There is also the danger that a machine breakdown or an industrial dispute elsewhere in the factory, or in a factory which supplies parts to another, could cause delays and the laying off of labour.

Another major disadvantage of division of labour, it is argued, is that the gap between management and employees tends to widen. Men and women doing a small job in a very big factory will tend to feel isolated so that pride in work and morale suffer. It is also said that because the work is boring, workers are more likely to become discontented. Because of division of labour, goods tend to be standardised to fit into the system. This eventually narrows choice and individual tastes cannot be met.

Exchange

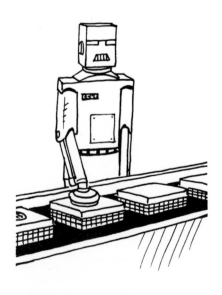

As explained previously, we are no longer self-sufficient as individuals and families, and instead we receive an income with which we acquire most of our goods and services. Our income is received in the form of money and we need to exchange this money for our requirements. If we were still self-sufficient, such exchange would not be necessary.

In the past, when families still produced most of their own needs, they exchanged goods on a very limited basis, but this was carried out, without money, through a process of *barter*. For instance, family X might have produced more clay pots than it needed and swapped them with family Y for some spears which it required. This swapping, or barter, had certain disadvantages, so that various forms of money came to be used as more convenient means of exchange.

Disadvantages of barter

- Each person has to want what the other is offering at the same time. What is more, they both have to know of each other's wants. This is referred to as the need for a 'double coincidence of wants'. If you want to exchange a sheep for a goat, then you need to find the owner of a goat who is interested in receiving a sheep. With money, the sheep can be sold to any interested person in exchange for money, and this money can then be used to buy a goat from someone else.

- Goods may be difficult to transport. If you want to swap a cow for three sheep, it is very difficult to carry a cow around, compared with carrying a bundle of £10 notes.

- Many goods are not divisible. If two clay pots can be changed for three spears, it must mean that one clay pot equals one and a half spears – though half a spear is very little use! Again, money can be used to make an adjustment, for example by replacing the value of half a spear.

Barter has its disadvantages

The importance of commercial services

As we can now see, the ways of producing our goods and services have become very complex and involve widespread exchange and distribution both within one country and all over the world. This is why commercial services have grown to such importance over the centuries, whereas they were not needed when families were self-sufficient.

We showed earlier how goods may pass through several stages of production before they are ready for use. Commercial services are important at all these stages. For example, when raw materials are extracted they need to be paid for and transferred to the factory at the secondary stage, so that commercial services such as banking and transport come into play. Once the materials have been manufactured into their final form, they then need to be distributed to the eventual users (the consumers). Wholesalers and retailers may have roles to play here, while various aids to trade such as banking, advertising and warehousing are also important. If goods are to be bought or sold abroad, then importing and exporting will be involved as well.

As an exercise, take a simple product, such as a chair, and trace it through all the stages of production (the chain of production) from the forest to the final user. Refer to the commercial services shown in the diagram on page 4, and then work out how each of these services may help at each stage of the chair's production. This exercise will help show you the importance of commerce in our economic system.

NOW TRY THIS

Write out the following sentences with a word inserted in the blank space. Choose from: *commerce, specialise, production, farmer, primary, wants.*

1 Human activity aimed at satisfying needs and wants is known as _____ .

2 Production can be divided into three types, and the first type is known as _____ production.

3 One type of occupation in the extractive industries is a _____ .

4 That branch of human activity involved in the distribution and exchange of goods and services is known as _____ .

5 What we would like, as opposed to what we need to survive, is known as our _____ .

6 People are said to _____ when they carry out one particular line of work.

SHORT QUESTIONS

1 What are the three broad types of production?

2 Name the main branches of commerce.

3 Give two examples of occupations which render a direct service.

4 What is the general purpose of production?

5 Why is barter little used now?

6 What does *interdependent* mean?

7 Explain the term *self-sufficient*.

8 How large is the working population in the United Kingdom?

9 Name the aids to trade.

10 What is the division of labour?

MULTIPLE CHOICE QUESTIONS

There are four possible answers to each of the following questions. Study the introductory words, and then decide which of the alternatives correctly answers the question or completes the sentence. Write down the question number and follow it with (A) (B) (C) or (D), according to your choice.

1 Into which category of production does farming fall?
(A) Service
(B) Extractive
(C) Industrial
(D) Commercial

2 Which of the following people are NOT considered to be part of the production chain?
(A) Typists
(B) Housewives
(C) Builders
(D) Fishermen

3 Dentists, pop stars and footballers are all examples of
(A) manufacturing occupations
(B) secondary occupations
(C) commercial occupations
(D) direct services.

4 Which of the following workers is engaged in a secondary occupation?
  (A) A teacher with an extra evening class
  (B) A fisherman who takes holiday-makers on boat trips in the summer
  (C) An ex-nurse who now teaches nursing in College
  (D) A joiner who works in homes as well as on a building site

5 Which of the following is NOT an example of a commercial occupation?
  (A) Bank clerk
  (B) Construction engineer
  (C) Car salesman/woman
  (D) Postman/woman

6 Division of labour occurs when
  (A) trade union members will not do work which properly belongs to another trade
  (B) each worker makes one small part of the whole product
  (C) all the work available is shared out
  (D) there are equal opportunities for men and women to do the same work.

7 Which of the following occupations is in a different category to the others?
  (A) Bricklayer
  (B) Hospital porter
  (C) Baker
  (D) Dressmaker

8 A travel agent is a/an
  (A) direct service occupation
  (B) commercial occupation
  (C) secondary occupation
  (D) industrial occupation.

9 Which of the following is NOT an aid to trade?
  (A) Advertising
  (B) Banking
  (C) Wholesaling
  (D) Insurance

10 A DISADVANTAGE of division of labour is that
  (A) each job becomes simplified
  (B) people employed need not have any qualifications
  (C) the employee's skill may be of use only to one particular employer
  (D) robot machines can do some of the work.

11 Which of the following contains examples of both primary and secondary industries?
  (A) Selling to the public jumpers knitted by hand by homeworkers
  (B) Growing wheat which is then made into wholemeal biscuits
  (C) Growing strawberries and inviting the public to pick and buy
  (D) Chopping and selling firewood

12 Aids to trade are essential because
  (A) they help to get goods from manufacturers to consumers
  (B) the middleman is needed in all branches of commerce
  (C) consumers are well-informed about the best buy
  (D) the quality of goods has to be controlled.

13 An example of trading is
  (A) manufacturing
  (B) banking
  (C) retailing
  (D) transport.

14 Barter is
  (A) exchanging goods for money
  (B) offering less than the asking price for goods
  (C) exchanging one item for another
  (D) offering services which do not have VAT added to the price.

15 An example of an extractive industry is
  (A) quarrying stone
  (B) tailoring
  (C) setting type for newspapers by computer
  (D) refining oil.

There are four possible answers to each of the following questions.

If you think (1) only is correct, write down A.
If you think (1) and (2) only are correct, write down B.
If you think (3) and (4) only are correct, write down C.
If you think (2), (3) and (4) only are correct, write down D.

16 Which of the following is an advantage of the division of labour?
  (1) An increase in production
  (2) Lower cost for each item produced
  (3) Less interesting work for those doing the job
  (4) A feeling of isolation by workers

17 Which of the following is NOT classified as industry?
  (1) Transporting goods
  (2) Selling second-hand cars
  (3) Moulding plastic
  (4) Making car-seat belts

18 When goods or services are exchanged directly without using money, this is called
  (1) barter
  (2) exchange and mart
  (3) direct trading
  (4) double coincidence of wants.

STIMULUS RESPONSE QUESTIONS

1 Read the following information and then answer the questions about it.

The productive worker is not only the worker who is engaged in manufacturing or construction industries, but anyone who is satisfying man's wants and needs. Services, as well as goods, satisfy a need and the shop-keeper, the DHSS clerk, the sailor and the nurse are just as productive as the car manufacturer, the house builder or the road construction worker.

In the first place, natural resources – the raw materials – are extracted and, secondly, they are used to make goods to satisfy our wants. After the goods have been made, they must be transported to the customer who is going to use them or distributed through wholesalers and retailers to the consumer.

Thirdly, workers need to be in good health to carry out their work properly; they need to be educated and to have recreational facilities. Law and order must be kept, and those who engage in this third category of productive service are as necessary to the economy as the other two.

  (a) Define a productive worker and give two examples. (6 marks)
  (b) Give two ways in which needs and wants can be met. (2 marks)
  (c) Suggest the stages of production through which a wool jumper must pass before you can wear it. (8 marks)
  (d) 'Those who engage in the third category of productive service are as necessary to the economy as the other two.' Give an example of an occupation in:
    (i) health;
    (ii) education;
    (iii) law and order;
    (iv) recreation. (4 marks)

2 Read the following information and then answer the questions about it.

Commercial activity can be defined as buying and selling: raw materials or finished goods can be purchased, moved to where they are needed and sold to those who want or need them.

At first, goods were sold by barter, which is the direct exchange of goods between people. Today, goods are sold to the middleman for money and are transported long distances to the consumer. One person may work as a clerk, and the money gained from this occupation is used to pay for food. The retailer who supplies the food buys it from the wholesaler, who may in turn purchase it from the farmer. The transactions may be paid for by cheques, with which the clerk deals during the course of his or her occupation. This is a simplified version of a complex process which needs many specialists who all work in commerce.

To maintain a high standard of living, Britain imports food and raw materials to make into goods which can be exported to pay for needs and wants. All these activities form marketing or commerce.

  (a) Explain the term 'commercial activity'. (6 marks)

  (b) Why are goods no longer sold by barter? (8 marks)

  (c) How does Britain maintain a high standard of living? (3 marks)

  (d) Name three specialists who work in commerce. (3 marks)

3 Read the following information carefully, and then answer the questions on it.

Simple ideas are best

Mohammed Salem left school in Morpeth, Northumberland, with few qualifications and little hope of a job. During that first summer of unemployment he decided to try to earn some money by washing and cleaning the insides of cars. To his surprise he found his services were very much in demand in the area in which he lived. Very soon he was having to use public transport to travel to jobs that his customers had recommended him for. The small advert he placed in the local newspaper meant that he was getting more cleaning jobs than he could cope with. He asked his friend Andrew Rowley to come into partnership with him and Andrew accepted.

Having Andrew with him meant that cars could be cleaned much faster and that Mohammed could, if necessary, use his typewriting skills to send bills and letters to the customers while Andrew cleaned a car. Despite this improvement Mohammed felt that the service was not as good as it could be as they wasted a lot of time waiting for buses which were too slow for their needs. Mohammed and Andrew are thinking about buying a small van as this will help them to get around much faster and improve the level of service for which they have become well known.

Since the business started earnings have gone in 12 months from £15 per month to £300 and look set to go even higher. Both young men now have to pay income tax of 27 per cent on what they earn but think the prospects for the future are good, even if research has shown that most small businesses fail to make it past the second year of operation.

(a) What sector of production does Mohammed Salem work in? *(1 mark)*

(b) Name TWO aids to trade used by Mohammed in his business. *(2 marks)*

(c) (i) What commercial service might he use to help pay for his van? *(2 marks)*
   (ii) What other commercial service will he be required by law to use if he buys a van? *(2 marks)*

(d) (i) If the business earned £300 per month for 12 months what would the annual earnings be? *(1 mark)*
   (ii) If the business had an annual income of £3600 what would the average monthly earnings be? *(1 mark)*
   (iii) How much income tax do Andrew and Mohammed each pay if they divide their most recent earnings of £300 equally between them? *(2 marks)*
   (iv) By what percentage has the earnings of the business increased in the last 12 months? *(2 marks)*

(e) If the business was to become very large
   (i) What *two* benefits might a customer notice? *(4 marks)*
   (ii) What *two* disadvantages might a customer notice? *(4 marks)*

ESSAY QUESTIONS

The following questions carry a mark of 20. Each section of a question shows the marks for the correct response.

1 (a) What does 'production' mean? *(4 marks)*

(b) Name two well-known firms involved in:
   (i) primary production; *(2 marks)*
   (ii) secondary production; *(2 marks)*
   (iii) tertiary production. *(2 marks)*

(c) Explain what is meant by:
   (i) commerce; *(5 marks)*
   (ii) direct services. *(5 marks)*

2 'Commerical workers produce nothing.' Examine the role of commercial workers in the light of this statement. *(20 marks)*
(Reproduced from the specimen GCSE Commerce examination paper of the LEA Group)

3 (a) What is the difference between needs and wants? *(4 marks)*
(b) Explain the advantages and disadvantages of the division of labour to:
   (i) employers; *(6 marks)*
   (ii) employees. *(6 marks)*

LEARN IT YOURSELF – ACTIVITY ASSIGNMENTS

1 Make a list of five businesses in your area and describe the goods or services they offer. Find out all you can about one business and prepare a talk for your class, using diagrams if necessary.

2 Refer to the diagram on page 4 and show how the five aids to trade are represented in your locality by finding the names and addresses of two firms engaged in each. You may find a Directory of Firms, such as *Kelly's Directory*, in your school or local library, a useful aid.

3 Choose a firm in your area or in your nearest large town which produces goods on a large scale. State the name of the firm, the locality and the reasons why the firm is situated there.

4 Prepare a series of interviews with friends and/or relatives to find out what their jobs entail. Classify your findings under the headings: industry, commerce and direct services. Arrange this material together with photographs and charts, etc. as a wall exhibition. This project is suitable for small groups of students to work on together.

5 Working in groups to ensure that the whole class does not send a letter to the same firm, write to one firm in each of the major branches of commerce asking about job opportunities for school-leavers. Prepare a chart showing the jobs about which you asked, and the qualifications which are needed to do that particular job.

ASSIGNMENT – THE WORLD OF COMMERCE

Design a questionnaire to interview the following people:

(a) People over 65.
(b) People of your parents' age.
(c) People from your own age up to the age of 30.

You wish to find out:

What job(s) they did (or are doing).
What the hours of work, conditions at work, and holidays were (or are).
Whether they held just one type of job or changed jobs.
What opportunities to train existed (or exist now) for people who wished to go on to other kinds of work.
What job opportunities there were (or are now) in your locality.
What old jobs have gone.
What new jobs have begun in the time in which your interviewee has been working: for example, someone who is retired might remember as a 'new' job that of a television repairer.

Present your findings neatly, under a, b and c (see above).
Look at the beginning of the chapter at the classifications of jobs.

Classify the jobs shown in a, b and c.

Get in touch with your local College of Further Education and ask for a brochure for the courses which they now teach. You may also wish to get in touch with a Polytechnic or University which has vocational courses. If possible, find out the courses which were once taught at these institutions but which are not taught now.

Present your findings about courses which used to be taught and which are taught now.

Can you draw any conclusions about the way work in your locality has changed? Do you notice any trends in training for work? Are there any differences in the classification of jobs in a, b and c? Can you draw a conclusion from the differences which you note?

CHAPTER 2

THE RETAILER

The work of the retailer

What is a retailer? A retailer is a person, or organisation, who buys goods in bulk and sells them in the small quantities which we, the customers, require to satisfy our needs and wants.

There is a *chain of distribution* for goods, and the retailer is an important link in that chain. Goods are made in a factory by the manufacturer, who has bought the raw materials from a supplier. These goods are then bought in large quantities by a wholesaler, who sells them to the retailer, or they are bought directly from the manufacturer by the retailer. Finally, the retailer sells goods to the consumer – the person who uses them.

Why do we need retailers? Surely it would be cheaper to buy straight from the manufacturer. However, if all our goods were made at the other end of the country, we would have to spend a lot of time and money going round various factories or sending away to buy every item we need. It is much simpler to go to a shop and obtain many different articles all at the same time.

The retailer buys in bulk from the wholesaler or manufacturer and sells in smaller quantities to individual customers. Buying in bulk means that the retailer pays the wholesaler less for each item than the charge which is made to the customer. The retailer adds to the wholesale price an amount known as the 'mark-up' on goods, and this is how a profit is made. This gross profit has to pay for the retailer's 'overheads', which are the expenses of running a business. For example, rent and rates need to be paid for the shop, and there are bills for lighting and heating, plus the wages of any assistants which must be met. The amount remaining after these expenses have been met is the retailer's *net* profit. Usually, the more goods a retailer sells, the more profit can be made.

One of the ways in which a manufacturer can tell which goods are most popular with the public is to note the articles bought most frequently by the retailer. Retailers provide a variety of goods locally for their customers. For instance, they may stock several different brands of washing detergent, and the retailer may offer advice about the best item to buy. Customers may be able to buy on credit: that is, they may be able to take goods away and pay for them when they

receive their wages. The retailer may also check goods to ensure that they work and offer an 'after-sale' service, such as repair and maintenance. Some retailers may open early and close late for the convenience of their customers.

Types of retailer

There are so many different types of retailer that it is difficult to place them in distinct categories. The following list shows most of the variations, but there is much overlapping between types. For example, co-operative retailers may operate mobile shops, and independent shops may be supermarkets. With this in mind, we will look at each type:

- Automatic vending machines.
- Street vendors.
- Itinerant traders.
- Mobile shops.
- Market stalls.
- Independent shops.
- Supermarket chains.
- Hypermarkets.
- Discount stores.
- Multiple shops.
- Variety chain stores.
- Department stores.
- Co-operative retailers.
- Mail order retailers.

Automatic vending machines

Automatic vending machines are economical because, once they have been bought or hired, they are labour-saving and provide a service for 24 hours every day of the week without the need for someone to be present (except for filling or servicing the machine from time to time). An example is a hot drinks vending machine in a leisure centre.

Street vendors

The 'barrow' which can be wheeled with its load of goods from the wholesale market to a pavement where many people pass by can provide a cheap source of goods – often fruit and vegetables. The overheads of the trader are low because instead of paying rent there is only a licence fee of some kind to be found.

Itinerant traders

These are people selling 'door-to-door', either by prior appointment or without invitation. They may work as individuals or for larger businesses. Examples of goods sold include double glazing, cosmetics and household cleaning items.

Mobile shops

The mobile shop includes the van selling bread and milk, groceries and greengroceries, the ice-cream van and the mobile fish-and-chip shop. Such vans can reach isolated areas where there are no shops. They are also very useful to people who have difficulty in getting out to the shops. The trader may find that the overheads are quite high for such items as petrol, road tax and insurance.

Market stalls

Most towns hold open-air markets on certain days and the rent for a market stall is low compared with that for a shop. Many stall-holders occupy the same stall every week, so that it is possible to exchange goods or even get a refund if the goods are faulty. However, some stall-holders come and go, and if anything goes wrong it may not be possible to get a refund or exchange. Articles for sale in markets are usually cheaper than those in shops, but they may be 'seconds' and the customer should check carefully. Trade can be brisk in good weather, but the stall-holder may find that people do not bother to come to the market if it is cold and wet. There are, however, also permanent indoor markets.

Independent shops

Independent shops are often run and owned by individuals and are therefore sometimes known as *sole traders*. This does not mean that they work alone, as they may employ full-time or part-time assistants, but that they take all the risks and gain all the profits.

Independent shops may have several branches, but generally there is only one. Independent shops are known as *unit retailers*. They usually have their business near their customers. As they control their own hours of work, some shops, such as newsagents, may be open early in the morning and late at night for the benefit of their customers. If the customers are known to the trader, the unit shop will sometimes allow credit and may deliver goods for the customers or give other personal services. For example, you could order a birthday cake to your own requirements from a small shopkeeper, or order something not normally available.

Some small shopkeepers, particularly those who sell food, join with wholesalers to form voluntary chains such as MACE or SPAR. Together with other members of the group, they are able to buy in greater bulk from the manufacturers and pass on their savings to their customers. The group might advertise nationally, with slogans such as 'Buy where you see this sign!' or 'MACE for value!', and such groups might loan money to their members to extend or buy new fittings for their shops. Disadvantages to members could be that they lose some freedom of action. They have to sell goods bought from the wholesaler by the group instead of items they might prefer, and there is a measure of central control over what they sell.

CHECK THIS OUT

Write out the following sentences, filling in the missing words:

1 The person who buys goods from the wholesaler and sells to the consumer is a _____ .

2 The retailer has expenses which are known as _____ to pay before the net profit can be calculated.

3 An example of an item commonly sold by a mobile shop is _____ .

4 An 'independent' shop is one which is often owned and run by an individual called a

_____ _____ .

5 Some small shopkeepers join with others to buy goods in bulk by forming a _____

_____ .

The number of independent shops has fallen greatly in recent years, despite their convenience, personal service and friendliness, mainly because of the growth of multiples (see page 19) which charge lower prices for their goods. The more units of particular goods sold, the lower the cost per unit. This enables the large-scale retailer, with national outlets, to buy in bulk and operate more economically than the independent.

The high sales (turnover) of goods experienced by large-scale retailers means that they can offer a wide range of goods which are kept up-to-date by sales and special offers. Independent shops cannot compete with this, nor can they afford expensive national advertising. In the last 20 years there has been a significant trend away from small-scale retailing.

Supermarket chains

The large self-service store with a sales area of at least 186 square metres which sells a full range of household goods and food is defined as a *supermarket*, and it is usually a part of a chain of such stores owned by a large company.

Supermarkets offer a display of ready-packaged goods which the shopper can choose from without the aid of a shop assistant. This has proved very convenient. Other advantages of supermarkets are that they stay open late on some evenings and provide customers with many needs in just one visit. This saves time. Perhaps the most important advantage, though, is that supermarkets can buy goods in greater bulk at advantageous prices and as a result sell to their customers at cheaper prices than small-scale retailers.

Supermarkets have developed their own techniques for tempting customers into buying additional products. For example, goods which customers would buy regularly (such as tea or sugar) are often put in less prominent positions. The eye-catching positions can then be filled with items which the shopper did not intend to buy. Another technique is the advertising of 'loss leaders'. These are goods which are sold at little or no profit, but which attract customers into the shop – in the hope that these customers will then buy other goods at the same time, on impulse.

The growth of supermarkets has also been influenced by various social changes. Married women now tend to have much less time for shopping, because the number of women working full-time has increased greatly in recent years, and with the growth of private transport, shopping locally or having goods delivered is no longer necessary. Weekly one-stop shopping by car for basic needs is now very common.

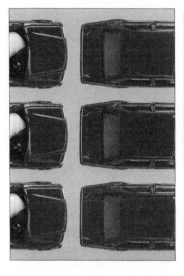
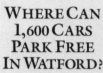

WHERE CAN 1,600 CARS PARK FREE IN WATFORD?

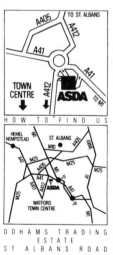

One trip and you're laughing.

A modern supermarket. This advertisement stresses the advantages of shopping by car

Hypermarkets

A hypermarket is often defined as a store with at least 4650 square metres of selling space. Hypermarkets are so large that they are usually situated out of town. They are visited by shoppers in cars who may wish to buy large quantities (for example, food for the freezer) weekly or monthly, and they sell, besides food, *consumer durables* such as furniture, electrical goods, etc. Some people oppose the building of hypermarkets. They argue that hypermarkets take away trade from local shops which may then be forced to close. This then causes a decline in the nearby traditional shopping areas.

Discount stores

Discount stores sell consumer durables at low prices and are often situated in old warehouses or mills out of the town centre, so avoiding high rents and rates. Prices of goods may be as much as 10 to 15 per cent below the normal selling price, but customers often have to pay by cash or credit card only. They operate on the self-service principle with few assistants.

Multiple shops

Multiple shops are often defined as those which are one of at least ten owned by the same organisation. Specialist multiple shops concentrate only on a narrow range of goods. For instance, C&A sells clothes, Timpsons sells shoes, and Mothercare sells items for babies and young children. Although each shop has a manager, a central office decides the store policy, and buys the goods. The shops are uniform and the decor in each is the same, so they can be easily recognised by customers. Buying in bulk keeps down the cost of the goods, but this means that individual tastes, shapes and sizes may not be catered for. Although the customer can be sure of the same standard whichever branch goods are bought from, many people will be wearing, for example, the same style of jumper. Most multiple shops rely on cash payment and goods small enough for the customer to carry home, but the use of credit cards and budget accounts is growing.

A cross between the multiple and the independent shop is the *franchise*, such as Kentucky Fried Chicken, where each shop has the same decor and type of goods for sale, but where each shop is owned separately from the franchise operator. The owner of the shop has the exclusive right to use the name and product in a certain area, and has to pay for this right, but any remaining profits go to the owner. This is a rapidly growing area of retailing in the 1980s.

Variety chain stores

Variety chain stores combine cheapness and convenience by offering a wider range of goods than the multiple shops, and they have branches all over the country. They are usually found in town centres and shopping precincts and all branches look alike so that the customer can recognise them. Marks and Spencer is an example of a variety chain store, and others include Littlewoods and BHS. Like multiple shops, variety chain stores usually rely on cash payment and customers transporting their own goods home, but they do accept credit cards in payment.

Department stores

A department store is usually found in the centre of a city or large town. It consists of many different shops or departments under one roof, all owned by one firm. Examples are Harrods and Debenhams. This type of store is run by a general manager and each department has a manager or buyer who tries to make his or her department a profitable one. At one time the individual buyer had responsibility for purchasing goods for the department, but with the growth of chains of departmental stores owned by single companies, much more buying is now done centrally for all the stores controlled.

Department stores often arrange extended credit for expensive goods, and they will deliver large items such as furniture. Customers may also have a budget or credit card account with the store which they settle at the end of each month. This is very useful if people want to buy items but do not have enough money until their monthly pay-day. Stores sometimes provide services in the store, such as an exhibition hall and their own banking service, which is open when other banks are shut. There are also public telephones, theatre and holiday booking offices, restaurants and toilets. Parts of the store may be rented out to independent 'concessionaires' for the sale of their individual products, such as cosmetics.

CHECK THIS OUT

Write out the following sentences, filling in the missing words:

1 A very large store selling a full range of food, household and other goods through self-service is known as a _____ .

2 An argument against _____ is that they may take away trade from town-centre shops.

3 Shops which sell a narrow range of goods only and have branches all over the country which look alike are called _____ stores.

4 A _____ chain store has branches all over the country and offers a wider range of goods than a multiple store.

5 A store consisting of many different shops which are under one roof and are all owned by the one business is known as a _____ store.

The co-operative retailer

Co-operative retailing is organised by separate societies which operate in different parts of the country. The most famous co-operative society is the Rochdale Equitable Pioneers Society, begun in 1884 by a group of weavers who each provided £1 to start a store in Toad Lane, Rochdale. They began trading in basic foodstuffs and household goods, and profit was distributed as a *dividend* twice a year to members who bought the goods. In time the range of items grew. Many customers bought all their food, clothes, footwear, coal and even furniture from the 'Co-op' and received a dividend of as much as 12½p in every £1 spent.

In the early 1970s many co-operative societies started to issue dividend stamps with purchases instead of the half-yearly money dividend. These stamps could be exchanged for cash or goods, but more recently stamps have become less popular. In fact, because of competitive price-cutting by other retailers and very low profit margins, co-operatives often dropped the dividend or stamps on some goods, and now many are considering stopping the dividend completely.

Co-operative retail societies vary greatly in size, but the larger ones offer a range of goods covering every item which people would normally want, in different types of shop, including small food shops, departmental stores, supermarkets and hypermarkets.

Through the Co-operative Wholesale Society and associated organisations, they also offer a range of services, including travel, banking and insurance.

Goods sold by the co-operative societies are often produced by the Co-op at each stage of production. In the primary stage, raw materials are grown on the Co-op's own plantations and farms. These raw materials will then be delivered by the Co-op's own transport to their own factories for manufacture. From there the goods pass to the Co-operative Wholesale Society (CWS) and out into the shops.

Anyone over 16 years old can become a member of a co-operative retail society by purchasing at least one £1 share. Each society is controlled by its members, who each have one vote at any meeting they attend and who determine the policies which the salaried manager will follow. Notice of all meetings is posted in Co-op retail stores so that shoppers know about them. Recent amalgamation has reduced the number of local societies, and although they operate the dividend scheme and finance educational and social activities, they are now often thought of as just another retail outlet (see also Chapter 5).

Mail order retailers

Mail order retailing takes various forms. A common way is to use part-time agents, often housewives, who show a large, colourful catalogue to family and friends and who place orders on their behalf with the company issuing the catalogue, for example John England. For this work, the agent receives commission on sales, often 10p in the pound cash, or 12½p in the pound in goods. A similar alternative method is to advertise and issue booklets or smaller catalogues to prospective purchasers without going through an agent, while a third variation is to advertise *individual* products and ask for direct orders.

Although mail order has become very popular, there is the disadvantage that the goods received may not be what was expected as they were bought unseen, but they can usually be returned if unsatisfactory. The high cost of packing and postage or transport costs is another disadvantage as the cost is added to the goods, and sometimes the customer is expected to pay when returning unsuitable goods.

A particular attraction is, however, that easy credit for up to a year or more is obtainable from catalogue companies, and short periods of credit are often free. Credit cards are also commonly acceptable in mail order. Another advantage is that goods are delivered to the door, and for the elderly or infirm, or people with little time to shop, it can be a convenient way of acquiring goods.

An advantage to the mail order firm of this kind of shopping is that they can locate their warehouse out of town in an older building, with low rental and rates compared with a high street shop. The firm does not need shop assistants, display counters, carpeted floors and fittings and this is also a saving on overheads.

E CAPTAIN CLUB RANGE. Weather-proof furniture. Five-position chair has resin frame, seat and back. Back has metal tubular support. The cushion is cotton, rayon-covered, with foam filling. Oval table is made from mineral-reinforced polypropylene, with smooth finish and high stability. Top measures 52 × 36 ins, with centre hole for parasol. One leg is adjustable. ▲

KS 061 Table. White. £74·99 20 wks £3·75; 38 wks £1·98

KS 062 Chair. White. £32·49 20 wks £1·63

KS 063 Parasol. Modern-floral or peach. £29·99 20 wks £1·50

KS 066 Parasol base. White. £7·50 20 wks 38p

KS 067 Cushion. Modern-floral or peach-stripe. £17·50 20 wks 88p

Special offer – buy table, four chairs, four cushions, parasol and parasol base together and **save £20·00 KS 070 Garden furniture set.** Order must state **modern-floral or peach-stripe.** £292·44 20 wks £14·63; 38 wks £7·70 **100 wks cat no KS 073** Interest £67·48 **(APR 24·8%)** Total price £359·92 100 wks £3·60

£**32·49** CHAIR ONLY

CAPTAIN CLUB RANGE

SAVE **BUY THE SET:** • TABLE (OVAL) • PARASOL • 4 CHAIRS • PARASOL • 4 CUSHIONS BASE **AND SAVE £20·00 ON M.R.P.**

A page from a mail order catalogue

Computers in retailing

Computers help retailers to process and record their financial accounts, in the same way as many other businesses, but they are also becoming a valuable aid within the shop itself, enabling a business to keep track continuously of sales and stock changes. For instance tags are sometimes detached from goods when a sale is made. A computer then processes them to give daily sales results and indicate where restocking is needed. A further development is the making of many items with bar codes, which can be read by special pen or scanner. These pens are being linked to check-out tills, which are themselves computer terminals. Each commodity has its own bar code and its details are fed into the terminal which produces the till receipt according to prices operating on the day.

Besides providing information for the customer on the receipt, the terminal can record the items which have been sold and this information can be passed on to a central computer, sometimes over a telephone line. The retailer then knows very quickly which goods to re-order, which goods are not selling very quickly and which goods have a very high turnover. There is no need to hold large stocks at the shop – when stocks of a certain item become low, the computer can quickly relay this information to a central warehouse to replace the goods. In this way, stocking costs can be reduced and sales are less likely to be lost because customers cannot find the goods they want.

The same system can be used similarly at the central warehouse itself, for re-ordering from manufacturers or wholesalers, and a further development is the fully automated warehouse where computerised trucks run between the shelves extracting the quantities of different goods required for delivery in a particular shop.

Shoppers may soon buy their goods by means of plastic cards which have a magnetic strip, instead of using money. These cards can be inserted in the check-out computer terminal when goods are bought and a communication link to the shopper's bank account allows the appropriate amount to be debited and then credited to the retailer's account. No cash will change hands, and the shopper should find it a speedy, accurate and convenient process.

A light pen in use

AIDS TO MEMORY

Learn This

Mail order firms sell by post, and discount stores sell cheaper,
Department stores sell many goods, but prices may be steeper.
Multiple store branches look alike, they sell one kind of thing,
Variety chains have a wider range, from motor parts to string.

SHORT QUESTIONS

1 Name *two* items often sold by mobile shops.

2 Give one reason for *not* buying from an open-air market.

3 What is a *sole trader*?

4 Give *two* reasons for the popularity of supermarkets.

5 Name *two* services which the customer might receive from a retailer.

6 What is a *loss leader*?

7 Explain the term: *high turnover*.

8 Name *two consumer durables*.

9 What is the difference between a multiple store and a variety chain store?

10 Why are discount stores often located out of town centres?

MULTIPLE CHOICE QUESTIONS

There are four possible answers to each of the following questions. Study the introductory words, and then decide which of the alternatives correctly answers the question or completes the sentence. Write down the question number and follow it with (A) (B) (C) or (D), according to your choice.

1 Which of the following is an example of a sole trader?
(A) The local branch of a chain of hairdressers
(B) A variety chain store
(C) A shop with one owner and two assistants
(D) A painting and decorating partnership

2 The retailer MOST dependent on advertising to contact customers is
(A) a multiple shop
(B) the corner shop
(C) a street trader
(D) a mail order firm.

3 Marks & Spencer PLC is an example of a/an
(A) department store
(B) variety chain store
(C) independent store
(D) partnership.

4 If the rate of stock turnover is high, the advantage to a retailer is that
(A) there are lower storage costs per item sold
(B) fashions change so quickly stock is left on the firm's hands
(C) more capital is needed to buy more goods
(D) goods may be damaged and have to be sold cheaply.

5 Which of the following is NOT essential to a supermarket?
(A) Many check-out tills
(B) Branded goods ready packaged
(C) Separate home bakery section
(D) A variety of goods on offer

6 An example of a mobile shop is
(A) a fish-and-chip shop
(B) a van selling ice-cream
(C) a kiosk in the market
(D) a lorry delivering bread from the baker.

7 A voluntary chain is one where
(A) assistants give their services free and the profit goes to charity
(B) members sell whatever they wish
(C) members band together to buy goods more cheaply from the wholesaler
(D) all branches of the shop have the same owner

8 Which is NOT an advantage of shopping at a supermarket?
 (A) being able to buy a 'loss leader'
 (B) late night opening
 (C) cheaper prices
 (D) being tempted to buy goods on impulse

9 An example of a multiple shop is
 (A) Harrods department store
 (B) a corner shop
 (C) a single newsagent's shop run by members of the family
 (D) Mothercare.

10 Which is NOT an example of a variety chain store?
 (A) Marks & Spencer
 (B) Debenhams
 (C) Littlewoods
 (D) Bhs

11 Department stores do NOT provide
 (A) toilets
 (B) some credit facilities
 (C) restaurants
 (D) late-night opening every night of the week.

12 Which of the following is NOT an example of mail order?
 (A) Part-time agents showing a catalogue and placing orders
 (B) Developing and printing photographs and sending through the post
 (C) Sending off for goods advertised in a newspaper or magazine
 (D) Advertising literature received through the post

13 Which of the following is NOT a retail outlet?
 (A) A supermarket
 (B) An automated vending machine
 (C) A stall in the local market
 (D) An estate agent

14 Which of the following is NOT an example of the use of computers in retailing?
 (A) Processing daily sales and indicating re-stocking
 (B) Providing information for customers on till receipts
 (C) Providing a delivery service to customers
 (D) Showing which goods have a high turn-over

15 Which of the following is NOT a feature of a discount store?
 (A) Operating on the self-service principle
 (B) Prices 10 per cent or more below normal selling prices
 (C) Operating as a small retail establishment which relies on advertising
 (D) Being usually situated out of the town centre in large premises

There are four possible answers to each of the following questions.

If you think (1) only is correct, write down A.
If you think (1) and (2) only are correct, write down B.
If you think (3) and (4) only are correct, write down C.
If you think (2), (3) and (4) only are correct, write down D.

16 A disadvantage of mail order to the customer can be that
 (1) the goods may be ordered by telephone
 (2) the firm may be situated out of the town centre
 (3) there are no shop assistants to help the customer
 (4) the goods received may not be what was expected.

17 Which of the following features apply to department stores?
 (1) Many different products are sold under one roof
 (2) They are usually found in town centres
 (3) They may have small branch shops in many parts of the country
 (4) They may be part of a voluntary chain such as MACE or SPAR

18 A feature of an independent shop is that
 (1) the owner has to work alone
 (2) there is only one branch
 (3) the owner takes all the risks and gains all the profits
 (4) the business is usually situated near the retailer's customers.

STIMULUS RESPONSE QUESTIONS

The following questions carry a mark of 20. Each section of a question shows the marks for the correct response.

1 Read the following information and then answer the questions about it.

Department stores are usually located in the centres of large towns and are so-called because they are made up of a number of different departments, each dealing with a particular type of commodity, all housed under one roof. The shopper can buy almost anything from the store without going outside, and there are often services such as hairdressing, banking, a travel agency and a restaurant for the customer. Some department stores have now added the facility to buy stocks and shares.

The department store deals in good quality commodities. Features are: an elegant window display and comfortable premises, allowing the shopper to look round without being urged to buy; the provision of toilets; the delivery service offered for furniture and other large goods and often hire-purchase facilities for consumer durables. There is a wide variety to choose from in each different department.

(a) Where are department stores usually located?
    (1 mark)
(b) Why are these establishments called 'department stores'?
    (1 mark)
(c) What other services might a department store offer to the customer, apart from the sale of goods?
    (8 marks)
(d) What differences would you observe in the premises of a department store compared to a variety chain store?
    (6 marks)
(e) Why do department stores appeal to their many customers?
    (4 marks)

2 Read the following information carefully and then answer the questions about it.

Shopping centres

Redevelopment in city centres in Britain, and special developments in other parts of large cities have, in recent years, taken the form of building new enclosed shopping centres. These shopping precincts are made up of a large number of different shops in one locality. The precinct is enclosed, so that shoppers can go from shop to shop untroubled by rain, wind or snow. There is usually an adjacent or enclosed car-park so that the centre is easy to get to for shoppers who want to use their own transport.

Local traders sometimes object to the building of large shopping precincts that can adversely affect their trade, and local authorities cannot give permission for such proposals without first referring them to the Department of the Environment, which will probably hold a public enquiry to allow the local community to thrash out the pros and cons.

(a) What new developments have taken place in recent years to attract shoppers? *(2 marks)*
(b) What are the features of the new shopping precincts? *(5 marks)*
(c) Why might local traders object to the building of new shopping centres? *(2 marks)*
(d) What advantages do these precincts hold for shoppers? *(3 marks)*
(e) What restrictions are placed on local authorities who want to give permission to building shopping centres? *(3 marks)*
(f) As a local trader, list some objections you might make to the Department of the Environment at a public enquiry about the possible building of a new shopping centre.
    (6 marks)

3 Read this information carefully and then answer
the questions on it.

THE NORTHTOWN NEWS

NEW SUPERSTORE FOR TOWN

SMALL RETAILERS FEAR LOSS
OF TRADE (Reporter Sue Jones)

'Nortrading', who own
superstores throughout the
country, want to open the first
superstore in Northtown.

As you can see from the map,
the store is to be built on the
outskirts of the town, where
land is available, close to good
roads.

The local council are to meet
next week to decide whether
or not to give permission for
the store to be built.

Some local shopowners are
worried. Mrs Ann Smith, a
greengrocer, said that she may
have to close down because
she cannot cut prices the way
Nortrading does. A member of
the local Chamber of
Commerce thought that in
general it would be a good
thing for Northtown because it
would give the town more
jobs, and attract customers
from out of town.

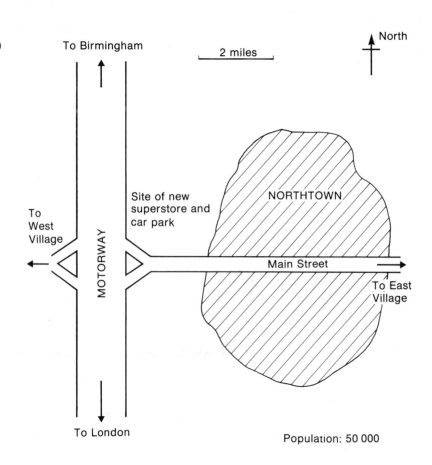

(a) (i) What type of retailer fears the building
of a superstore? *(1 mark)*
(ii) Why does this type of retailer fear the
new superstore? *(2 marks)*
(b) Why does Nortrading wish to open a new
superstore in Northtown? *(6 marks)*
(c) How will the following people be affected by
the coming of the superstore?

(i) couples with children *(8 marks)*
(ii) pensioners *(8 marks)*
(iii) a local fruit and vegetable wholesaler
(6 marks)

(Specimen question from the Commerce GCSE
paper of the Northern Examining Association)

4 Read this information carefully and then answer the questions which follow:

Fashion co-ordinates by mail

Dear Customer

It is with great pleasure that we send you our new Fashion Collection brochure, in which you will find details of our latest offers. I'm sure you will agree that these goods represent the very best in quality and value – particularly if you compare them with other companies. The goods represent unbeatable value and you will note that some are available to you at a SPECIAL LOW PRICE. You will know from your previous custom that if you are not satisfied with any of the items we send you, they can be returned at once and we will refund any money paid without question.

(a) What type of business would write this letter?
(2 marks)

(b) Why has the letter been written to this particular customer? *(2 marks)*

(c) What kind of items are on offer? *(2 marks)*

(d) How does the firm try to persuade the customer to buy the goods? *(6 marks)*

(e) What happens if the customer receives the goods and then is disappointed and does not want to keep them? *(2 marks)*

(f) What might be the advantage to the customer of buying goods in this way? *(4 marks)*

(g) What other disadvantages to the customer, besides possible disappointment when the goods are seen, are there to buying goods by this method? *(2 marks)*

ESSAY QUESTIONS

1 (a) (i) What is the basic function of a retailer?
(2 marks)
(ii) Name TWO retail outlets other than shops. *(1 mark)*
(b) Describe and contrast the chief characteristics of TWO of the following types of retail outlets: retail co-operative stores, department stores, supermarkets, multiple shops. *(6 marks)*
(c) Despite charging higher prices than large scale retailers, some independent traders still continue to compete successfully. How do you explain this situation? *(15 marks)*

(Reproduced from the specimen paper of the LEA Group for GCSE Commerce examination)

2 (a) How are retail co-operatives organised? *(10 marks)*
(b) What differences are there between co-operative and other retail outlets? *(7 marks)*
(c) What other services, besides retail establishments, are offered by the Co-operative Society? *(3 marks)*

3 (a) To what marketing techniques do you attribute the success of supermarkets? *(12 marks)*
(b) What disadvantages to the customer might there be in shopping at a supermarket? *(4 marks)*
(c) What social changes have influenced the growth of supermarkets? *(4 marks)*

4 (a) What economic advantages do variety chain stores enjoy compared with the small trader? *(4 marks)*
(b) What are the advantages and disadvantages to the customer of shopping at
(i) a variety chain store;
(ii) a shop in your locality owned by a smaller trader? *(8 marks)*
(c) Do you agree with the view that small shopkeepers should enjoy some protection against competition from multiple or chain stores? Give reasons for your answer. *(8 marks)*

LEARN IT YOURSELF

1 List TEN items of groceries bought for your household each week. Make a survey and find their prices in
   (a) a small local shop;
   (b) a supermarket;
   (c) a market stall.
   Comment on the quality and value of the goods, and present the results in an attractive and clear form.

2 Look round your local Co-operative store. Roughly, what proportion of items bear the Co-op brand name? (Choose from: 75%, 50%, 25%, 10%.)

3 Imagine you are a unit retailer selling newspapers, cigarettes, cards and sweets. Design a window display to attract people so that they stop and look in your window.

4 Design the floor lay-out for a large supermarket. Give reasons why you have put goods in a certain place. Remember to put some items by the check-out desk.

5 Visit a large department store and make a list of at least ten departments and the floors on which they are located. Before you make a visit, choose an item which you might buy there. Afterwards, make a list of the departments you would have to walk through first (if any) before reaching your chosen item. Why do you think the particular departments on the ground floor have been located there?

NOW TRY THIS

The following questions must be answered verbally but without using the words 'YES' or 'NO'. The teacher may ask the questions round the class or groups may ask each other in turn.

Each person keeps score of their own answers, provided they have been made correctly without using the words 'YES' or 'NO'. At the end of a round of questions, the scores are totted up to find the winner(s). The players MUST USE FULL SENTENCES.

An example of a question might be:
'Is Marks and Spencer a department store?'
An example of a correct answer would be:
'Marks and Spencer is not a department store.'
A wrong answer would be:
'No, it's not' or 'Yes, it is'
as these answers use the forbidden words.

If two teams are formed, a time limit can be put on the questions and answers, to see which group manages to answer correctly the most questions in a given time.

Questions to start you off:

1 Does a retailer pay cash to the wholesaler?

2 Is the profit which a retailer makes counted only after the bills have been paid?

3 Can you tell me if retailers give credit to their customers?

4 Is it true that retailers only stock one brand of goods?

5 Has the number of sole traders grown over recent years?

6 Can you count a street vendor as a retailer?

7 Do market stalls have high overheads?

8 Is it true that members of voluntary chains such as SPAR and MACE operate quite separately from each other?

9 Do supermarkets buy goods in such bulk that they can sell to the consumer more cheaply than other food shops?

10 Do discount stores sell on credit?

11 Are hypermarkets smaller than supermarkets?

12 Is a multiple store one with many branches?

13 Does a variety chain store sell a narrower range of goods than a multiple store?

14 Does mail order run on the credit system?

15 Is a department store usually situated out of the town centre?

16 Does the retailer buy in bulk from many different manufacturers?

17 Is an ice-cream van classed as a mobile shop?

18 Does the sole trader work alone?

19 Are discount stores often situated out of the town centre?

20 Is Kentucky Fried Chicken an example of a franchise?

21 Do department stores usually deliver large items such as furniture?

22 Did co-operative retail societies begin by trading in basic foodstuffs?

23 Do mail order firms have to have a showroom for their goods?

24 Can a check-out till sometimes be linked to a computer?

25 Will a plastic card inserted in a check-out computer terminal allow money to be transferred from the customer's bank account?

RETAILING ASSIGNMENT

Work with other people in a small group to complete this assignment.

Each member of the group should make out a sample shopping list of food requirements for a family. Decide on how many members of the family the food is required for. The list should cover requirements for one week. Members of the group can have different food requirements so that a wider range of goods can be included.

Price the items on your list at:
(a) a supermarket;
(b) individually owned shops;
(c) a local retail market or street traders.

Look at the same retail establishments and note what other facilities are offered to shoppers. Include items such as delivery of goods, taking special orders, access for shoppers with prams or handicapped people with wheelchairs and toilet facilities.

Compare the retailers investigated and show:
(i)   the best prices obtainable;
(ii) the best service obtainable;
(iii) the easiest and most convenient way to shop.

Present your findings neatly in the form of a report.

Conclude with your recommendations to a person doing the shopping for a family in your area. You may conclude that different establishments are recommended for different purposes if this is what you find out.

CHAPTER 3

THE WHOLESALER

Channels of distribution

Channels (or chains) of distribution are the means by which goods are transferred from the producer, for example a farmer or manufacturer, to the eventual user who is called the consumer. The various means of transport involved are dealt with in Chapter 9, but there are also the 'intermediaries' through whose hands the goods may pass on their way between producer and consumer. The retailers we looked at in the previous chapter are intermediaries, but in some channels of distribution wholesalers are also very important.

In simple terms there are four possible channels for distributing home-produced goods within the country:

1   Producer → Wholesaler → Retailer → Consumer
       Examples: clothing and meat.

2   Producer → Retailer → Consumer
       Examples: bread and furniture.

3   Producer → Wholesaler → Consumer
       Examples: carpets and building materials.

4   Producer → Consumer
       Examples: vegetables and double-glazing.

In reality the channels used are very varied and often complex, and there is also much overlapping. For instance, you may have noted that the examples given above are often sold through one or more of the other channels as well, and deciding which channel is being used is often difficult. Is a wholesaler who sometimes sells to consumers also a retailer? If a manufacturing firm such as Boots sells its products through its own shops, is it classified as channel 2 or channel 4 above?

The work of the wholesaler

The basic role of the wholesaler is to act as an intermediary (or middleman), generally between producer and retailer. This usually means buying large quantities of goods from the producer and breaking them down into the smaller quantities required by the retailer. In carrying out this work, the wholesaler provides many services which greatly help producers and retailers, and in turn the consumers. These include:

- paying cash to the manufacturer for the goods instead of asking for credit;
- providing storage for the goods and keeping them safe until required;
- taking the risk that goods held in the wholesale warehouse may not be wanted;
- keeping prices steady, by having supplies of goods on hand to meet any rising demand or by holding surpluses;
- storing goods in warehouses and stacking for easy access;
- obtaining and displaying a large variety of goods from which retailers can choose what they need;
- arranging transport of goods to the retailer;
- giving credit (that is, allowing payment to be made later on) to the retailer;
- informing the manufacturer when there is a change in the demand for a particular product;
- informing retailers of new trends in products.

Leaving out the wholesaler

Is it possible to leave out the 'middleman'? If so the work still has to be done by someone, probably the producer. The risk-bearing and costs of storage must be met, together with those of transport and employing office staff. As this work must be done and the expenses must be borne, the price of an article need not necessarily be cheaper when the wholesaler is cut out. In fact, it would possibly be dearer, as the wholesaler's specialist skills and knowledge are lost.

In some channels of distribution, the wholesaler *is* left out and the manufacturer *does* sell the goods straight to the retailer. This often occurs in the case of large, expensive items which are difficult and costly to store, for example furniture. But it is also common in branded goods, such as confectionery, where the manufacturer wishes to ensure that the products are marketed properly in as many retail outlets as possible. Some retailers buy from manufacturers and put their own brand name on the goods.

In other cases the retailer may be left out as well as the wholesaler. One example is mail order, where manufacturers sell direct to consumers. More commonly, they operate their own retail outlets to sell their own branded products, such as shoes and clothing.

Cash-and-carry wholesalers

Retailers who use this type of wholesaler find that goods are cheaper because the retailer pays cash and has to transport the goods to his or her shop. This means a saving in the cost borne by the wholesaler, some of which can be passed on to the retailer. The wholesaler's warehouse has goods displayed in a similar way to the supermarket, but packed in bulk, and the retailer uses a large trolley or skip on wheels to move chosen goods to the checkout. The till works out the VAT due on the goods, lists each item by name and gives the price so that the retailer has a check list of all purchases made. This type of wholesaler is particularly important to small retailers who cannot buy in very large quantities, as it helps them to compete with the low prices charged by supermarket chains, especially in pre-packed food products and general household items.

A cash and carry warehouse

Wholesale markets

Items which perish quickly, such as fruit and vegetables, meat and fish, are often bought through wholesale markets where retailers and wholesalers go first thing in the morning to obtain produce. Examples are New Covent Garden at Nine Elms (fruit and vegetables), North Quay, West India Docks, Isle of Dogs (fish) and Smithfield (meat).

CHECK THIS OUT

Write out the following sentences filling in the missing words:

1 The wholesaler buys from the _____ and usually sells to the _____ .

2 Some special items such as office machinery go from the _____ to the _____ and do not need the services of the wholesaler.

3 The wholesaler stores and transports goods and keeps a variety of items for the _____ to choose from.

4 The job of a wholesaler is to buy goods in _____ quantities and to sell in _____ quantities.

5 Perishable items such as _____ and _____ are often bought through wholesale markets.

Commodity markets

Another type of wholesaler deals with raw materials such as cotton and copper ore, and the less perishable foodstuffs, such as grain and tea. Commodity markets are often known as *exchanges*. Some deal in only one commodity, such as sugar or cocoa, while others deal in several products. Most commodities have a controlling association which makes its own rules and governs its own membership, which is not open to the public. Deals are often made verbally, and a high degree of trust is given to the spoken word, which is regarded by everyone as binding.

Contracts can be made for immediate delivery of raw materials (termed *spot*) or for delivery at a stated future date (termed *futures*). Spot prices are those agreed now for goods to be delivered immediately and paid for right away, that is, 'on the spot'. Futures markets developed because the price and availability of commodities can vary greatly. A futures contract agrees that required supplies will be available in the future, at a price agreed on now. The buyer does not have the expense of storing goods until they are needed, and if prices rise and shortages develop, supplies are already guaranteed at the lower contracted price. Three of the commodity exchanges are described below.

The London Commodity Exchange

This deals in a very wide range of commodities including tea, rubber and spices. Commodities can be sold by sample or by description if they can be accurately graded. Deals are arranged by auctions or more commonly by *private treaty* – an arrangement made privately between broker and dealer. Since the makers of, for example, rubber gloves will want to know what price to charge for their product, it is possible to trade in futures for the rubber which will be used. Graded goods are guaranteed to fit the quality implied by the grade. Futures contracts are registered with the International Commodities Clearing House which guarantees completion of the contracts.

The Baltic Exchange

The main business transacted through the Baltic Exchange is the chartering of ships or shipping space, although there is also trading in items such as grain and oils. *Tramp ships*, which are ships carrying cargo to any port in the world, do not run on scheduled routes and timetables and usually carry full commodities of one cargo. They may pick up another cargo at their destination and then go to wherever that cargo is needed. A *cargo liner* is one which runs to schedule between specified ports and has room for a small number of passengers. The Baltic Exchange also provides a number of shipping services such as ship repairs and is the world's largest market for buying and selling ships. *Chartering agents* are firms who specialise in placing cargoes by hiring ships or space in ships. They act for producers and try to arrange the cheapest and fastest delivery for their goods. *Owners' brokers* are firms which act for the ship-owners. They are in touch with the chartering agents and arrange for the charter of ships, or for cargo space in them. The Baltic Exchange also arranges cargo space in aircraft: both state and private airlines carry freight chartered through the Exchange.

The London Metal Exchange

The London Metal Exchange is the largest market in the world for metals such as copper, lead, tin and zinc. Numbered seats are arranged in a circle around the rostrum and this is known as the *Ring*. Members assemble and five-minute periods are allotted to each metal several times a day. Bids are made verbally, and the clerks standing behind the dealers record the transactions. Dealing is mainly in futures.

Dealing in the London Metal
Exchange ring

Kinds of wholesaler

This chapter shows that the term 'wholesaling' covers a wide range of different activities and businesses. Many wholesalers have warehouses or other storage facilities and they deal physically with one or more commodities. Others may never handle the goods (or may deal in services such as shipping) and merely bring buyers and sellers into contact, often conducting business by telephone. There is also the distinction between those wholesalers who actually buy and sell on their own behalf (the merchants) and those who act only on behalf of others (the brokers and agents). The former hope to make a profit by selling for more than the buying price, while the latter receive a rate of commission based on the value of a transaction. A special type of agent is the *del credere*, who guarantees payment to the business for whom goods are being sold, even if a buyer fails to pay.

Write out the following sentences, filling in the missing words:

1 Ships can be chartered through the _____
   _____ .

2 Ships which carry goods regularly between
   certain ports are called _____ _____ .

3 Goods such as tea and rubber are dealt with on
   the London _____ _____ .

4 Some wholesalers never handle the goods, but
   bring _____ and _____ into contact.

5 The type of wholesaler who guarantees payment
   to the supplier of the goods is known as a
   _____ _____ agent.

Wholesale transactions

How does the retailer buy from the wholesaler? The retailer may do
one or more of the following:

- buy through an agent;
- pay a personal visit to the wholesale warehouse;
- order by telephone or post;
- order from the wholesaler's travelling representative.

The wholesaler can help the retailer in his choice of goods by
warehouse displays, catalogues with price lists, advertising in trade
journals and direct mailing of advertising leaflets. When an order is
given, the wholesaler will pack the goods in one consignment and
forward them to the retailer. An invoice will follow, and the retailer
is usually given time in which to pay, that is, credit is allowed.

In order to encourage early payment, a cash discount is allowed if
the goods are paid for within a certain time. A discount of 5 per cent
in seven days means that the retailer need only pay £95.00 for every
£100.00 if he pays within a week. Payment within a month might be
encouraged by a 2½ per cent discount, which means paying £97.50
in every £100.00. After that time, the full price must be paid. The
retailer will already have received a trade discount, for example 20
per cent, which gives him a good profit margin when he resells the
goods to his customers. In addition, some wholesalers give higher
trade discounts for buying in bulk and vary the discount according
to the quantity purchased.

---

1 Name two types of goods which are generally
  not sold through the wholesaler to the retailer.

2 What is the basic role of the wholesaler?

3 Name two commodity exchanges.

4 What is the difference between *spot* and *futures*
  contracts?

5 What are the four possible channels through
  which home-produced goods are distributed
  within the country?

6 Give two reasons why the manufacturer might sell direct to the retailer.

7 What is the difference between an ordinary agent and a *del credere* agent?

8 What is a cash-and-carry wholesaler?

9 Give two advantages to the manufacturer of selling goods through a wholesaler.

10 Give an example of an organisation which has integrated manufacturing, wholesaling and retailing.

NOW TRY THIS

Choose the correct words from a, b or c to complete each sentence, and then write out the whole sentence.

1 The function of the wholesaler is to buy from
   (a) the market
   (b) the manufacturer
   (c) the retailer.

2 The wholesaler usually pays the manufacturer
   (a) through banker's order
   (b) after the goods have been sold
   (c) as soon as the goods are delivered.

3 At his warehouse, the wholesaler
   (a) re-packs goods in quantities required by retailers
   (b) sells to the public
   (c) only sells to the retailer for cash or a cheque.

4 The wholesaler may be left out by a manufacturer who
   (a) has a factory a long way from the wholesaler
   (b) sells goods like bread and cakes
   (c) brings all his goods from abroad.

5 Cash-and-carry wholesalers are different because they
   (a) sell goods in bulk
   (b) ask the retailer to transport the goods to his shop himself
   (c) charge VAT.

6 Commodity exchanges deal with goods such as
   (a) machines sold by the manufacturer
   (b) goods bartered for each other
   (c) coffee, tea, cocoa and sugar.

7 The Baltic Exchange is
   (a) a special telephone line to Russia
   (b) a place where shipping space can be chartered
   (c) a market for perishable foodstuffs.

AIDS TO MEMORY

The Retail Chain

A manufacturer makes the goods,
The wholesaler will buy them,
To put them in a warehouse
Where retailers can try them.

A retailer who likes the goods
Will sell them in the shops
Consumers buy and use them:
The retail chain then stops.

MULTIPLE CHOICE QUESTIONS

There are four possible answers to each of the following questions. Study the introductory words, and then decide which of the alternatives correctly answers the question or completes the sentence. Write down the question number and follow it with (A) (B) (C) or (D), according to your choice.

1 The basic role of the wholesaler is to
   (A) produce goods from raw materials
   (B) sell goods to the consumer
   (C) retain a large staff of sales persons
   (D) act as an intermediary or middleman.

2 The services which a wholesaler provides to a
   manufacturer include
   (A) credit
   (B) information on the way new products are
       selling
   (C) adding components to basic goods
   (D) insurance facilities.

3 Which of the following statements about
   wholesalers is incorrect?
   (A) They will transport goods to the retailer
   (B) They will store goods in their warehouse
       until needed
   (C) They will pass on information from
       manufacturer to retailer
   (D) They only sell direct to the public

4 A cash-and-carry wholesaler does NOT provide
   (A) goods packed in bulk
   (B) check-out till with VAT worked out on the
       invoice
   (C) delivery service
   (D) a list of the items bought, together with
       itemised prices.

5 Which of these problems might arise for the
   retailer who decides to buy from the
   manufacturer and by-pass the wholesaler?
   (A) The goods cost less
   (B) The price of the commodity can be held
       steady
   (C) The goods may be in large quantities
   (D) Faulty goods may not be returnable

6 If a buyer pays within a week, a discount of 5
   per cent, 7 days on £100.00 means that the
   amount paid will be
   (A) £93.00
   (B) £95.00
   (C) £97.50
   (D) £90.00

7 An example of a commodity dealt with by a
   commodity wholesaler is
   (A) shoes
   (B) clothing
   (C) cars
   (D) tea.

8 Which one of the following is NOT an example
   of a wholesaler?
   (A) A firm which buys and sells goods which
       they never physically handle
   (B) A firm which makes wedding cakes to order
   (C) A firm which makes and stores new cars
   (D) A firm which brings buyers and sellers into
       contact

9 The channel of distribution refers to the
   (A) way goods are transported to retailers
   (B) transfer of goods from the manufacturer to
       the consumer
   (C) retailer's work in getting goods ready for
       customers
   (D) packaging of goods in the warehouse.

10 Which of the following is NOT the way the
   retailer buys from the wholesaler?
   (A) Making personal visits to all the
       manufacturers who make the goods
   (B) Ordering from the wholesaler's
       representative
   (C) Ordering by telephone
   (D) Buying through a personal visit to the
       warehouse

There are four possible answers to each of the
following questions.

If you think (1) only is correct, write down A.
If you think (1) and (2) only are correct, write down B.
If you think (3) and (4) only are correct, write down C.
If you think (2), (3) and (4) only are correct, write
down D.

11 A retailer using a cash-and-carry would have to
   (1) order through a visiting representative
   (2) make arrangements for credit
   (3) visit the wholesaler to choose the goods
   (4) transport the goods to his/her shop.

12 The wholesaler's function includes
   (1) selling in small quantities to consumers
   (2) breaking bulk into smaller units
   (3) sending a sales representative to the retailer
   (4) offering credit to the retailer.

13 The retailer may prefer to deal with a wholesale
   firm because
   (1) there is less likelihood of loss through
       damage
   (2) they offer a large choice of goods from
       different manufacturers
   (3) they break bulk and re-pack the goods
   (4) they provide storage for goods until the
       retailer needs them.

14 Wholesale markets sell
   (1) grain
   (2) fruit and vegetables
   (3) fish
   (4) meat.

STIMULUS RESPONSE QUESTIONS

The following questions carry a mark of 20. Each section of a question shows the marks for the correct response.

Trade journals, such as *The Grocer*, are full of advertisements directed at retailers by wholesalers, who are then able to make enquiries and compare samples and delivery dates for the goods offered. The wholesaler buys goods in bulk from the manufacturer, who needs to sell them quickly in order to buy more raw materials to continue producing goods. The product is stored by the wholesaler, thus sparing both the manufacturer and retailer the expense of keeping large quantities of goods. The retailer who wishes to buy a variety of goods from different manufacturers need not make a tour of the country in order to meet his or her requirements. Instead, a visit to a wholesaler to choose goods saves what might otherwise be a time-consuming and expensive business. The commercial traveller or representative will visit the retailer in order to take note of his or her requirements and persuade them to buy from a particular wholesaler.

(a) Name a trade journal? *(2 marks)*

(b) Who pays for the advertisements in the trade journals mentioned in the extract? *(2 marks)*

(c) At whom are the advertisements intended? *(2 marks)*

(d) What is the next step for a retailer who is interested in several competing advertisements? *(4 marks)*

(e) Why does the manufacturer need to sell goods quickly? *(2 marks)*

(f) What expense does the wholesaler spare both the manufacturer and the retailer? *(2 marks)*

(g) What disadvantages might a retailer face in buying direct from different manufacturers? *(4 marks)*

(h) What does a commercial traveller do? *(2 marks)*

ESSAY QUESTIONS

1 (a) What are
   (i) the advantages
   (ii) the disadvantages
   to the retailer of the cash-and-carry type of wholesaler? *(8 marks)*
  (b) Describe how the retailer buys from the cash-and-carry type of wholesaler. *(6 marks)*
  (c) Why does a retailer buy from a wholesaler, and not from the manufacturer or importer of the goods? *(6 marks)*

2 (a) Give an example of a commodity exchange. *(2 marks)*
  (b) Explain what is meant by the following terms:
   (i) spot;
   (ii) futures. *(8 marks)*
  (c) Explain how deals are carried out in a named commodity exchange. *(8 marks)*

3 (a) What are the basic functions of a wholesaler? *(10 marks)*
  (b) What advantages might be gained if a retailer left out the wholesaler? *(8 marks)*

(c) Suggest two commodities which might be sold by the manufacturer to the customer without using a wholesaler or a retailer. *(2 marks)*

4 (a) Name one wholesale market and describe the main commodity sold there. *(2 marks)*
  (b) (i) Why does the wholesaler offer discounts? *(2 marks)*
   (ii) John Jopling buys goods costing £100 from wholesaler A. He then takes advantage of 5 per cent cash discount. Donna Dobson buys goods costing £200 from wholesaler B. She then receives a 3 per cent discount. Which of the two, John or Donna, has made the biggest *cash* saving? *(3 marks)*
  (c) Why do you think the rise in the number of large retailers has led to a decline in the number of wholesalers? *(7 marks)*
  (d) George Dunkley runs a small newsagents on his own. Sales vary very little from week to week, even though the shop is open long hours. Which ways of buying his stock is he likely to find cheapest and most convenient? *(6 marks)*

LEARN IT YOURSELF

1 Using a trade directory such as *Kelly's Directory*, make a list of the names and types of wholesaler in the nearest business area to your school or college. Obtain a map of the area. Mark the wholesalers on the map, using a different symbol for each type of wholesaler. Find which wholesalers are most prevalent, and comment on the reasons for this.

2 Name two manufacturers whose transport you have seen delivering goods to local retailers. Suggest reasons why this happens.

3 Write to one of the Commodity Exchanges for information about their work and prepare a display of the information you obtain.

4 Using the *Financial Times* or a similar newspaper, chart the spot and futures prices of tea, coffee, sugar or any other commodity of your choice over the course of a week. You will find newspapers in your local library or possibly in the school/college library.

5 Look in your local trade directory for the names and addresses of cash-and-carry wholesalers in your nearest business area. Telephone and ask if you may visit to find out answers to a questionnaire. Design a questionnaire to find out: the kinds of items sold there; restrictions on people shopping there (do they have to have a card?); do they advertise by advertisements in trade journals, newspapers, leaflets through the mail to customers; the size of the wholesaler; the number of people employed; if it is part of a larger chain; etc. Draw up a short report on the wholesale warehouse from your information.

ASSIGNMENT – THE WORK OF THE WHOLESALER

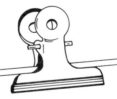

Consider setting up a small business in which you will sell products bought from a wholesaler.

Keep the idea simple, for example, a stall on your local market (details of rent from your local authority), a snack bar, a mobile sandwich service or any other idea which appeals to you.

Read anything you can find on running a small business. You will find information from banks, your local authority, books in the school and/or the public library. Some services of this nature are advertised on television.

Before you investigate setting up as a retailer, you need to decide
(a) What goods or services you might offer.
(b) Whether there is any training offered, of which you might take advantage.
(c) Who might buy your goods or services.
(d) Where you will locate your retail outlet.
(e) What overheads, such as rent, heating, lighting, you might have to pay.
(f) Whether there is any local competition in your line.

Look in *Yellow Pages* or in your local trade directory for the wholesalers of a chosen local product, or of a commodity which is in demand almost everywhere, such as catering food, drinks and snacks, baby clothes, children's wear or other ideas which appeal to you.

Ring up the wholesaler and ask if it would be convenient for you to visit them and ask questions

- about the wholesale firm itself;
- about a project investigating the possibilities of setting up as a retailer using the wholesaler's services and products.

Questions about the wholesale firm might include:

(i)   Name of company?
(ii)   Name and position of the person granting an interview?
(iii)   Does the wholesaler obtain goods from several different manufacturers?
(iv)   Are the manufacturers local firms, or do goods come from a distance?
(v)   Are any of the goods imported?
(vi)   Does the company employ sales representatives who keep in touch with the retailer?
(vii)   How does the company advertise its products?
(viii) What type of invoice does the retailer receive?
(ix)   Is the wholesaler part of a larger company?
(x)   Does the wholesaler have large storage facilities?

Questions about retailing which you might ask the wholesaler could include:

(1) Whether credit would be offered to a new retailer?
(2) Whether a new retailer would need references?
(3) What would be the minimum amount of stock the retailer could buy?
(4) What is the usual mark-up added to the goods or services as the retailer's profit?

Present all your findings neatly.

Draw any conclusions you can about the possibility in your locality of running your own business along the lines which you have investigated.

CHAPTER 4

BUSINESS DOCUMENTS

Introduction

As we have already found out, commerce is about buying and selling and all the other activities which help buying and selling to take place. Because all businesses vary in the documents they use, it is impossible to say that *all* business transactions happen in one particular way, although generally they follow the *stages* shown in this chapter. Things like the type of goods, how often the two firms do business together, how payment is made and whether the goods are for export or not affect the documents used.

Because of the millions of transactions which take place every day, it is important to write down (that is, to document) what is going on at each stage of the buying and selling process. Accurate records are essential, but keeping them is quite simple. Business transactions may be easier to understand if you think of them in terms of buying something such as a pair of jeans.

The enquiry

If you were given money to buy some new jeans, you would probably look round for the best jeans available at the price you were prepared to pay. You might find this out through posters, leaflets or television advertisements. Another way would be going from shop to shop enquiring about the price of jeans.

When businesses want to buy goods, it is not always possible to go and visit suppliers who might be hundreds of miles away. Usually a letter of enquiry is written asking about which goods are available, sizes, costs, delivery dates and whether or not discounts and credit will be given. Several suppliers will be asked and the answers compared. A transaction based on the following letter of enquiry on page 44 can be followed through as an example.

Price list or quotation

When you are looking round for your jeans, you will receive information about the prices of jeans, and you will then be in a position to make a decision on which pair to buy.

Tel: 064-888-7654	**CASTLE CARY PLC** **5 Barlow Street** **HANLEY'S FORD** **HA5 2RD**	**Telex No:** **202769**

# ENQUIRY TO Brookside PLC Mosstown MANCHESTER	DATE 17 February 1988 ENQUIRY NUMBER D186/719 DELIVERY ADDRESS: 5 Barlow Street HANLEY'S FORD HA5 2RD

Please quote your price and delivery date for the following goods or services as specified:

Quantity	Description
50	Teddy bears
25	Soldier-boy

_____ (Signed)
for Castle Cary PLC

A firm employs a *buyer* who will receive price lists and catalogues from the suppliers who received the enquiry. These will give answers to the questions asked. If the trade is one where prices change very often (for example fruit, wines and vegetables), a *prices current* is issued. This is a way of telling buyers that prices on the list apply only at the present time.

As you will probably do when buying your jeans, a sensible buyer compares the prices which the sellers have quoted and then chooses the most suitable one. This leads to the placing of the order.

PRICE LIST

Brookside PLC
Mosstown
MANCHESTER M1 9GJ

Telephone 061 689-1234
Telex MNCR 12323

Description	Price per 100	Recommended retail price
Teddy bears 45 cm high, velvet paws	£1000	£24.99
Soldier-boy, blue or red uniform	£1000	£24.99
Keep-Fit Lindy doll	£1500	£29.99
Thomas the Tank Engine train set	£2000	£39.95
Teary Tina baby doll	£2250	£44.99
Doll's perambulator, blue/mink	£2500	£49.99
Desk and four chairs (set)	£2750	£54.95
Pedal car, orange or peacock	£3000	£59.95

Delivery: transport to own premises

Terms: trade discount 10%
cash discount $2\frac{1}{2}$%

The order

The order is sent on the firm's specially printed order forms and clearly explains what quantity and type of goods the buyer requires. Sometimes the order will contain a request for a particular delivery date. Note that the total price is not shown. At least one copy will be kept for reference. The order will have a reference number to identify it from all the other documents and orders which the firm might have to deal with, and it will be signed and dated.

Tel:	CASTLE CARY PLC	Telex No:
064-888-7654	5 Barlow Street	202769
	HANLEY'S FORD	
	HA5 2RD	

ORDER FORM

Date ...... 24 February 1988 ......

To

Brookside PLC
Mosstown
MANCHESTER

Order number   39876

PLEASE SUPPLY AND DELIVER TO THE
ABOVE ADDRESS THE FOLLOWING GOODS

Description	Quantity	Unit price	Total
Teddy bears	50	£10.00	£500.00
Soldier-boy	25	£10.00	£250.00
			£750.00

GOODS WILL ONLY BE ACCEPTED
ON PRODUCTION OF AN OFFICIAL
ORDER NUMBER

Terms of payment: $2\frac{1}{2}\%$ one month, 5% 7 days

Signed .... Purchasing Officer
Castle Cary PLC

If you were purchasing jeans, this is the stage which is equivalent to
going into the shop and asking for the jeans you have decided to buy
(giving your order).

Acknowledgement

A seller will sometimes write to the buyer confirming that the order has been received and is being attended to. If the goods are to be sold on credit to a new customer, it is at this stage that the seller will check the buyer's *creditworthiness*. This means that the seller will ask the buyer for some kind of reference, perhaps from a bank, which shows that the firm has been conducting its financial affairs in a proper manner.

If you buy jeans and pay by cheque rather than cash, the seller will probably ask if you have a cheque card, with which your bank guarantees payment of that cheque.

CHECK THIS OUT

Write out the following sentences, filling in the missing words:

1 Many transactions involving buying and selling take place every day in business. It is important to keep accurate _____ and write down what happens.

2 The first move in buying and selling is to send an enquiry to various firms asking how much goods will _____ and when they can be _____.

3 The seller gives a _____ to the person enquiring about the cost of goods.

4 If the quotation is acceptable, the buyer places an _____ with the seller.

5 When an order is being attended to, the seller sends the buyer an _____ to show the order has been received.

Advice note

Once the seller is satisfied about the buyer's creditworthiness, an advice note will be sent telling the buyer that the goods have been despatched. As this document is usually a copy of what is on the invoice, it provides an opportunity for the buyer to spot any mistakes, which can be corrected quickly, and to prepare the necessary space for the goods when they arrive.

If you were buying jeans by post, the use of an advice note would be unlikely unless there was some delay in completing your order.

Invoice

The invoice can be sent with the goods, it may be sent in advance to act as an advice note or it may follow the goods separately. The invoice shows in detail what quantity and type of items have been sent. As well as this, the invoice shows the price of each item and the total cost of a number of items. If any cash discounts are given, this is usually shown as 'Terms . . .' (see Chapter 3, page 37).

The buyer can see by glancing at the bottom of the invoice how much the total price for the goods will be. The invoice will be checked against the buyer's copy of the order, which is particularly important for a complicated order. The goods will also be checked against the invoice to make sure that everything charged for has been sent.

In the case of your jeans, if a cash transaction took place in a shop, then there would be no invoice as such, but the amount rung up on the till would indicate how much you owed. However, if mail order were used, you would receive a separate invoice in the case of payment after receipt of the goods.

INVOICE

Brookside PLC
Mosstown
MANCHESTER M1 9GJ

Telephone 061 689-1234
Telex MNCR 12323

DATE   1 March 1988

TO: Castle Cary PLC
        5 Barlow Street
        HANLEY'S FORD
        HA5 2RD

INVOICE NUMBER   K82/498

YOUR ORDER NUMBER   39876

Quantity	Description	Unit Price	Total Price
50	Teddy bears	£10.00	£500.00
25	Soldier-boy	£10.00	£250.00
	GOODS TOTAL		£750.00
	PLUS VAT @ 15%		£112.50
	INVOICE TOTAL		£862.50
	E & OE		
	Terms of payment: $2\frac{1}{2}\%$ one month 5% 7 days		

Statement

A statement is usually sent out at the end of each month from the seller to the buyer. It sums up all the transactions which have been made in a month (but individual items are *not* indicated) and shows any amount still outstanding from the previous statement. The statement gives the total amount of money due on each invoice and whether or not any payment has been received or credit notes issued (see page 50). The final total takes payments (credits) away from the various amounts owed (debits) and shows the final figure remaining to be paid. The statement usually reminds the buyer of the advantages to be gained by prompt payment by showing 'Terms...' again.

STATEMENT

Telephone 061 699-1234
Telex MNCR 12323

Brookside PLC
Mosstown
MANCHESTER M1 9GJ

TO: Castle Cary PLC
5 Barlow Street
HANLEY'S FORD HA5 2RD

Account Number 12323

Date 30 April 1988

Date	Goods	Debit	Credit	Balance
1988				
1 March	Goods supplied on Invoice No K82/498	£862.50		£862.50
6 March	Returns 3 items Credit Note CN82/498		£30.00	£832.50
	VAT		£ 4.50	£828.00
	E & OE			

The amount now due is the last figure in the column headed 'Balance'.

If you were buying jeans from a shop, the statement of account is the bill which is either written out on a pad or produced by the till.

Discount

Traders will often use various methods to attract custom. Two long-standing methods in the reduction of prices by giving discounts are used, and there are two main types of discount:

- *Trade discount* – this is usually given by the seller to buyers who buy in large quantities. Buyers will normally be told that orders over a certain minimum will receive a reduction of *x* per cent. This brings down the cost of each item and so helps shops, particularly large ones, to sell goods cheaply.

- *Cash discount* – this is a discount given by the seller to buyers who pay quickly. Details of the cash discount available may appear as 'Terms $2\frac{1}{2}\%$ one month' on the invoice and statement. The terms may vary, and in this particular case it means that if payment is made in one month, $2\frac{1}{2}$ per cent will be taken off the amount owed. This encourages the buyer to pay promptly.

Payment

Once the buyer has received the statement, he or she will realise that payment should be made quickly if the firm is to get the benefit of cash discount. Usually a cheque will be sent through the post but a bank giro credit might be used.

If you were buying jeans, you would normally pay by cash, cheque (with cheque card) or credit card over the counter.

Receipt

In business, receipts are important as they provide proof that payments have been made. They are issued by creditors (sellers) and show the date, amount paid and type of goods. A receipt is not always issued for payment by cheque. This is because a cheque works its way quickly through the banking system and appears on the buyer's bank statement as proof of payment. Receipts will usually be issued for any payments not passing through bank accounts.

In the case of your jeans, the till print-out will often act as a receipt as well as a bill, but a written bill might be used and signed as paid. If any dispute arises the receipt is proof that the goods have been bought and paid for on a particular day at a particular shop.

Credit note

Suppose you took your jeans home and found a stitching fault that you had not noticed in the shop. You could take them back to the shop and ask for a refund of your money. Alternatively the shopkeeper might offer a credit note which you could (if you wish) accept. You could spend the credit note on another pair of jeans or on other goods in the same shop, but if you did not see anything else which you wanted, you could return some time in the future to use it.

Likewise in business, goods may sometimes be delivered in an unsatisfactory condition, or in smaller quantities than shown on the invoice. If this happens, the buyer will contact the seller, who will issue the buyer with a credit note to the amount owed. Credit notes are also used for returned packing cases, 'empties', etc., and where goods wrongly supplied are sent back. The value of such credit notes will be set against the buyer's debts when the next statement is sent. As the credit note is given by the seller to the buyer to represent money, it is often printed in red to make it stand out.

CREDIT NOTE

Telephone 061 699-1234
Telex MNCR 12323

Brookside PLC
Mosstown
MANCHESTER M1 9GJ

TO: Castle Carey PLC
     5 Barlow Street
     HANLEY'S FORD HA5 2RD

Credit Note   CN82/498
Invoice Number   K82/498
Date   8 March 1988

Quantity	Description	Unit Price	Total Price
3	Teddy bears Packing damaged and returned	£10.00	£30.00
	VAT		4.50
	TOTAL PRICE		£34.50
	E & OE Carriage paid		

Debit note

This is the opposite to a credit note. If the buyer is undercharged, a debit note will be issued to claim the extra money outstanding. The seller has a right to do this if the letters 'E & OE' are printed on the invoice. This means 'Errors and Omissions Excepted', so if delivered items are left off or pricing errors are made on the invoice, the seller can charge the extra amount later. In these circumstances, a debit note will be issued. In practice, it usually takes the shape of an extra invoice for the extra amount of money involved.

DEBIT NOTE

Telephone 061 699-1234
Telex MNCR 12323

Brookside PLC
Mosstown
MANCHESTER M1 9GJ

DR TO: Castle Carey PLC
        5 Barlow Street
        HANLEY'S FORD HA5 2RD

Date   10 February 1988

1988		£
3 February	To 3 cases, charged on your Invoice Number K82/470 and returned by own transport.	4.50

CHECK THIS OUT

Write out the following sentences, filling in the missing words:

1 In business, if the buyer receives broken goods or a smaller quantity of items than has been invoiced, then a _____ note is sent to the buyer from the seller.

2 If the buyer receives more goods than those ordered and invoiced, and decides to keep them, the seller will issue a _____ note for the extra money involved.

3 A _____ sums up all the transactions in a given period between a buyer and a seller.

4 After receiving a statement, _____ is made by the buyer to the seller.

5 In business, the buyer can prove that goods have been paid for by producing a _____ for the money.

AIDS TO MEMORY

First an enquiry, second a quote
Send off the order, get advice note.
After the goods come, check that they're right
Invoice, then statement, pay it tonight!

Credit note is red
Use as cash instead.
Debit note is black –
You must pay it back.

SHORT QUESTIONS

1 Complete the missing words in the following sentence to show the correct sequence of business documents: 'The sequence of business documents is: enquiry _____ _____ acknowledgement _____ _____ statement.'

2 Briefly describe the work of a buyer in a business.

3 Why is a statement sent out to businesses?

4 Which method of payment does not need a receipt? Why is this?

5 Why will a seller take copies of an invoice?

6 What two things are special about a credit note?

7 When would a *prices current* be used?

8 When might a receipt for payment not be given?

9 What is the difference between a statement and an invoice?

10 Give two instances where a firm might issue a debit note.

NOW TRY THIS

Each person in the class works with a partner.

• Partner A sends a short, written letter of enquiry to Partner B.

• Partner B replies with a quotation.

• Partner A then sends a written order, using a form if preferred.

• Partner B sends an invoice for the goods given on the order.

STIMULUS RESPONSE QUESTIONS

The following questions carry a mark of 20. Each section of a question shows the marks for the correct response.

1 Study the following document and answer the questions on it:

CHARLESTOWN GARAGE

Motor Engineers
381 Dunkerley Road
CHARLESTOWN

TO: Miss J Martin

DATE: 28 February 19..   INVOICE NUMBER 616833

TO: Amount

    carrying out full service to motor vehicle
SVU 315Y:

Changing engine oil
Fitting new filter (oil)
Fitting new filter (air)
Reset brakes   £42.30

ADD: VAT at 15%   ─────────

                                               ─────────

(a) What type of document is this?   (*2 marks*)

(b) What kind of firm sent out this document
                                         (*2 marks*)

(c) Is the firm working in industry or commerce
                                         (*2 marks*)

(d) How much would VAT at 15 per cent be
     (to the nearest penny)?   (*7 marks*)

(e) What would be the total price
                                         (*7 marks*)

2 Study the following document and answer the questions on it:

ORDER NUMBER 98317			A T Jackson & Son Ltd Ashton Road East LEICESTER DATE _____
TO J Munro PLC 22 Gilmartin Drive LEICESTER			Please supply the following goods:

Cat. No.	Quantity	Description	Unit price £
R29	10	Quilt cover, cream/pink 54 × 78	32.99
R28	10	Fitted sheet, cream/pink 54 × 78	28.99
R27	20	Pillow cases, cream/pink 19 × 29	9.99 (pair)

(a) What type of document is this? *(2 marks)*

(b) What would be the total price for each item? *(6 marks)*

(c) What would be the total price for all the goods? *(3 marks)*

(d) Take away 20 per cent Trade Discount from the total goods price. *(3 marks)*

(e) Add 15 per cent Sales Tax (VAT). *(3 marks)*

(f) A T Jackson & Son took advantage of the 5% discount 7 days by paying at once. How much did the firm pay? *(3 marks)*

3 (a) Design an invoice form from J Munro PLC (see Question 2) and send it to A T Jackson for supplying the goods on their order number 98317. *(12 marks)*

(b) Add the letters 'E & OE' and on a separate piece of paper, state what this means. *(4 marks)*

(c) One of the quilts has been returned by the buyer, as it has a fault. What discount would now be issued, and for how much? *(4 marks)*

ESSAY QUESTIONS

1 (a) Name four documents which might be used in a business transaction. *(4 marks)*

(b) Explain why each document is used. *(10 marks)*

(c) (i) Why are receipts important to a customer? *(2 marks)*

(ii) What does a receipt show? *(2 marks)*

(iii) Why are receipts not always issued when payment is made by cheque? *(2 marks)*

2 (a) Explain the difference between:
(i) an enquiry and an order; *(4 marks)*
(ii) a credit note and a debit note; *(4 marks)*
(iii) a price list and a quotation. *(4 marks)*

(b) How does the seller persuade the buyer to pay promptly? *(4 marks)*

(c) A supplier may issue a catalogue and separate price lists. Suggest reasons for this. *(4 marks)*

3 You are employed as a buying clerk by J Munro PLC.

(a) Explain the purpose of the following business documents which you use:
(i) price list with catalogue; *(2 marks)*
(ii) enquiry form; *(2 marks)*
(iii) order form. *(2 marks)*

(b) When an order has been placed, what business documents would you expect to receive? *(6 marks)*

(c) Explain the following two statements which may appear on an invoice:
(i) E & OE; *(2 marks)*
(ii) 5% 7 days, 2% one month. *(4 marks)*

(d) When the invoice has been received, what steps will the buyer take to check that the goods are as required? *(2 marks)*

4 (a) Explain how an advice note is issued.
(5 marks)

(b) What details appear on an invoice? *(5 marks)*

(c) An accounts department clerk is notified that some goods stated on the invoice were not despatched. How would the clerk put this right? *(4 marks)*

(d) The same clerk finds that the price of an item has been left off the invoice and omitted from the total of goods. The buyer has already paid for the goods. How would the clerk put the mistake right? *(4 marks)*

(e) What document would the accounts clerk send to the businesses being dealt with to show the transactions for the past month and any amounts outstanding? *(2 marks)*

LEARN IT YOURSELF

1 Collect samples of business documents (marking each one 'SAMPLE') by writing, telephoning or visiting firms and asking for examples. Make a display of business documents in the order in which they would be used to buy and pay for goods.

2 You are going to start your own business. Design the documents you will need. Give your firm a name and perhaps a 'logo' (a design to suggest the business you are in).

3 Design a wall chart to show the course of a business transaction from start to finish.

4 Collect leaflets from your local post office and local bank on the methods of payment they offer. Suggest which methods might be most useful for (a) someone starting up in business; (b) an established business.

5 Design a list of rules for office staff to remember when sending business letters and forms to other firms. You may need to read up information on business letters in books in the library. You may use the headings 'DO' and 'DO NOT' for your rules.

CHAPTER 5

BUSINESS OWNERSHIP

The two sectors

There are essentially two different ways of organising a system of business enterprise:

- A *capitalist* system in which most aspects of business are the responsibility of *private enterprise*. The owners of businesses take the risk of investing their own money, and any profit (after taxes and debts have been paid) belongs to them.

- A *socialist* system in which the State runs the main business enterprise. The profit then belongs to the people.

In fact no country has a system that is completely capitalist or completely socialist. In the United Kingdom we have what is known as a *mixed economy*: that is, a system with a mixture of private and state control. The two groups are referred to as the private and public sectors. they are subdivided as follows:

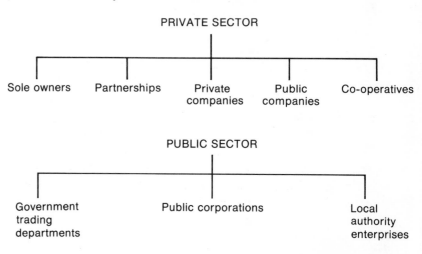

The United Kingdom is usually called a capitalist economy because a large proportion of business enterprise is under private control, but a number of important areas, such as coal mining and the railways, are under public control. Since 1979 the Government has reduced the public sector by selling shares in businesses previously owned by the State. These have included British Telecom, British Gas and British Airways. As the ownership of these concerns was transferred to private individuals and organisations the process was called 'privatisation'.

People who favour 'privatisation' believe that the private sector is able to provide goods and services more efficiently than the public sector. People who hold this point of view believe that the private sector is able to respond more quickly to the needs of the consumer and so provide greater choice. Opponents of privatisation argue that State assets are owned by rich and poor alike and so should not be sold to only those who can afford it as this is unfair. A further argument is that large organisations like British Telecom are so important that the State should control them rather than a group of people seeking to make money for themselves. Some people fear that the unprofitable services provided by companies in the public sector will disappear if they are privatised. An example is the concern over the future of telephone boxes in rural areas. These are needed by the public, but because they make little money there is some concern that they might be removed.

The State continues to provide many services that might not be provided for those unable to afford them, such as health care, and some services (such as railways) benefit from State control as unprofitable services can be maintained to satisfy public demand.

To understand fully how the public and private sectors exist together it will be easier to consider each one separately and look closely at each sub-group within it. Before this is done, the meanings of two phrases used to distinguish the various business units must be understood.

1   Limited liability

This means that a business owner's loss is limited to the amount he or she invests in the business, should it become insolvent. If an owner had 'unlimited' liability, he or she would then be liable for all the debts of the business, even to the extent of selling personal possessions. A person with limited liability does not have this worry. A firm where the owners have limited liability must put PLC after its name if it is a *public* limited company. A private limited company must either have Limited, or its abbreviation Ltd., after its name. This acts as a warning to the firm's creditors that, if the firm goes bankrupt, they may not receive all that is owed to them.

If the owner of a business has limited liability then they must be liable for any debts

2   Body corporate

If this term applies to a business, it means that in the eyes of the law it is recognised as being separate from its owners. For example, if a business had four shareholders, the law would recognise the business as a separate legal entity, existing apart from the four shareholders.

The first Boots shop

The private sector

The sole owner

We begin with the *sole owner*, sometimes called the *sole proprietor*. The sole owner is the only person who owns the business, and he or she does not have any other boss. There may, however, be other employees working in the business. The sole owner is, in fact, the oldest and most common type of business unit. A famous example is Boots, the Chemist, which started as a business with a sole owner in 1850. It expanded into a large limited liability company and now employs many thousands of people, doing business in many countries. Although many people think of a corner shop as a typical business with a sole owner, there are many other businesses, such as small building firms, joiners, plumbers and electricians who only have one owner and a number of employees. Small engineering firms, hairdressers and travel agents can also be businesses with a sole proprietor.

Advantages of the sole owner

- It is easy to set up in business.
- The owner can give the business personal attention and make decisions quickly.
- All the profits belong to the owner, so the owner has a greater interest in the success of the business.

Disadvantages of the sole owner

- The business is not a separate legal entity and the owner has unlimited liability (see page 57).
- The owner has to provide the money to start the business, whether his or her own savings or by borrowing from a bank or friends.
- The firm ends when the owner dies.

The partnership

A way for a sole trader to expand is to form a *partnership*. This is governed by the Partnership Act of 1890. While a partnership is still easy to establish, it is recommended that a *partnership agreement* is drawn up. This document, sometimes known as the *partnership deed*, gives details such as the amount of salary to be paid to the partners, the amount of money (capital) invested and the firm's trading name. It also states the type of trade in which it is engaged; whether or not interest is to be paid on the capital invested; and how profits and losses are to be shared.

The partnership is not a popular form of business organisation but is often used by doctors, dentists, solicitors and other professional people.

Advantages of the partnership

- Although a partnership can have a personal flavour, it is able to draw on more capital than a sole owner.

- Any losses can be spread among the partners and not be the responsibility of one person.

- A person with flair for a particular aspect of the business can concentrate on that one aspect, creating greater efficiency.

- Even in small partnerships, if one person is ill or on holiday, there is still someone to carry on the business.

Disadvantages of the partnership

- Decisions may be delayed by disagreements because a number of people are involved.

- Partners have unlimited liability (but see 'limited partnership' below).

- Capital in a partnership could be fairly limited.

- If the partners change or one of them dies, a new partnership agreement is required.

- One partner's decisions can be binding on the other partners.

Under the 1907 Limited Partnership Act, a *general* partnership (as described above) may be transformed into a *limited* partnership, in which some partners may only put up capital. Their liability for loss is then limited to the amount of capital which they subscribe. These partners can share the profits but have no say in the running of the business. Partners who take no part in managing the business, whether they are limited or general partners, are sometimes referred to as *sleeping partners*. In all limited partnerships, at least one partner must still be a general partner with unlimited liability. However, limited partnerships are very uncommon, as the private limited company has become the preferred type of organisation for smaller businesses owned by two or more persons.

The private company

The private company fills the gap between the partnership and the large public company. Private companies first came into being under the Companies Act of 1907, which allowed companies with a minimum of two members and a maximum of 50, although the 1980 Companies Act removed this upper limit. The private company is popular because it is both a separate legal entity (i.e. it is a body corporate – unlike sole proprietors and partnerships) and it can offer limited liability to all its members (shareholders), although unlimited companies do exist. Because it is a separate legal entity, it has greater continuity than other units so far described, and with its large membership is able to raise more capital. Private companies are not allowed to advertise shares for sale to the general public and their internal rules (Articles of Association) *can* restrict the shareholders' freedom to transfer shares to anyone outside the company. Limited private companies are always required to submit accounts annually to the Registrar of Companies, but *unlimited* private companies are not. Private companies do not require a trading certificate to commence business, as public companies do, and there is no minimum £50 000 capital requirement which applies to public companies. If a company feels that it needs to expand further, it becomes a *public company*: for example, Marks & Spencer PLC.

The public company

The largest businesses in the private sector are controlled by public companies. The minimum number of shareholders is two and there is no maximum (as in private companies), but the most important difference is that they can raise finance from the public by advertising shares. The shares are freely transferable, and in the case of many of the larger companies they can be bought and sold by shareholders through the Stock Exchange (see Chapter 6). Shareholders in *all* public companies have the benefit of limited liability, and full accounts have to be sent annually to the Registrar of Companies. The Registrar controls closely the setting up of public companies and will allow them to commence by issuing a trading certificate only when he or she is satisfied that adequate finance has been raised from the sale of shares. Certain minimum qualifications or experience are also required for public company secretaries (such as an accountancy qualification or a law degree: these 'secretaries' do not type letters), and there are strict laws about 'insider' dealings in company shares. Such dealings occur when persons closely involved in the operation of a company, for example directors, use inside information to make gains for themselves or others from deals in the company's shares. An instance of this might be a director who knows that his firm's shares will go up when it announces, say, the discovery of a new oil well, but cannot legally buy or advise his or her friends to buy shares while they are cheap in anticipation of the rise. Company directors are elected to the board of directors by the shareholders, and the board is then responsible for running the business.

The advantages of the public company

- The business is a separate legal entity with limited liability for all shareholders, which encourages the public to invest.
- The business can sell shares and debentures (loans) to the general public, which raises a lot of financial capital.
- Banks are normally more prepared to lend money to public companies as they are a 'good risk'.
- The business has the money to attract specialists to work for the company in such fields as marketing, accounting and personnel.

The disadvantages of the public company

- A public company is expensive to set up because of all the legal requirements.

- Decisions are delayed because of the amount of administration involved, whereas the sole owner could take decisions 'on the spot'.

- A feeling may arise in employees and customers of being out of touch because the business is so large, and efficiency and sales may suffer.

- The directors have to account for the business performance to the shareholders each year at the Annual General Meeting.

NOW TRY THIS

Complete the following sentences by choosing (A) (B) or (C) and write out the whole sentence:

1 In the United Kingdom we have what is known as a
   (A) mixed economy
   (B) capitalist system
   (C) socialist system.

2 If a business owner's loss should the business become insolvent is limited to the amount he or she invests in the business, it is known as
   (A) a private limited company
   (B) a body corporate
   (C) limited liability.

3 The sole owner is
   (A) a term applied only to the owner of a corner shop
   (B) the only person who owns the business
   (C) a business in which only one person, the owner, works.

4 A partnership is a type of organisation where
   (A) there are only two partners in the business
   (B) each partner must work in the business
   (C) professional people expand from being sole proprietors.

5 A private company
   (A) must have more than 55 members
   (B) fills the gap between the partnership and the large public company
   (C) can advertise shares for sale to the general public.

6 A public company
   (A) is a separate legal entity with limited liability for all shareholders
   (B) has no minimum number of shareholders
   (C) is inexpensive to set up.

Starting a company

Two documents must be drawn up in order to set up a company: the Memorandum of Association and the Articles of Association.

The memorandum of association

The memorandum of association governs the company's relationship with the outside world. The main contents are:

- the name of the company, ending with PLC for a public company, or Ltd., where relevant, for a private company, warning anyone dealing with the company that they cannot claim against any individual shareholder's private possessions;

- a statement, where relevant, that the company is to be public;

- the location of the company's registered office;

- the objects of the company – claims may be made against the company if it goes beyond these stated objects;
- a statement of limited liability for its shareholders (where relevant);
- the amount of capital to be raised by issuing shares (the authorised capital), showing the minimum of £50 000 in the case of a public company.

Articles of association

The articles are concerned with the internal running of the company and may include such matters as:

- the procedure for calling a meeting of shareholders;
- the rights and obligations of directors;
- how the directors, chairperson and managing director of the company are chosen;
- the borrowing powers of the company;
- the allocation of voting rights to shareholders.

The Companies Acts, 1948 to 1980

Company Limited by Shares

Articles of Association

Of

B.E.C. Company Limited

Preliminary

1   Regulations 2, 3, 24, 53, 75, 88, 107, 108, 110 and 134 of Part I of Table A (hereinafter referred to as "Part I of Table A") shall not apply to the Company, but the Articles hereinafter contained together with the remaining regulations of Part I of Table A of the First Schedule of the Companies Act 1948 as amended by the Companies Act 1980 subject to the modifications hereinafter expressed, shall constitute the regulations of the Company.

Capital

2   The initial share capital of the Company is £1000 divided into 1000 shares of £1 each.

3   The shares of the Company, whether forming part of the original capital or any increased capital, may be allotted or otherwise disposed of to such persons and for such consideration and upon such terms as the Directors may determine subject, in the case of any shares forming part of any increased capital, to such directions as to the allotment or disposal thereof as may be given by the Company in general meeting at the time of the creation of such shares.

Extract from an articles of association document

Certificate of incorporation

The memorandum and the articles are forwarded to the Registrar of Companies, together with a statutory declaration by the company's promoters that they have complied with the requirements of the various Companies Acts. If the Registrar agrees and all the documents are in order, a *certificate of incorporation* is issued. This establishes the company as a separate legal entity and it becomes a body corporate.

Issuing shares

The company will need some finance to start business which it obtains by issuing shares. In the case of a private company, this is usually only a matter of selling shares to the persons who have agreed to set up the company. Public companies are often set up by converting private companies and additional shares may not be issued. However, if more finance is needed, or if it is a completely new company, then a prospectus issue or an 'offer for sale' may be arranged (see page 67). Advertisements are placed in newspapers such as the *Financial Times* or *The Guardian*, and people apply to buy the shares offered. More details on the issuing of shares are given on pages 64–7.

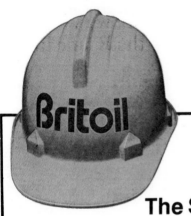

As mentioned above, many public companies have their shares quoted on the Stock Exchange, but this is not automatic and they must apply for the privilege. The Stock Exchange will carry out a thorough investigation of the company, in order to offer some protection to prospective shareholders, and even then the new shares cannot be sold directly on the Exchange. They are first purchased by investors, but can then be resold on the Exchange if desired (see Chapter 6). If a company has requested a quotation, then its shares will be more popular as they can be readily sold.

It is only when the Registrar is satisfied that the public company has raised enough money to have a reasonable chance of starting successfully that a trading certificate is issued, allowing it to commence business.

What are shares

When investors buy shares in a company, they receive a *share certificate* indicating the number of shares they own and, in return for the finance they have provided, they may receive a *dividend* on the shares yearly or twice yearly. There are different types of share which appeal to different types of investor. Some individuals may choose to take a share with more risk attached, but with the prospect of large returns; whereas others prefer a more secure, steady income.

CERTIFICATE NUMBER	TRANSFER No.		DATE OF REGISTRATION	NUMBER OF SHARES
1659	00711	671	20MAY80	---10---

CERTIFICATE FOR ORDINARY SHARES

MANCHESTER UNITED
FOOTBALL CLUB LIMITED
(INCORPORATED UNDER THE COMPANIES ACTS, 1862 TO 1900)

This is to Certify that ROBERT DEREK CALROW ESQ

is/are the Registered Holder(s) of TEN---

Ordinary Shares of £1 each in the Company, subject to the Memorandum and Articles of Association thereof

Given under the Common Seal of the said Company

Exd........

NOTE: NO TRANSFER OF ANY OF THE SHARES COMPRISED IN THIS CERTIFICATE WILL BE REGISTERED UNTIL THE CERTIFICATE HAS BEEN SURRENDERED TO THE COMPANY'S REGISTRARS, NATIONAL WESTMINSTER BANK LIMITED, REGISTRAR'S DEPARTMENT, PO BOX 82, 37 BROAD STREET, BRISTOL BS99 7NH

CE/874/A/--

BURRUP, MATHIESON & CO. LTD. LONDON S526944B

An example of a share certificate. This one is for ten ordinary shares in Manchester United Football Club

1   Ordinary shares

These are sometimes called *equities*. There is considerable risk attached to them, as they may not be repaid in full if the company closes down and the dividend is not fixed. The dividend income is paid only when all other claims on the profits have been met, but this income can be quite high if the company is doing well. The price of the shares on the Stock Exchange may also climb rapidly if the earnings are high, until it is much higher than the nominal (par) value as shown on the share certificate. Shares which are less secure are sometimes called *risk capital*. Ordinary shares generally carry voting rights, unlike most other shares, and there is normally one vote per share, so that someone holding more than 50 per cent of these shares would control the company. Companies do not have to declare a dividend, for example in cases where a company makes a loss or only a small profit.

2   Preference shares

The owners of these shares receive preference over ordinary shareholders when the dividend is being paid, and also in the repayment of their capital if the company closes down. Normally, these shares carry a fixed rate and are useful for people who want a steady income. Preference shares are therefore safer than ordinary shares, but the share price does not increase very much because they do not have the chance of high earnings. Generally they have no voting rights. There are special versions of these shares:

(a) *Cumulative* have the right to any arrears of dividends from previous years when profits were insufficient. The fixed rate of dividend paid for each year means that the shareholders are normally certain of receiving a return on these shares unless the company goes into liquidation.
(b) *Non-cumulative* do not have any right to arrears of dividend.
(c) *Redeemable* will be repaid by the company in the future, and they can be bought back from the shareholders either out of accumulated profits or from the money received from a fresh issue of shares. This type of share is used to help to start a company.

3   Deferred shares

Deferred shares are sometimes issued to the promoters or founders of a company. A family business may use them to give special rights and privileges to members of the family to ensure that they keep the controlling voting rights over ordinary shares. They may also ensure that their share of the profits is very favourable. These are also known as *founders' shares*.

New issues

Going public

Companies which wish to expand and develop must consider ways of raising extra finance. Sometimes it may be sufficient to re-invest profits in the company or take out a loan, but for any substantial expansion it is usually necessary for the company to issue shares.

Private companies are not allowed to advertise shares for sale, and this prevents them from raising money in this way. For this reason, an expanding private company may decide to convert to becoming a public company, or *go public*, as it is known. At the same time it may apply to the Stock Exchange to allow its shares to be dealt in on the Exchange. This will help to make the shares more popular, as people know that they can sell them easily through the Exchange and that the company's background has been thoroughly investigated. Many companies, which are already public, are not listed on the Exchange, and these companies sometimes apply for a quotation which will make a new share issue attractive to investors and allow them to expand more readily.

Before the Stock Exchange Council will approve a new quotation, the company will first have to show evidence of a good trading record and sound financial prospects. The company must usually be worth at least half a million pounds before the Stock Exchange is likely to grant a quotation, as it is uneconomic to advertise small issues of shares.

The actual issue of new shares is a complex and expensive undertaking. Firms will usually employ the services of a merchant bank which specialises in new issues. These *issuing houses*, as they are called, undertake full responsibility for the issuing of the new shares and collecting payment for them. There are five basic methods which can be used when issuing new shares:

1   Rights issue

A rights issue allows existing shareholders in a company to buy up the new shares in proportion to the number of shares they already hold – for example, the right to buy one new share for every ten shares already held. An *open offer* does not limit the number of shares which can be bought by individual shareholders. Issuing by 'rights' has the advantage of being more economical to administer. Details of the share issue are sent to all existing shareholders, and they apply to purchase them directly from the company or through an issuing house.

2   Placing

If an issuing house believes that the shares on offer can be placed with a few large institutional investors or other clients, it will circulate details of the shares to them, often using the services of a stockbroking firm. As these institutional investors tend to buy shares in very large blocks, the issue can be disposed of, and finance raised, quickly and economically.

3 Prospectus

A prospectus can be drawn up and circulated, for example through stockbrokers to their clients, and it will often be published in the national press as well. A prospectus gives details of the company's development, past profits and prospects for the future. An application form is included, and if members of the public feel they wish to subscribe, they can apply. All applications are opened on the same day, *issue day*. This must be at least three days after the prospectus has been published.

4 Offer for sale

In this method, the issuing house first buys the shares and then resells them using a prospectus as in method 3 above. The advantage to the company is that it receives its finance without having to worry whether the share issue will be fully subscribed. This is now more usual than the prospectus method.

When methods 3 and 4 are used, the public also have the benefit of comments in the financial press as well as the information contained in the actual prospectus, before the issuing of the shares.

5 Tendering

Very often the newly issued shares are sold again very quickly by speculators who wish to make a quick profit. These *stags*, as they are called, buy the shares at the issue price in anticipation that the price at which they are then quoted on the Stock Exchange will be significantly higher.

In order to limit this, the issuing house can invite tenders. The offer for sale or prospectus is again used, but it invites applications, not at a fixed price, but at or above a stated minimum price. This means that potential shareholders have to offer a price which they think is reasonable and which is high enough to obtain some of the shares. When all the tenders or bids have been received, the issuing house looks at the prices offered and fixes a suitable price (the *striking price*) which will allow all the shares to be disposed of. Those people who *tender* at or above the striking price receive some of, or all of, the shares they wanted. Those whose bid is too low receive their money back. By using this method, the company ensures that the highest possible price at the time is obtained. This means that the financial benefits which the 'stags' might have had will come, instead, to the company.

Speculators

A speculator is a person who deals in shares with the intention of making a profit by buying and selling in a short period. Apart from the stags mentioned above, there are two other kinds of speculators, known as bulls and bears.

Bulls are speculators who believe that the price of certain shares will soon rise, and they buy shares so that they can be sold later at a profit.

Bears are the opposite of bulls and they sell shares for delivery at a future date, hoping that the price will fall. Since the bear does not actually possess the shares, but is hoping to buy some at a lower price in time for delivery, he can be said to be selling the bearskin before he has caught the bear!

CHECK THIS OUT

Write out the following sentences, filling in the missing words:

1 The dividend on ordinary shares is not _____ and is paid only when all the other _____ on the profits have been met.

2 The owners of preference shares receive preference over _____ shareholders when the dividend is being paid.

3 Ordinary shares do not have a fixed dividend and the income can be _____ if the company is doing well, or _____ if the company has had a poor year.

4 Preference shares carry a fixed rate of dividend and are useful for people who want a _____ income.

5 A special version of preference shares is cumulative shares, which carry the right to any _____ of _____ from previous years when profits were insufficient.

6 Another version of preference shares is non-cumulative shares, which do not have any right to _____ of _____.

7 Because private companies are not allowed to advertise shares for sale and raise money in this way, an expanding private company may decide to become a _____ company.

8 A merchant bank, or _____ house will undertake full responsibility for issuing new _____ and collecting payment for them.

9 A prospectus gives details of the company's development, past profits and _____ for the future.

10 A _____ is a person who deals in shares with the intention of making a profit by buying and selling in a short _____.

Other sources of finance

1   Debentures

These are *not* shares, but are stock certificates showing *loans* to a company; people who buy them rank as creditors and not as part owners of a company. A firm can obtain finance from the investing public by this means, usually for a fixed number of years. A fixed rate of interest is paid each year to those who hold debentures. If the company should go into liquidation, debenture holders have a preferential right over shareholders to the repayment of their money.

'Mortgaged' debentures are secured against particular items of property. This means that they are an even safer method of investment. Debentures are usually redeemed after a number of years, for example twenty.

2 Other external sources

Other methods of raising finance from outside a company include:

- borrowing from banks by means of loans or overdrafts;
- loans from specialist finance corporations, such as Finance for Industry Ltd.;
- government loans and grants, for example regional development grants;
- buying vehicles or equipment on hire purchase or credit;
- mortgaging property;
- leasing or renting property or equipment;
- obtaining trade credit from suppliers;
- private loans, for example from directors of the company.

All these are methods by which the company can obtain money, or items which it does not have to pay for at once, thus enabling it to expand and make more profits from which it can repay its debts.

3 Internal finance

Where a company has an adequate level of profits, it may decide not to distribute all of it to the shareholders and instead retains it in the company to pay for expansion or to hold as a reserve. This is called the *ploughing back* of profits.

CHECK THIS OUT

Write out the following sentences, filling in the missing words:

1 *Limited liability* means that a shareholder in a company which becomes insolvent only loses the amount _____ in the business.

2 One disadvantage of a partnership is that capital can be fairly _____ and one advantage is that any losses can be spread among the _____.

3 A private company fills the gap between the _____ and the _____.

4 The largest unit in the private business sector is the _____ _____.

5 One of the items given in a company's Memorandum of Association is the name of the _____.

6 Articles of Association are concerned with the _____ _____ of the company.

7 The certificate of incorporation establishes a company as a separate _____ _____.

8 When a company is being formed, shareholders reply to advertisements in _____ and receive a prospectus.

9 Members of the public may buy shares in a company and receive a _____ in return when the firm makes a profit.

10 The owners of _____ shares receive priority when the dividend is being paid.

The co-operative

Co-operatives carry out a wide range of activities, for example there are worker co-operatives in agriculture and manufacturing industry. But co-operatives have usually been associated with the distribution sector – in wholesaling and retailing. The idea behind all co-operatives is that there is no profit-making by investors. This makes them different from the other private sector organisations mentioned in this chapter since any profits not used within the business are distributed to the work force, or to the customers.

To become a member of a co-operative retail society, such as the Royal Arsenal in London, you purchase at least one £1 share (with maximum of 5000) and this money is used to finance the business. Fixed interest is paid on these shares which can be cashed in when desired, and additional shares may be bought over the counter. Some of the profits of these co-operatives is ploughed back to expand and improve the business, and some is used for social and political purposes. For example, educational grants are provided and donations are made to the Co-operative Political Party.

However, the best known way in which profits are used is in the payment of 'dividends' to customers according to the value of purchases which they make from a society. Members control their society on the basis of one vote per share, so that no single person could take over and control a society, as could happen in the case of a company (see also Chapter 3).

The public sector

Much of the public sector is not concerned with business activity as such, but manages the administration of the country and essential services such as the National Health Service. The main part of the State's business activity is covered by the public corporations, but some government departments have trading activities, as do some sections of local authorities, and in addition the State has shareholdings in other businesses.

The public corporation

As you can see from the name, a public corporation is a body corporate, that is, a separate legal entity. A number of these corporations control some of the United Kingdom's major industries. Examples are British Coal, the British Steel Corporation and the Atomic Energy Authority. All these are sometimes referred to as the nationalised industries, but this term is sometimes used more narrowly to cover only those industries which were compulsorily taken over by the Government from the private sector in the late 1940s. It therefore excludes bodies such as the British Broadcasting Corporation and London Regional Transport.

Each corporation is controlled by a board, which is responsible to a Government department and to a minister in that department who has to answer to Parliament, which has the final say. Any losses made by the corporations have to be subsidised by the State. The finance is generally raised via the Treasury, but external borrowing is sometimes allowed.

As usual, there are various arguments for and against operating these industries as single units under State control. Industries such as water and electricity supply can be regarded as too important to leave to private enterprise. There would also be a great deal of waste if lots of different firms were all laying their own pipes and cables to supply different factories and houses in an area. The latter point also applies to railway lines. State control also helps to prevent private monopolies exploiting the public by charging high prices, while at the same time allowing the industry to benefit from operating as a single large unit. For instance, it can buy in bulk at favourable rates, it can afford to employ highly skilled specialist staff, and it has access to large-scale finance for expansion and modernisation.

On the other hand, the large size of these corporations can cause inefficiency through delays in making decisions and there may be communication difficulties between different parts of the organisation. Waste can occur because financial loss does not automatically result in closure, as might happen in private enterprise. An industry might be prevented from taking certain decisions because of political considerations. An example of this is the operation of a loss-making railway route because its closure might result in much higher unemployment and the loss of an essential public service for that area.

The local authority enterprise

Most of the work of local authorities is not concerned with business activity, but with the provision of education, roads, parks and libraries, but some sections may be operated on a business footing. For example, Hull has its own telephone service and other authorities, such as Bristol, operate docks. Services of a more social nature may also be provided, such as indoor sports centres, where direct charges may be made at a level which will cover all costs. Apart from collecting money from these charges, local authorities receive income from the local rates and from central government grants, and they also borrow by selling interest-bearing bonds to investors.

The Government department

Most of the work of Government departments is concerned with the administrative work of running the country, but some do carry out limited trading activities. Two examples are Her Majesty's Stationery Office, which charges for a wide range of publications, and the Export Credits Guarantee Department which covers certain overseas trading risks by providing insurance.

Local government and public corporations together provide almost one-third of the jobs in this country and are some of the largest employers.

CHECK THIS OUT

Write out the following sentences, filling in the missing words:

1 Public corporations are controlled by a _____which is responsible to a Government department and to a minister.

2 Local authority enterprises are concerned with providing _____ and _____.

3 Local authorities receive income from _____ and _____ _____.

4 The State holds shares in _____ _____.

MULTIPLE CHOICE QUESTIONS

There are four possible answers to each of the following sentences. Study the introductory words, and then decide which of the alternatives correctly answers the question or completes the sentence. Write down the question number and follow it with (A) (B) (C) or (D), according to your choice.

1 A public limited company
  (A) must have a maximum of more than 20 shareholders
  (B) may raise finance from the public by advertising shares
  (C) may be owned by two or more partners
  (D) is not required to submit accounts annually to the Registrar of Companies.

2 Rules for the internal conduct of a company are known as the
   (A) certificate of incorporation
   (B) memorandum of association
   (C) articles of association
   (D) certificate of trading.

3 Which of the following is NOT part of the public sector?
   (A) public companies
   (B) public corporations
   (C) Government trading departments
   (D) local authority enterprises.

4 The most likely of the following businesses to operate as a partnership is
   (A) large factory
   (B) dental practice
   (C) supermarket
   (D) small newsagent.

5 A shareholder getting part of a firm's profits will receive
   (A) a bonus
   (B) interest
   (C) commission
   (D) a dividend.

6 Which of the following is an advantage of being the sole owner of a business?
   (A) No other people are employed
   (B) All the profits belong to the owner
   (C) Owners can work unlimited hours
   (D) No income tax is paid.

7 Which Act of Parliament removed the upper limit on the number of shareholders a private company might have?
   (A) 1980 Companies Act
   (B) 1907 Partnership Act
   (C) 1890 Partnership Act
   (D) 1983 Shareholders Act

8 An advantage of a partnership is that
   (A) any losses are the responsibility of one partner
   (B) there is someone to carry on the business, even if one partner is away
   (C) delay in decisions is possible if a number of people are involved
   (D) capital could be fairly limited.

9 It is NOT true to state that the private company
   (A) fills the gap between a partnership and the large limited company
   (B) is a separate legal entity
   (C) is allowed to advertise shares for sale to the general public
   (D) needs a minimum of £50 000 to start trading

10 Advantages of a public company include
   (A) selling shares and debentures to the general public
   (B) being such a large business that employees and customers may feel 'out of touch'
   (C) being expensive to set up
   (D) being liable for debts in the event of closure.

11 Which of the following is NOT usually included in a memorandum of association?
   (A) The name of the company ending in PLC
   (B) The names of all the directors
   (C) The location of the company's registered office
   (D) The objects of the company.

12 An investor who is prepared to risk a low dividend but hopes for a high dividend if the firm does well would choose
   (A) cumulative shares
   (B) ordinary shares
   (C) non-cumulative preference shares
   (D) gilt-edged securities.

13 Debentures are
   (A) shares issued to promoters or founders of a company
   (B) loans from specialist finance corporations
   (C) shares which pay a dividend twice yearly
   (D) stock certificates indicating loans to a company.

There are four possible answers to each of the following questions.

If you think (1) only is correct, write down A.
If you think (1) and (2) only are correct, write down B.
If you think (3) and (4) only are correct, write down C.
If you think (2), (3) and (4) only are correct, write down D.

14 The public sector includes
   (1) the National Health Service
   (2) the education service
   (3) British Coal
   (4) British Rail.

15 Which of the following is NOT a local authority enterprise
   (1) An independent school
   (2) The Parks Department
   (3) The local library
   (4) The Environmental Health Department.

16 Which of the following is a public corporation?
   (1) Central Electricity Generating Board
   (2) British Steel Corporation
   (3) British Assets Investment Trust
   (4) Department of the Environment.

17 A government department which carries out limited trading activities is
   (1) Her Majesty's Stationery Office
   (2) the Office of Fair Trading
   (3) Her Majesty's Customs and Excise
   (4) the Department of Health and Social Security.

SHORT QUESTIONS

1 State *one* advantage and *one* disadvantage of being a sole owner.

2 Name *two* industries owned by the State.

3 What is the basic difference between the public and the private sector of industry?

4 A public limited company is a corporate body. What does this mean?

5 Briefly, distinguish between Articles of Association and Memorandum of Association.

6 Give *two* advantages which a public limited company has over a partnership.

7 Name two services often run by local authorities.

8 Who owns a public limited company?

9 How do nationalised industries raise capital?

10 How is a public corporation controlled?

STIMULUS RESPONSE QUESTIONS

The following two questions have been taken from the specimen examination paper of the Northern Examining Association.

Each section of the question carries marks for the correct response.

1 Below are the trading results of Smith Brothers (makers of candles) and Bright House PLC (makers of lampshades) for the year ending 31 December 1986:

	Smith Brothers	Bright House
Capital employed	£36 000	£50 000
Turnover	£60 000	£100 000
Gross profit	£20 000	£30 000
Net profit	£12 000	£10 000

(a) Which firm has the biggest turnover?
   (1 mark)

(b) What does the term turnover mean?
   (2 marks)

(c) Which is more important to a firm, Gross Profit or Net Profit? Give reasons for your answer. *(3 marks)*

(d) Calculate the value of expenses for:
   (i) Smith Brothers *(1 mark)*
   (ii) Bright House *(1 mark)*

(e) Calculate the Net Profit as a percentage of turnover for:
   (i) Smith Brothers *(2 marks)*
   (ii) Bright House *(2 marks)*

(f) Say which of the two firms you consider was the more successful during 1986, giving reasons for your answer. *(4 marks)*

2 Read the following interview between a local reporter and Mr Alan Hull, Managing Director of Snob Clothes PLC. Snob Clothes are makers, wholesalers and retailers of fashion jeans in Britain.

Reporter: Is it true you are being asked to resign your job because shareholders are worried by falling profits? They seem to think change of management would help.

Mr Hull: Not at all! but obviously the shareholders want us to make better profits.

Reporter: Why have your profits fallen in recent years?

Mr Hull: Like many firms we have generally been hit by depression. Young people without jobs don't have as much money to spend on clothes and don't forget we have more competitors, especially the increase in cheap clothing from the Far East.

Reporter: Many young people don't find your jeans as fashionable as your competitors' jeans.

Mr Hull: There may be some truth in this. Certainly we'll have to change some of our designs. Our market research people are out there now finding out what the young customer wants.

Reporter: There are also rumours that Snob Clothes plan to break into the American market.

Mr Hull: We are hoping to sell abroad. The USA may well be the place to try and sell our jeans. The British have a good name there for quality clothing and, of course, they have more consumers to spend on clothing such as our jeans. The depression has not been as bad there among young people.

(a) Give *three* reasons for Snob Clothes' loss of trade. *(6 marks)*

(b) How does Snob Clothes hope to increase its trade in Britain? *(2 marks)*

(c) Why does Mr Hull think Snob Clothes will be able to find buyers in the USA?
(2 marks)

(d) (i) Why should Snob Clothes' shareholders be worried about falling profits?
(2 marks)

   (ii) Can shareholders in a public limited company force a managing director to resign? Explain your answer. *(2 marks)*

(e) Snob Clothes have begun their market research to find out who the buyers of their jeans would be. What information do they need to know and why do they need to know it? *(2 marks)*

(f) Snob Clothes manufacture, wholesale and retail their own jeans. Suggest reasons why they do all three. *(4 marks)*

ESSAY QUESTIONS

For section (c) of this question, you are advised to turn to Chapter 2 on Retailing.

1 Sharon Wilson owns a self-service grocery store and wishes to expand by opening a similar shop in a different area.
   (a) (i) What is meant by self-service?
   (3 marks)
      (ii) State *two advantages* and *two disadvantages* to Sharon of selling through self-service. *(4 marks)*

(b) What factors should Sharon consider when choosing a site for the new shop? *(4 marks)*

(c) (i) Why might it be to Sharon's advantage to form a partnership before opening the new shop? *(5 marks)*

   (ii) How are profits allocated in a partnership? *(4 marks)*

(Reproduced from the specimen GCSE Commerce paper of the Southern Examining Group.)

2 (a) Choose three different types of business unit and explain how each of them provides
   (i) management   *(6 marks)*
   (ii) finance   *(6 marks)*
   for their business.
  (b) In what way is the liability of the owners for the debts of the businesses different? *(8 marks)*

3 Explain the ways in which a public corporation differs from a public limited company, giving suitable examples. *(20 marks)*

4 (a) Why do companies issue shares? *(8 marks)*
  (b) Describe *three* different types of share available, showing how they are different. *(12 marks)*

5 (a) Explain the difference between a private and a public company. *(4 marks)*
  (b) Outline the different types of business unit which exist in each of these sectors. *(10 marks)*
  (c) Explain how the types of business unit are controlled. *(6 marks)*

6 Explain how you would set up a public limited company. Include any terms you think are important, for example, prospectus, Registrar, limited liability. *(20 marks)*

7 (a) Name one public company. *(1 mark)*
  (b) Name one public corporation. *(1 mark)*
  (c) Give *two* reasons why someone with sufficient capital might prefer to invest in
   (i) their own business; *(4 marks)*
   (ii) a public company. *(4 marks)*
  (d) Your friend has a choice between buying an ordinary share or a debenture for a newly-formed Public Limited Company selling a new product. What would your advice be to your friend? *(10 marks)*

8 (a) Name *one* public corporation
   (i) which provides a service; *(1 mark)*
   (ii) which sells a commodity. *(1 mark)*
  (b) It is said that 'privatisation' is the opposite of 'nationalisation'. Explain what you understand by privatisation. *(4 marks)*
  (c) The Labour Party has said that British Telecom and other privatised firms should be taken back into public ownership and not remain as a public company. Put forward some arguments in favour of this. *(12 marks)*

LEARN IT YOURSELF

1 Write to either a public limited company or a public corporation asking if it is possible for a speaker to visit your group to give information on how the organisation is controlled and financed, or if a speaker is not available, if they will send you these details.

2 Find the share prices of two firms by looking in a newspaper. Write them down and check for at least a month to see what changes occur. Write a brief report on your findings.

3 Find an example of a small factory or mass-production factory and ask if it is possible for the group to visit the firm. Find out what kind of business unit it is, what is produced there, and (if applicable) the address of the head office. Obtain any advertising literature and write a short report, illustrated if possible, about your findings.

4 Write to a nationalised industry and ask for information about its product. Write a short report or project on the industry, explaining how it is controlled and financed, and illustrate it with the information you have obtained.

5 Write to or visit your local authority and ask for information on the services which it provides. Find out how these services are paid for: for example, rates, government grants and other income. Work out what proportion of income is spent on education.

NOW TRY THIS

1 Pair up the following and then write out each sentence in full:

(a) Private sector

(i) are given priority when a dividend is paid.

(b) Public sector

(ii) refers to a sole owner.

(c) Ordinary shares

(iii) are creditors, not shareholders.

(d) Preference shares

(iv) includes public corporations and local authority enterprises.

(e) Debenture holders

(v) can offer high dividends if the company is doing well.

2 Draw up a leaflet for a sole owner who is going to open a new unisex hairdressing salon in your area. Include the opening times of the salon, some special prices to encourage customers to try the new service, the name and address with the telephone number of the shop. If possible, illustrate with a drawing or a picture cut out and pasted on your leaflet.

CHAPTER 6

SHARE TRANSACTIONS

Providing a market

In the previous chapter, the Stock Exchange was mentioned as a way in which the Government and public companies can raise money. It should be stressed that the Stock Exchange DOES NOT GIVE MONEY to these institutions, but provides a market for second-hand shares through which they can raise money to finance themselves.

How did it all begin?

It is useful to look at the past history of the London Stock Exchange which shows how it all began.

Jonathan's Coffee House was a meeting place for merchants and shipowners in London during the eighteenth century. Here merchants could buy part shares in ships sailing to far-off lands which would, hopefully, on their return bring back goods which could be sold at a profit in England. Sometimes the merchants might need to raise money for some other business venture and, in order to get it, would sell their 'share' to someone else. Eventually other business ventures all over the country were paid for by using this method of 'shares'. When merchants wanted to pass messages to someone, perhaps in a different coffee house, they would get a waiter to carry the message for them. Even to this day, Stock Exchange attendants are still called *waiters*. In time it was decided that all the business should take place in one building, and in 1773 the first Stock Exchange building opened.

An eighteenth-century engraving of a London coffee house

Investing through the Stock Exchange

About nine out of ten people in the United Kingdom invest directly or indirectly through the Stock Exchange. Most of this investment is through the large institutions such as pension funds or insurance companies, but direct share ownership by individuals is also becoming more popular – it is estimated that today about seven million people own shares directly. The Stock Exchange must protect investors from mismanagement of their funds, because if they lost confidence and stopped investing, much of our economic activity would cease.

Any company which wishes to have its shares sold through the Stock Exchange must first get the approval of the Stock Exchange Council. Before a share can be *quoted* (bought and sold) on the Stock Exchange, the Council must be satisfied that the company is financially sound and that its directors are trustworthy. A company which is quoted on the Stock Exchange is referred to as a *listed* company. If at any time a company is seen to be breaking Stock Exchange rules or acting in a questionable way, its quotation will be suspended until matters are cleared up.

A large part of the business done on the Stock Exchange is the buying and selling of Government stocks (gilt-edged stocks). The Government issues these stocks as a way of borrowing money to pay for its spending programme, in addition to the money it raises through taxes.

How does it all work?

Until 27 October 1986, the only way shares could be purchased on the Stock Exchange was through a broker acting on your behalf. The broker would buy the shares for you from a jobber on the trading floor of the Stock Exchange, and charge a commission for this service. The jobber made his or her living by buying and selling shares and making a profit on the deal, and no single individual or firm could be both broker and jobber. The commissions charged by brokers were fixed by the Stock Exchange, and firms which acted as brokers or jobbers were not allowed to have other business interests. Most of the buying and selling of stocks and shares was carried out during opening hours on the trading floors of the Stock Exchange.

The activities of brokers and jobbers were restricted and separated so that investors always knew that brokers were giving them independent investment advice, as they had no financial interest in the shares they recommended. Jobbers, who did have such an interest, were not allowed to deal directly with the public.

During the 1980s, the Government became concerned that these arrangements were restricting competition and the Stock Exchange system for the buying and selling of stocks and shares was unnecessarily complicated and expensive. This meant that people were discouraged from investing, and that foreign investors would use overseas exchanges such as New York, with the result that Britain's earnings from abroad would suffer. For a time it looked as if the Stock Exchange would be taken to court under the Restrictive Practices Act by the Office of Fair Trading. (For more details of the Office of Fair Trading, see Chapter 14 on Consumer Protection.) In 1983, the Stock Exchange and the Department of Trade and Industry came to an understanding by which the Stock Exchange agreed to make some changes to its rules, and the Government agreed not to take the Exchange to court.

The 'Big Bang'

The Stock Exchange was given until the end of 1986 to make the changes. It was decided to make most of the changes together rather than phasing them in, so the phrase 'the Big Bang' was coined. The date chosen was 27 October 1986, and the main changes were:

- The distinction between Jobbers and Brokers was removed. Today, all members of the Stock Exchange are called Brokers/ dealers, and they are all allowed to deal with the public. Brokers/dealers can continue to act as agents for the public, or they can buy and sell shares on their own behalf. This ability to carry out both types of trading is known as 'dual capacity'. Brokers/dealers may also register with the Stock Exchange as 'market makers'. Market makers have much the same role as jobbers used to have: they undertake to buy and sell listed stocks and shares.

- Fixed rate fees were abolished. This means that the members of the Stock Exchange can compete with each other to offer the lowest charges in order to attract clients. The Government hopes that this will encourage people to buy shares and attract clients from abroad.

- Firms with other business interests are now members of the Stock Exchange. This 'corporate membership', as it is called, has been extended to overseas firms. This change was intended to increase competition and improve earnings from abroad. Japanese and American firms were among the first to take advantage of this change.

- As a result of these changes, it was realised that the old system of face-to-face dealing between buyers and sellers on the floor of the Stock Exchange was no longer the best. The increased use of computers and telecommunications has meant that up-to-the-minute share prices are now available at a distance, and deals can be conducted electronically without the need for face-to-face contact. Dealings on the actual floor of the Stock Exchange in London have therefore declined greatly.

Buying and selling

Firms who wish to deal on the Stock Exchange have to receive a licence from the Securities and Investments Board (SIB) or be an existing member of the Stock Exchange. It is hoped that by increasing the number of firms who can deal in stocks and shares, the public will be able to invest money more easily by approaching banks, building societies or firms established especially for the purpose in the areas where they live and work. This process will be made easier by the use of computers and advanced telecommunications which will enable deals to be arranged instantly from all over the world.

CHECK THIS OUT

Write out the following sentences, filling in the missing words:

1 Merchants who met in Jonathan's Coffee House in London bought part _____ in ships which would bring back goods from distant lands to sell at a profit.

2 Other business _____ all over the country began to be paid for by using this method of 'shares'.

3 About _____ out of every _____ people in the United Kingdom invest through the Stock Exchange, either directly or indirectly.

4 Any company which wishes to have its shares dealt in, on the Stock Exchange, must first get the _____ of the Stock Exchange Council.

5 The Government issues securities called _____ _____ stocks as a way of borrowing money to pay for its spending programmes.

6 During the 1980s the Government believed that changes to promote _____ were needed.

7 If foreign investors only used overseas exchanges, then the United Kingdom's _____ from abroad would suffer.

8 For a time it seemed that the Stock Exchange might be taken to court under the _____ _____ Act.

9 The Stock Exchange and the Government came to an understanding by which the Stock Exchange agreed to make some _____ to its rules.

10 Most of the changes were brought into operation on 27 October 1986 and the phrase '_____ _____' was coined to describe this.

Finding information

Information about shares is available from a licensed dealer through a computer system known as SEAQ (Stock Exchange Automated Quotes), as well as through newspapers and financial magazines. SEAQ gives up-to-date information about the buying and selling prices of shares and the quantities and prices which various traders are offering to buy or sell the shares at. Information of this type is only available on the most commonly traded shares (the Alpha group of shares) and the next most commonly traded group (the Beta group of shares). The least commonly traded groups (the Delta

A display from the SEAQ system

and Gamma groups) are also recorded but the information is not as detailed. Further details such as company announcements and exchange rate changes as well as share prices can be found through the TOPIC (Teletext Output of Price Information by Computer) computer systems. In return for an additional subscription, users of the TOPIC system can have access to further information which can help those firms which want to make a detailed analysis of particular share price movements. Share prices can also be found in newspapers and magazines, on the Ceefax and Oracle teletext services, and on the Prestel service. There is in addition a British Telecom price information service called Citycall.

Making a transaction

A transaction – buying or selling shares – can be arranged through a broker or any of the licensed dealers approved by the Securities and Investments Board (see below for details). Clearly, which dealer to use should be considered very carefully and the fees charged compared with those of other dealers. One of the features of the October 1986 changes is that shares have become easier to buy. One firm of dealers, Quilter Goodison, now has 'share shops' in some Debenham's department stores and similar developments on the High Street are becoming more common.

Computers in the Stock Exchange

Because the number of transactions has grown rapidly since the changes of October 1986 and because the London Stock Exchange has become more directly affected by changes elsewhere in the world, fast up-to-date and reliable information from all parts of the world has become increasingly important. This has meant greater use of computer systems and advanced satellite communications.

TALISMAN (Transfer Accounting Lodgement for Investors, Stock Management for Jobbers) is a computer system which has been used to record transactions in share ownership since 1979. This system continues to be used so that the growing number of transactions can be settled and paid smoothly. Despite the use of computers, share certificates (see previous chapter) still have to be exchanged by post and the details completed by operators. By 1989 it is envisaged that this task will be taken over by a computer system called TAURUS (Transfer and Automated Registration of Uncertified Stock).

It is now possible to carry out share transactions from home using a Prestel TV for information gathering from the systems described and a home computer-telephone line link for communication with the computers is available. Similar developments have taken place in the retailing of food and clothes.

How are we protected?

Investors are protected by the 1986 Financial Services Act, under which the Securities and Investments Board (SIB) was established to oversee the workings of all financial services businesses.

Firms which want to carry out investment business have to be authorised by the SIB, which delegates this responsibility to several Self-Regulatory Organisations (SROs) which can authorise their members as 'fit and proper persons' to carry out investment business.

When this system was first proposed, the Stock Exchange put itself forward to be an SRO. In addition, many of the large international banks and investment businesses trading in London proposed to set up their own SRO, to be called the International Securities Regulatory Organisation, ISRO. Eventually, however, the Stock Exchange and ISRO decided that it would be inefficient to have two parallel organisations in this way, and the two have decided to merge to form a single Self-Regulatory Organisation, to be known as the Securities Association.

Other SROs under the Financial Services Act are AFBD (Association of Futures Brokers and Dealers); FIMBRA (Financial Intermediaries, Managers and Brokers Regulatory Association); IMBRO (Investment Management Regulatory Organisation) and LAUTRO (Life Assurance and Unit Trust Regulatory Organisation). Each of these SROs oversees a different area of investment business, from insurance to financial futures.

Under the terms of the Financial Services Act, securities investment business must be carried out through a Recognised Investment Exchange (RIE). The Stock Exchange and ISRO have jointly set up such a Recognised Investment Exchange, conducting markets in United Kingdom and foreign company shares, government stocks, and traded options.

The Stock Exchange, and all the other SROs and RIEs, must have a number of independent members on their ruling bodies, to which members or claimants can appeal in the case of a dispute.

SROs act as watchdogs over the activities of their members

Individuals or firms who lose money through unfair practice on the Stock Exchange can claim compensation of up to £250 000 and take up the matter with an Ombudsman who deals with the Stock Exchange. Similar protection is available for disputes in other SROs such as that for insurance.

Only firms recognised by the Securities and Investment Board are allowed to trade in stocks and shares. A licence will only be granted after the firm's background, capital and resources have been investigated. Firms trading without a licence are prosecuted. Those firms which gain approval are required to gain the best possible deal for their clients – the principle of 'best execution' of instructions – and conduct their transactions in such a way that in the case of a dispute it is possible to follow the course of a transaction and find out who did what, when. Given that each firm dealing on the Stock Exchange will carry out thousands of transactions each day, this is not as straightforward as it seems. The Surveillance Division of the Stock Exchange employs over 50 people whose job it is to investigate complaints and ensure that investors are fairly treated. The Stock Exchange motto of 'My word is my bond' which relies on dealers to keep their word, should also afford some protection. The Quotations Department of the Stock Exchange looks at companies seeking to raise money by selling shares or debentures (see previous chapter – pages 64-9) and makes sure that investors get an accurate picture of the firm.

As a result of the 1986 Financial Services Act, Stock Exchange firms and other financial institutions have appointed compliance officers to ensure that their firms stay within the law. It is the job of the compliance officers to advise a firm's management about the law, help to train staff and devise methods of recording transactions which meet the requirements of the law. If, for example, a firm has dual capacity, it is possible that the part of the firm which acts as a broker on behalf of clients might persuade the client to buy shares which the firm's jobbing section wishes to sell. The result could be a profit for the firm. If the shares are not a good investment, this works against the best execution principle (see above) and the client loses as a result of the deal he or she was advised to make. The compliance officer is expected to ensure that those activities of the firm which might conflict are kept separate from each other. This has been called maintaining 'Chinese Walls' between sections of the firm where conflict might arise. Some firms have gone as far as using separate buildings in order that sections of the firm are apart, while others restrict access to areas where there is sensitive information which might affect how another part of the firm deals with a client.

SHORT QUESTIONS

1 In what establishment did the London Stock Exchange start?

2 What is an 'institutional' investor?

3 What *two* things must happen before a public company can have its shares sold through the Stock Exchange?

4 Give *one* reason for restricting the activities of brokers and jobbers before October 1986.

5 What was the main intention of increasing the number of firms who deal in stocks and shares?

6 What is the difference between the Alpha, Beta, and Gamma and Delta groups of shares?

7 Describe *one* way in which a person can transact a purchase of shares.

8 In what kind of 'non-financial' organisation can people buy shares 'over the counter'?

9 Why have computers become important to people wishing to buy shares on the Stock Exchange?

10 What task will the computer system TAURUS take over in 1989?

MULTIPLE CHOICE QUESTIONS

There are four possible answers to each of the following questions. Study the introductory sentence, and then decide which of the alternatives correctly answers the question or completes the sentence. Write down the question number and follow it with (A) (B) (C) or (D), according to your choice.

1 Merchants in the eighteenth century, meeting in Jonathan's Coffee House, could buy
(A) merchandise displayed in the window
(B) part-shares in ships sailing abroad
(C) land in the London area
(D) shares in retailing businesses.

2 Before 1986, individuals and firms could only buy shares using
(A) a broker
(B) Stock Exchange waiters
(C) a jobber
(D) a banker.

3 The ability of Stock Exchange firms to trade as brokers AND market makers is called
(A) dual capacity
(B) non-restrictive practice
(C) conflict of interest
(D) double dealing.

4 Fixed rates of commission for brokers in Stock Exchange dealings were abolished because
(A) incompetent traders disliked it
(B) of criticism by the Office of Fair Trading
(C) low charges would attract clients
(D) Stock Exchange members considered competition would be unfair.

5 Stock Exchange members now trade using
(A) only face-to-face dealing
(B) computers only
(C) telephones only
(D) a mixture of (A) (B) and (C).

6 Firms trading on the Stock Exchange must be members, or
(A) large banks with capital behind them
(B) building societies
(C) insurance companies
(D) authorised by the Securities and Investment Board.

7 The most commonly traded group of shares is called
(A) Alpha
(B) Beta
(C) Gamma
(D) Delta.

8 TOPIC (Teletext Output of Price Information by Computer) gives
   (A) only the buying/selling prices of shares
   (B) share prices and other details such as company announcements
   (C) an analysis of share price movements
   (D) names and addresses of stock market traders.

9 Share certificate transfers will be carried out totally by
   (A) SEAF
   (B) TALISMAN
   (C) SEAQ
   (D) TAURUS.

10 Firms licensed by the Securities and Investment Board to trade in stocks and shares must
   (A) have at least 18 shareholders
   (B) claim compensation if they lose money through unfair practice
   (C) have their background, capital and resources investigated
   (D) carry out thousands of transactions a year.

11 The Stock Exchange motto of 'My word is my bond' means
   (A) no written record need be made of any transaction
   (B) if a deal has been offered and accepted, it will be kept to
   (C) a witness to bond every deal is needed
   (D) there are never any complaints about Stock Exchange deals.

12 The 1986 Financial Services Act states that
   (A) activities of a firm, which might conflict, must be kept separate
   (B) separate buildings for brokers and market makers working in one firm must be provided
   (C) brokers must not give advice to clients
   (D) firms which have dual capacity must not profit from deals.

There are four possible answers to each of the following questions.

If you think (1) only is correct, write down A.
If you think (1) and (2) only are correct, write down B.
If you think (3) and (4) only are correct, write down C.
If you think (2), (3) and (4) only are correct, write down D.

13 The Stock Exchange provides
   (1) a market for selling stocks and shares
   (2) a market for raising company finance
   (3) money which is given to companies
   (4) a meeting place for merchants.

14 The Government was concerned that Stock Exchange arrangements up to October 1986 were
   (1) promoting competition
   (2) discouraging investors
   (3) unnecessarily expensive
   (4) causing Britain's earnings from abroad to suffer.

15 Changes in Stock Exchange arrangements from October 1986 include
   (1) the Government making Stock Exchange rules about trading
   (2) stockbrokers and market makers only trading face-to-face on the floor of the Stock Exchange
   (3) firms being able to trade as both stockbrokers and market makers
   (4) fixed rate fees for buying and selling shares being abolished.

16 Now that computing and telecommunication equipment is used, this means that
   (1) deals can be arranged immediately all over the world in various Stock Exchanges
   (2) anyone with access to Viewdata systems can see share prices listed
   (3) dealing on the floor of the Stock Exchange has stopped
   (4) all Stock Exchanges must be open 24 hours every day.

17 Information for investors concerning shares is available from
   (1) local government
   (2) newspapers
   (3) magazines
   (4) the computer system known as SEAQ.

18 Nine out of ten people in the United Kingdom invest in the Stock Exchange through
   (1) buying goods from a firm whose shares are quoted on the Stock Exchange
   (2) putting money into a firm's pension fund
   (3) taking out an endowment policy with an insurance company
   (4) buying shares from a broker.

STIMULUS RESPONSE QUESTIONS

The following questions carry a mark of 20. Each section of a question shows the marks for the correct response.

1 Read the following passage carefully, and then answer the questions on it.

PERSONAL EQUITY PLANS

A scheme announced by the Chancellor of the Exchequer in his March 1986 budget was designed to encourage more investment in British industry by small savers. The scheme came into existence on 1 January 1987 and offers tax concessions to be received by small investors in PEPs (the name given to the plan).

There are two types of PEP. In the first, the investor makes all the decisions about the choice of investment, with the Plan Manager simply carrying out the instructions. In the second, the Plan Manager decides which shares to buy or sell.

The advantages to be gained in tax concessions are: first, anyone who makes a capital gain large enough to pay tax on will not be liable for Capital Gains Tax, and secondly, any dividends which are re-invested will not be liable for income tax. In fact, there is no need for the investor to have any contact with the Inland Revenue at all about PEP.

(a) Why did the Chancellor of the Exchequer announce the PEP scheme? *(1 mark)*

(b) Why might small investors take advantage of one of these plans? *(2 marks)*

(c) Who chooses the shares in which to invest? *(2 marks)*

(d) Would this be a suitable investment for two people whose only income, at the moment, is a state pension? Give reasons for your answer. *(15 marks)*

2 Read the information in the following passage and answer the questions about it.

People who wish to invest in shares for the first time often find that putting capital into investment or unit trusts is less risky than buying shares. The reason for this is that the investor is protected from excessive losses in the stock market because the risk is spread over a wide range of shares.

An investment trust is a publicly-owned company which has the sole function of investing its money in a wide range of stocks and shares. Investors can buy shares in the trust itself. The funds are managed for the investor, and when the managers see a good company, they invest in it. There is a flow of dividends and capital gains from these investments back into the trust fund, which enhances the value of the trust company, and this produces a rise in the share price of the trust itself, together with dividends on its shares.

A unit trust is also a fund of money invested by the public, who are given units (not shares) in proportion to the amount of money they pay in. The price of the units goes up or down with the value of the underlying stocks and shares that the fund has invested in and dividends are received, usually half-yearly, by unit holders. New units can be issued as more investors come into the pool. The trusts are run by management companies who charge an annual fee, but the trusts themselves are not listed on the Stock Exchange. Since they do not hold shares in the trust, investors have no say in their operation.

(a) What are the *two* less risky ways mentioned in the passage, of investing shares for the first time? *(2 marks)*

(b) Why is an investor in a trust more protected compared with buying shares in companies directly? *(2 marks)*

(c) How is an investment trust controlled? *(2 marks)*

(d) How are the unit trust funds administered? *(2 marks)*

(e) Explain what can cause a rise in the share price of an investment trust. *(5 marks)*

(f) What is the fundamental difference between investing in a unit trust and in an investment trust? *(2 marks)*

(g) What *two* benefits can investors gain from putting money into investment trusts? *(5 marks)*

ESSAY QUESTIONS

1 (a) Describe how the general public can find out
        information about shares.   (*8 marks*)

   (b) State how they are protected when buying
        shares.   (*6 marks*)

   (c) How can the general public purchase the
        investments they require?   (*6 marks*)

2 The introduction of computers and
   telecommunications is very important to firms
   dealing on the Stock Exchange. Describe

   (a) the ways in which these systems are used;
                                          (*12 marks*)
   (b) how they help people in share transactions.
                                          (*8 marks*)

LEARN IT YOURSELF

1 Look through the *Financial Times* or the financial
   pages of a daily newspaper and see how many of
   the following special terms, often used in
   connection with the Stock Exchange, you can
   find:

   *par, discount, premium, nominal value, blue chip,
   gilt-edge, bulls, bears, dividends.*

2 Choose a large retailer where you like to shop
   and follow their share price for two weeks in the
   listings in the *Financial Times* or another
   newspaper. Can you give any reasons for any
   movements in the share price?

3 Read the business pages in your local newspaper
   and make a collection of items about the Stock
   Exchange.

CHAPTER 7

ADVERTISING

Introduction

The idea of advertising goes back a long way into history. Archaeologists have found an advertisement cut into stone in Roman times offering a reward for a runaway slave. Street sellers in eighteenth-century London used to cry their wares, so that people would come and buy from them. Nowadays, the ice-cream van chimes in our streets so that we know that ice-cream is available. These are all methods of advertising, but most advertising is now done through the mass media, such as newspapers and television. Every day millions of pounds are spent in the United Kingdom on advertising by individuals, the Government, manufacturers, retailers and many other businesses.

The advertising media

The media are the various means by which advertisements are channelled to the public. The medium chosen will depend on the cost and the kind of audience the advertiser is trying to reach. For example, textbooks are often advertised by sending leaflets to schools where teachers may wish to buy them. Toys may be shown on television during early evening in the weeks before Christmas when young children may see them and ask for them as presents, while retailers will advertise their annual sales in the local press.

The main advertising media are:

A London street crier

Newspapers, magazines and journals

The advertiser needs to know what kinds of people read which newspapers and magazines, in order to choose the most suitable ones. It is important that the advertisement should reach the people he or she wants it to. Included under this heading are trade journals which are used for advertising *within* particular trades, for example by manufacturers wishing to sell particular lines of goods to retailers.

Television

Television advertising is a very effective method because it reaches into people's homes when they are relaxing and it makes a very strong impact through colour, movement and sound.

However, any company considering TV advertising needs to consider the time of day, the size of the audience for the programme and the high cost involved.

Radio stations

Radio stations such as Radio Luxembourg have a young audience at which the advertisements are aimed. Many areas now have a local commercial station which caters for all ages. These stations carry local and national radio advertisements.

Direct mail

Previous customers and potential new customers are sent price lists, catalogues or leaflets and sometimes samples may be included. We all have these delivered to our homes and we may be tempted to take advantage of special offers made without having to visit the shops.

Cinemas

Cinema audiences are small, but cinemas are useful for local advertisements and for some national products, especially those aimed at younger people who go to cinemas more frequently.

Point of sale displays

These include displays inside shops and window displays which are aimed at the passer-by who may then be tempted to enter the shop and buy the object or service. Attractive packaging of goods helps here and many manufacturers supply a range of display material, including signs.

Posters and signs

Different sizes of posters are used in many varying locations, for example on roadside hoardings, on stations, on buses and bus shelters. Neon signs on theatres, cinemas and shop fronts are a specially attractive method. All of these come to our attention regularly as we travel from place to place.

Posters are a popular form of advertising – even long ago as this nineteenth-century picture shows

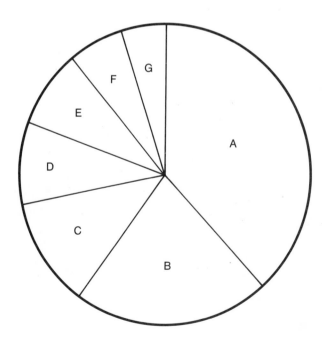

KEY

A   Television

B   Newspapers, magazines, journals

C   Hoardings

D   Direct mail

E   Point of sale

F   Cinema

G   Radio

A pie chart showing the proportions spent by advertisers on each advertising medium

Advertising techniques

Some advertising can easily be categorised as persuasive and some, such as advertisements for jobs, as informative.

Persuasive advertising is used to appeal to all our emotions and instincts, and often refers to a particular branded product. For example:

An educational toy for babies is said by the manufacturers to be 'stimulating' and to 'encourage the development of intelligence'. Parents often want their children to be better than others and give them the 'best possible chance in life'.

A television advertisement shows smart, successful-looking people in a beautiful setting. Suddenly you notice that they are drinking Fizzo and smiling happily. All the smart people drink Fizzo these days. And, of course, you are a smart person, aren't you?

Kenny Kicker, England's top goalscorer, uses Surefire football boots. Gosh, he's wonderful! If only I could use them, I might score some goals!

Clare sees advertisements for Cleeraspot Cream, Slimnow Aids, Molly's Tights, Aromo Bath Oils and Newmint Toothpaste. Soon she will look as beautiful as a Mayfair model. After dark she will be whisked off in her evening gown by a stranger in a dinner-jacket hovering outside her front door!

Is this the real world? Maybe not. Although this sort of advertising can be harmful, perhaps we all like a bit of romance. We all daydream sometimes.

All sorts of clever techniques are used in the designing of advertisements in order to create the greatest impact on our minds by appealing to our various senses. Colour, movement, sound and layout are all used in an attempt to make the product memorable and desirable, and repetition ensures that the message is regularly reinforced.

Some advertisements are simply informative, telling the public what is available. Examples of this kind of advertisement are posters explaining what is on at the local cinema or leisure centre. In newspapers there will be announcements about houses for sale, football matches, jumble sales and other events. In these cases the advertisers are hoping that the public will respond to the information given, but often they will try to use persuasion as well.

Sometimes firms will band together to put out a general (or *generic*) advertisement, such as 'Buy where you see the Woolmark' or 'Tea, the best drink of the day', to promote their products and save the cost of advertising separately.

CHECK THIS OUT

Write out the following sentences, filling in the missing words:

1 Most advertising is now done through the mass _____ , in particular _____ and _____ .

2 The kind of advertising medium chosen depends on the _____ and what kind of _____ the advertiser seeks to reach.

3 Any company considering TV advertising needs to consider three things: the _____ of _____ , the _____ of _____ and the high _____ .

4 Price lists, catalogues or leaflets and sometimes samples are sent to _____ customers and _____ _____ customers by direct mail.

5 Posters on hoardings and neon signs on _____ , _____ and _____ _____ bring products to our attention regularly as we travel from place to place.

6 Persuasive advertising is used to appeal to all our _____ and _____ .

7 Colour, _____ , sound and _____ are all used in an attempt to make a product appear _____ and _____ .

Branded goods

Branded goods help manufacturers in their advertising campaigns. Manufacturers want the public to buy their goods again and again, so they give their goods a brand name which makes them easy to identify. Consumers then recognise the brand name and expect such goods to be reliable and of a standard quality. If they find this to be true, they are often loyal to one brand.

When goods are manufactured under a brand name, the manufacturer has a monopoly (sole use) of that name and it cannot be used by anyone else. Makers of similar goods sold under different brand names compete for sales and each promotes their goods by using their brand names. The pre-packaging of most goods these days also helps in this respect, as the brand name can be included in an attractive package design.

Why do firms advertise?

Firms advertise in order to:

- bring a product to the attention of prospective customers throughout the intended market area, whether nationally or locally;
- give information on a product, for example on use, price and quality;
- create a demand for a product by persuading people to buy it on a large scale;
- expand sales and therefore the size of the business, in order to increase profits;
- allow output to expand so that the cost and price per item can be reduced, thus increasing sales and profits again;
- ensure that competitors do not take away sales through their own advertising;
- establish a reputation for good products and become a household name.

How do we benefit from advertising?

Firms benefit from advertising if increased sales and profits more than cover the cost of carrying out the advertising, but we also benefit as consumers and citizens.

Advertising:

- lets us know what goods are available and provides information about them;
- allows us to compare different makes of goods in order to make the best choice;
- increases the size of firms and competition between firms, bringing greater efficiency and lower prices;
- helps to raise the quantity and quality of goods produced, so raising living standards;
- gives indirect benefits, such as keeping down the cost of newspapers and magazines, providing free commercial television and generally making our lives more interesting;
- creates jobs in the advertising industry itself and through greater sales in general.

Is advertising a bad thing?

- Advertising puts up the cost of goods, and the consumer may have to pay more for the product;

- Advertising is used just to keep the advertiser's share of the market steady, and people working in advertising would make a better contribution to the economy if they manufactured goods instead;

- The information may not be needed by the consumer who is interested only in the job a product does and not the information contained in the advertisement;

- Advertisements can make consumers want items they do not really need and some people may get into debt unneccessarily;

- Advertising may be used to influence people to buy articles which are not suitable for their purpose;

- Advertising can encourage greed in people, encouraging them to become too concerned about the material things in life;

- Advertising harms people by encouraging bad habits;

- People's emotions are played upon too much by advertising;

- Advertising can be misleading, creating wrong impressions in people's minds and causing them to buy goods which turn out to be different from what was expected;

- Much money is spent on advertising and it could be used in more beneficial ways.

Appoint one person to read out each of the arguments which may be used *against* advertising. The rest of the class can act as business people who support advertisements and think of reasons why they disagree with the points made.

Look at these benefits of and arguments against advertising and discuss them in small groups. Choose a spokesperson to sum up in a sentence or two the views of your group in a report back to the class.

Advertising agencies

An advertising agency is a firm which specialises in creating or maintaining a demand for products. Persuading people to part with their money for a product requires considerable specialised skill and experience. This is why advertising agencies are employed by companies. These agencies have the ability to make the advertising effective. The agency takes responsibility for the advertising of the product, leaving the producer free to concentrate on production.

The advertising agency will choose the 'image' it wishes to create for the product. It will decide, for example, on whether the advertisement should appeal to a person's sense of insecurity and whether it should feature someone famous or 'Mr or Mrs Average'. When the decision on image has been made, the agency must choose from all the media available a method of advertising that suits it best: television, newspapers or cinema, for example. They may also use sales promotion methods, such as competitions and free samples, to promote the product. 'Money off next purchase' coupons are often used to entice the customers to buy. Skilled writers and artists then design the posters and advertisements and the product is 'launched'.

Advertising rules and regulations

Because it is possible for advertising to be harmful and misleading, various arrangements have been introduced in order to prevent the worst abuses. For example, the Government has introduced laws, especially through the 1973 Trade Descriptions Act, so that advertisers cannot make untrue claims about goods and services. Some advertisements are completely banned, for example cigarette advertisements on TV, and all cigarette advertisements in magazines, etc. must carry a Government health warning. (Have a look to see what this warning says.)

Apart from the law, various organisations have rules about advertising. The Advertising Standards Authority, set up by the advertising industry itself, has posters asking 'Is it legal? Is it decent? Is it honest? Is it truthful?' and they ask advertisers to conform, voluntarily, to these standards. Advertising is also controlled by the media, for example, by the Independent Broadcasting Authority which can ban advertisements from TV, and press editors who can refuse to accept unsuitable material (see Chapter 14). No longer can 'Wonder Medicine' claim to cure anything from an aching toe to loss of hair, and false claims such as 'Reduced for the Sale' cannot be made unless a reduction *has* been made – items bought in cheaply for sales cannot be advertised as reduced goods.

Market research

Before a firm produces and advertises a product, it usually carries out investigations into whether people are likely to want the product and in what quantity. The company will try to find out which group of people is most likely to buy it (this is called the 'target population'). This could be teenagers, housewives, motorists and so on. A decision is made about what form the presentation of the product should take, for example the design and colour, and the type of packaging. All this 'pre-launching' investigation is called 'market research'.

This research does not, however, stop there. It can continue after the product has been launched and is selling. It may take the form of a study of people's reactions to the product and an investigation of any complaints they may make. The firm may then decide that it is necessary to improve the product or its image, or the advertising techniques used. Competitors are always changing their products, and people's tastes change, so that even long-established products continue to have market research carried out on them.

Large businesses have their own market research departments, but firms often hire the services of specialist companies to carry out the general research, or specific tasks such as surveys. The advertising agencies mentioned earlier sometimes carry out this research in addition to designing advertisements. There are different methods of conducting market research:

1   Interviews

Shopkeepers, wholesalers and the general public are interviewed to find out their reaction to a product or a proposed product. Questions may be asked about its price, colour, size and so on. Sometimes members of the public may be given some of the product to try and then asked to fill in a questionnaire. The answers to all the questions are then analysed (sometimes using a computer). The results will show whether changing the product in any way would increase sales or whether a new product is likely to be successful.

" SAME HERE— I CAN'T FIND AN ORDINARY MAN IN THE STREET ANYWHERE ! "

2   Test marketing

Before trying to advertise and sell goods nationally, many firms will advertise and sell them only in a certain area. This reduces the possible losses if the goods do not appeal. Such an approach is called *test marketing* and it often takes place in an area covered by one of the commercial television companies (such as Tyne-Tees, Granada or Thames). The firm can look at the sales returns to see how their product is being received, and can calculate reactions on a national scale and make any product or advertising improvements that are needed. Test marketing is usually backed up by surveys and questionnaires.

3   Desk research

Firms also research markets and products by looking at statistics and other published information, such as details about changes in people's spending habits and the sales of similar products of other businesses. This will help firms to decide what market to aim for and how to beat their competitors.

Sales promotion

The term sales promotion refers to any method used by businesses in order to increase or maintain sales. Advertising is a very important method of sales promotion, although many of the others rely on advertising in order to be effective. Some examples of sales promotion are given below.

- When shoppers buy an item, they are offered a coupon which can be used in part-purchase of the item next time they buy it.

- There may be a free gift with a purchase, such as the dishwasher offered by a kitchen specialist if the shopper buys kitchen units, or free entry into a competition for valuable prizes, such as a car or a holiday, if the consumer buys the product on offer.

- An obvious way of promoting sales is to make special offers such as half-price fashion goods at certain times of the year, including winter and summer sales.

- Some firms persuade the motorist to buy *their* petrol rather than *another* petrol by offering tokens for free gifts, so that when enough tokens have been collected, they can be exchanged for a gift. The motivation to purchase petrol where tokens can be collected towards a gift means that sales of petrol improve.

- Newspapers sometimes promote sales by offering prizes. One example of this type of sales promotion is a 'bingo' game. Each number has a box underneath it with a symbol, and the symbols are covered by a substance which can be scratched off. When numbers appear in the paper, the buyer scratches the symbol box to show the symbol. When a certain number (usually nine) of identical symbols has appeared on the card, the newspaper buyer can ring up and claim a prize.

- Sales representatives for double glazing, kitchen equipment and bathroom suites are often found in large supermarkets where there are busy shoppers, offering leaflets or asking for names and addresses so that their experts may visit the shoppers and persuade them to buy their product.

- Celebrities, such as TV personalities and football players, are frequently used in various forms of advertisement, in order to persuade people that the product concerned must be good if they use it.

SHORT QUESTIONS

1 Why do consumers tend to buy branded goods from well-known manufacturers?

2 Through which medium is most money spent annually on advertising?

3 What is
   (a) persuasive advertising;
   (b) informative advertising?

4 Give *three* ways of advertising which were used in the nineteenth century.

5 Name *two* media used for advertising purposes.

6 Give *two* reasons why advertising can be beneficial.

7 Give *two* arguments against advertising.

8 Name *two* publications which carry advertisements aimed specifically at women.

9 What is market research?

MULTIPLE CHOICE QUESTIONS

There are four possible answers to each of the following questions. Study the introductory words, and then decide which of the alternatives correctly answers the question or completes the sentence. Write down the question number and follow it with (A) (B) (C) or (D), according to your choice.

1 Which of the following methods of advertising would you advise a person about to set up a small painting and decorating business to use?
   (A) Leaflets to 500 000 houses
   (B) Independent television
   (C) An advertisement in the local newspaper
   (D) Neon lighting in the city centre

2 Persuasive advertising does NOT appeal to
   (A) our common sense
   (B) our desire to do our best for our children
   (C) our sense of humour
   (D) our daydreams of a fantasy world.

3 The term which means that different firms band together to advertise a common product is
   (A) competitive advertising
   (B) generic advertising
   (C) informative advertising
   (D) persuasive advertising.

4 Branded goods are
   (A) packaged for use by several manufacturers
   (B) used by one manufacturer to build public loyalty
   (C) similar goods with not much to choose between them
   (D) only goods which have become a 'household name'.

5 Advertising can be criticised because
   (A) some people may be tempted to buy goods they cannot afford
   (B) it tells people about new products
   (C) it keeps the cost of magazines down
   (D) it helps people to make the best choice of goods.

6 The rule that all advertisements must be legal, decent and honest comes from
   (A) a consortium of firms which use advertising
   (B) an Act of Parliament
   (C) the Advertising Standards Authority
   (D) commercial radio stations.

7 Market research is
   (A) finding the way to the local market
   (B) a way of finding out if people are likely to buy a new product
   (C) advertising goods for sale in a market hall
   (D) launching a new line of goods.

8 Test marketing involves
   (A) a firm testing a product in certain areas only
   (B) asking people passing by if they will test a product
   (C) asking how much people spend when shopping at a market
   (D) asking people which of two products they like best.

9 Which of the following advertising media is likely to be the most effective for marketing a new toy?
   (A) Leaflets to teachers in junior schools
   (B) An advertisement at the local cinema
   (C) An advertisement in a comic bought by children in the age range
   (D) An advertisement during children's programmes on television.

10 An example of informative advertising is
   (A) a television advertisement showing smartly-dressed people using a certain product
   (B) a newspaper advertisement showing a famous cricketer using a branded cricket bat
   (C) a newspaper advertisement showing what is on at the local cinema
   (D) a magazine advertisement showing a soap-opera star wearing clothes which consumers can obtain through mail-order.

11 Which of the following is not a commercial TV station?
   (A) Thames Television
   (B) BBC Television
   (C) Tyne-Tees Television
   (D) TV-South

There are four possible answers to each of the following questions.

If you think (1) only is correct, write down A.
If you think (1) and (2) only are correct, write down B.
If you think (3) and (4) only are correct, write down C.
If you think (2), (3) and (4) only are correct, write down D.

12 Radio advertisements are aimed at
   (1) small children of pre-school age
   (2) teenagers
   (3) people who listen to the radio at home
   (4) people who listen to the radio at work.

13 Advertising can be said to be of benefit to the consumer because
   (1) the customer pays more for the product
   (2) it plays upon people's emotions
   (3) it helps to raise the quality of goods produced
   (4) it gives information about new products being marketed.

14 Which of the following is/are point-of-sale advertising
   (1) A leaflet giving information about a new shop
   (2) A full page in a newspaper giving details of a store's annual sale
   (3) Sweets on sale at the check-out desk
   (4) Window display.

15 Clever techniques used to create the greatest impact in advertising include
   (1) giving information in small print
   (2) using colour
   (3) using movement
   (4) repeating the message in different ways.

16 People buy branded goods because
   (1) they are not sure what to expect
   (2) they are loyal to a brand
   (3) they have been satisfied with the goods in the past
   (4) they know that the quality will not vary.

17 Which of the following would be used in desk research
   (1) Face-to-face interviews
   (2) Free gifts
   (3) Government statistical journals
   (4) Trade magazines

18 The medium which the advertiser chooses will depend on
   (1) the time it takes the advertising agency to decide on ideas
   (2) whether the goods have a 'brand name' to use
   (3) the cost of the advertisement
   (4) what audience the advertisement is trying to reach.

19 Which of the following statements about advertising is/are untrue?
   (1) The Advertising Standards Authority has been set up by Act of Parliament to make advertisers conform to the law.
   (2) Press editors can refuse to accept unsuitable advertising material.
   (3) Some advertisements, such as cigarette advertisements on TV, have been banned.
   (4) It is possible for advertising to be harmful and misleading.

STIMULUS RESPONSE QUESTIONS

The following questions carry a mark of 20. Each section of a question shows the marks for the correct response.

1 Read the following information and answer the questions about it.

Stylish Living

of City Centre, Newtown,

a-n-n-o-u-n-c-e

WINTER SALE!

There is up to 50% off all suites, carpets, beds, bedroom and dining-room furniture – and instant credit to help you to make the most of these STYLISH LIVING offers.

Mariane 3-piece suite –
save one-third of the price!

Michelle dining-set –
four chairs, Welsh dresser, drop-leaf table – save £150!

Leonie divan beds
complete with headboard and storage drawers – save £100!

WE ARE OPEN ON NEW YEAR'S DAY UNTIL 8 pm –
You can't buy cheaper anywhere!
(Goods subject to availability)
Credit available, subject to status.

(a) Where would you expect to see an advertisement similar to this? *(1 mark)*

(b) What inducements in this advertisement are there to persuade the consumer to purchase goods? *(12 marks)*

(c) How does the advertisement suggest that the consumer should hurry to make purchases? *(3 marks)*

(d) How does the name of the firm help to suggest to the consumer that the goods on offer are desirable? *(2 marks)*

(e) Why does the firm consider it necessary to advertise that it will be open on New Year's Day? *(2 marks)*

2 Read the following advertisement and answer the questions on it.

EASISHOP

Make the right choice from this new catalogue. Easy shopping for all the family – just call FREEFONE 108695 to get your FREE CATALOGUE – and when you spend your first £10 with us, we will send you a fabulous FREE GIFT of your own choice. There's no agency to run, no complicated forms to fill in – it's the Easiway to Easishopping with new EASISHOP!

(a) What is the advertisement offering? *(2 marks)*

(b) How does the prospective customer obtain the offer? *(2 marks)*

(c) Give *two* inducements offered by the advertisement. *(4 marks)*

(d) What kind of shopping is the 'Easishopping' which is being offered? *(2 marks)*

(e) Indicate whether you consider the advertisement to be mainly persuasive or mainly informative, and give a reason for your answer. *(6 marks)*

(f) Give *one* advantage and *one* disadvantage of shopping in the manner suggested by this advertisement. *(4 marks)*

ESSAY QUESTIONS

1 (a) What is market research? *(4 marks)*

(b) Describe *two* methods of carrying out research for a new chocolate bar to be produced by a large company. *(8 marks)*

(c) Why are businesses willing to spend large sums of money on market research projects? *(8 marks)*

2 State the advantages and disadvantages of market research to
(a) the consumer *(10 marks)*
(b) the advertiser. *(10 marks)*

3 (a) Define the term mass media. *(4 marks)*
  (b) What factors will an advertiser consider in selecting the most appropriate advertising medium for a product? *(12 marks)*
  (c) Why is the press (newspapers, magazines and journals) the most popular advertising medium? *(4 marks)*

4 (a) Describe *four* advertising media. *(4 marks)*
  (b) What is an advantage of each to
    (i) the consumer; *(8 marks)*
    (ii) the manufacturer? *(8 marks)*

5 Three companies wish to advertise the following:
Company A – a new geography textbook
Company B – a new margarine
Company C – winter holidays in Portugal.
Suggest the most suitable medium of advertising for each company, giving the reasons for your choice in each case. *(20 marks)*

6 'Advertising does not benefit the public and may in fact cause harm.' Discuss this statement, giving arguments for and against it. *(20 marks)*

7 What legal restrictions are there are on advertising? What other controls over advertising exist? *(20 marks)*

8 (a) Explain why business firms advertise. *(8 marks)*
  (b) What would be an appropriate method for advertising:
    (i)   services of a local plumber;
    (ii) a sale at a department store in the centre of town;
    (iii) a new breakfast cereal.
    Give reasons for your choice in each case. *(12 marks)*

LEARN IT YOURSELF

1 Assume that a full-page advertisement in a national magazine costs £10 000. Use a copy of a magazine and calculate roughly how much income that magazine obtains from advertising. State whether or not you think the income affects the price of the magazine, and give reasons for your answer.

2 Look through newspapers, magazines and journals and choose different advertisements in various categories. Write a report using the advertisements to show how they
  (a) create a desirable image;
  (b) play on a person's emotions;
  (c) give information;
  (d) make it easy to obtain what is offered;
  (e) persuade people to buy.

3 Your school/college is producing a play such as *The Boy Friend* at the end of the summer term,
and a group from the Commerce class has been asked to advertise it. Draw up an advertising campaign to promote production, and allocate jobs between the members of the group. Show draft copies of advertising matter such as leaflets, notices, posters and so on, taking into account who will want to see the play and how they will get tickets, and what if anything the group would do to contact the media.

4 A small business such as a Unisex hairdresser or mobile fish-and-chip van is setting up in your area. Design a leaflet to inform people locally and to persuade possible customers to use the service offered.

5 With a group of fellow students, choose a product, prepare a 30-second television advertisement to promote it, and then act it out.

NOW TRY THIS

Choose from A, B or C to complete the following sentences, and write them out in full.

1 TV advertising showing famous people using branded goods is trying to sell goods by using
  (A) hero-worship
  (B) instinct
  (C) the approval of your friends.

2 Advertising which is used to tell people what is on at the local cinema is
  (A) persuasive
  (B) informative
  (C) generic.

3 Advertising in newspapers and magazines
  (A) cuts their cost to the consumer
  (B) wastes money because it does not reach the people it is intended for
  (C) is used only for goods obtainable locally.

4 An advantage of advertising is that
  (A) consumers are tempted to make a purchase
  (B) it is not needed for well-known products
  (C) manufacturers of branded goods do not build up a reputation for a dependable product.

5 Direct mail advertising is done through
  (A) a leaflet obtainable when you visit a shop
  (B) a slogan printed across envelopes which come through the post
  (C) sending price-lists, catalogues or letters to customers by post.

6 A disadvantage of advertising is that
  (A) it does not help people to find where to buy the goods they want
  (B) it may create a demand by some people for goods which they do not really need and cannot afford to buy
  (C) it is a complete waste of manufacturer's money.

ASSIGNMENT – ADVERTISING STANDARDS

Send off for the booklet about rules for advertising standards from:

Advertising Standards Authority
Department A
Brook House
Torrington Place
LONDON WC1E 7HW

Collect a selection of advertisements from newspapers, journals, magazines, holiday brochures, catalogues, photographs of posters, neon signs and point-of-sale advertisements and from any other sources of advertising which occur to you, such as displays in the windows of estate agents.

Classify your advertisements as far as possible into:

(i) persuasive
(ii) informative
(iii) generic

and show examples of each. (Note that some may fall into more than one category.)

Check each advertisement against the booklet of rules.

Write a report on the advertisements in each section which you consider comply with the rules, and on any advertisements which you find faulty. Mention what is wrong with these advertisements, according to advertising standards.

Try to find some old advertisements (look in your school or local library, local history centre or museum) and see what examples you can find of advertisements which break today's rules. If you use books, make a list at the end of your report and do not forget to include them in your bibliography of course work.

Draw conclusions about the standards of the advertisments you have selected, including any old advertisements, according to the rules for advertising issued by the Advertising Standards Authority.

CHAPTER 8

BANKING

Introduction

The word *bank* comes from *banca*, which means a bench, and it refers to the bench on which Italians, who came to London from Italy, sat to conduct their lending transactions many years ago. The origin of our modern banking system lies, however, with the activities of the London goldsmiths in the Middle Ages.

In the late sixteenth century merchants who wanted somewhere safe to keep their cash left their money and valuables in the goldsmiths' strong-rooms. The goldsmiths lent some of this money to others for a charge called 'interest', and paid the merchants who had left the cash up to 6 per cent of the value for the loan of their cash.

By charging borrowers more than they paid to depositors, the goldsmiths made a profit by lending money that was not even theirs. This idea still forms the basis of modern banking. Banks take deposits of money, calculate how much they can expect to pay out on any one day (plus a good margin for error) and then lend out the rest. If a bank lends out too much and cannot repay its depositors when they want their money back, it is *insolvent*. This is known as a bank 'crashing'.

Another development came from the receipts which were given by the goldsmiths to the merchants for their money, promising to 'pay on demand'. These receipts were sometimes passed on by merchants to other people in payment of debts, so that they could claim the deposit instead. These receipts form the basis of our present bank notes which still bear the words 'I promise to pay the bearer on demand the sum of . . .' followed by the number of pounds the note is worth. The wording on cheques is also similar to the written instructions which people once gave to the goldsmiths to pay out their money to someone else.

Savings banks

Savings banks keep money safe until it is needed. The savings bank operated by the Post Office on behalf of the Government is called the *National Savings Bank* and has the advantage of being open during post office hours (including Saturday mornings). It has

BANKING

ordinary savings accounts which pay interest to the saver, and for the person who does not want money out in a hurry, a special 'investment' account which carries a higher rate of interest.

The *National Girobank* is dealt with separately in Chapter 11.

There is also the *Trustee Savings Bank*. It once operated simply as an institution for holding savings but now offers a wide range of services to customers, such as cheque accounts, credit cards, travellers' cheques, bank giro credits and personal loans. Like the National Savings Bank it has ordinary and investment accounts for savings.

There used to be a large number of separate groups of these banks scattered across the country. In 1987 the Government changed the legal basis of the TSB, allowing the public to buy shares without first having to open a savings account.

Barclays

The clearing banks

The *commercial (or joint stock) banks*, owned by shareholders and working for profit, have names which can be seen in every high street. They include:

National Westminster
Barclays
Lloyds
Midland

The major commercial banks are also called *clearing banks*, because they are members of the London Clearing House, where cheques are exchanged and debts settled (see page 120). The members of the Clearing House are:

Barclays
Lloyds
Midland
National Westminster
Coutts and Co. (a subsidiary of National Westminster)
Bank of Scotland
Clydesdale
Royal Bank of Scotland
Trustee Savings Bank
Co-operative Bank and four branch banks in Northern Ireland

Those commercial and other banks, which are not members of the Clearing House, have their cheques 'cleared' by one of the member banks. The services provided by the commercial banks are discussed in detail later in the chapter.

Lloyds

National Westminster

Midland

Merchant banks

The work of these banks is in many ways different from that of the commercial banks, not least that they deal mainly with businesses, and examples are N.M. Rothschild and Hill Samuel. Their services include:

- issuing shares for companies (see Chapter 5);
- assisting companies with take-overs and mergers;
- arranging international payments and finance;
- making large loans to UK and foreign businesses;
- taking large deposits from businesses;
- managing investments for businesses and other organisations.

Some merchant banks which finance international trade are termed *accepting houses* (a house in this sense means a company). They accept bills of exchange by signing them on behalf of reliable traders and thereby guarantee to pay against such bills if traders fail to honour their debt. Bills of exchange are common in international trade and they arise when traders wish to delay payment for goods bought from other traders. If a bill has been accepted by a merchant bank, the trader selling the goods can easily obtain his money immediately (less a small percentage) by *discounting* (selling) the bill at another bank. His customer then pays the bank at the agreed future date, often three months later (see Chapter 15).

Some merchant banks are termed *issuing houses*. They float new issues of shares and debentures on the capital market, both at home and overseas (see Chapter 5). The reasons for proposed issues are thoroughly investigated and finance is raised from the public for both new and existing companies.

The Bank of England

The *Bank of England* was originally a private bank founded in 1694 by Royal Charter. It was nationalised in 1946 and now belongs to the State. It acts as the bank for the Government and works in close co-operation with the Government and with the clearing banks. The clearing banks all have an account and keep part of their reserves with the Bank. At one time, the commercial banks used to issue their own bank notes, but now the only bank which does so in England is the Bank of England. It also issues the coins which are made at the Royal Mint. Some Scottish banks still produce bank notes for use in Scotland, although they can also be accepted in the rest of the United Kingdom. The Bank of England also takes the lead in fixing interest rates and is used by other banks as a guide to the interest they charge.

Other activities of the Bank include:

- settling inter-bank debts by transfer between the clearing banks' accounts;

- managing the National Debt on the Government's behalf – borrowing or repaying money and paying interest due;

- acting as a *lender of last resort* if the banking system is short of funds;

- controlling, on the Government's behalf, the amount of money in the country;

- holding the country's reserves of gold and foreign currency;

- supporting the value of the pound, as necessary, on the foreign exchange market.

Commercial bank services

The commercial banks offer many services. People usually become customers by opening a bank account, which could be a *current account* or a *deposit account* or perhaps both.

Current or cheque accounts

A current or cheque account can be opened by paying into a bank any sum of money, and cash withdrawals can be made only by means of cheques (which are issued in 'books' to the account holder) or by a cash card (see page 110). Payments out of the account can also be made to other persons by means of cheques or through other services linked to the current account (see below). Cash, cheques or other payment methods can be used to put money into the account, and many people often have their salary paid directly into their banks, and usually no charges are levied for operating the account provided that it is kept in credit, possibly with a minimum of £50 or £100. In competition with building societies and merchant banks, some commercial banks are now, however, offering *special* current accounts which yield interest, but require a large minimum deposit and allow only large cheque payments and in-payments.

Cheque guarantee cards

These are issued only to current account holders and are used when payments are made by cheque where a trader wants a guarantee that the cheque is genuine and will not 'bounce', because there is no money in the account for example. The card number is written on the back of the cheque and the bank will guarantee payment if the sum is not more than a specified figure, for example £50. The guarantee depends on the account holder's specimen signature on the card matching that written on the cheque in the presence of the trader. This arrangement is very advantageous, as cheques backed by a card are now accepted by most traders, and there is less need to carry around large sums of money when shopping. The card can also be used to obtain cash up to £50 from banks and branches where one does not hold the account. Special cards are issued for use abroad.

Overdrafts

Overdraft facilities may be granted on the current accounts of individuals or businesses by arrangement with the bank. Under this agreement, more money may be drawn out than is actually in the account, but interest is charged on the amount overdrawn. This is a cheaper way of borrowing money, because interest is only charged on money outstanding for the time it is overdrawn. As soon as it is repaid, interest charges stop. This differs from a loan, where the sum borrowed is paid into the person's current account and interest is charged immediately on the full sum whether or not it is used.

Statements

Midland Bank plc

L J TOYPEN ESQ

39 TOTTENHAM COURT RD. BRANCH
39 TOTTENHAM COURT RD LDN W1P 0AR

Statement of Account

1986	Sheet 4 Account No. 01205358	DEBIT	CREDIT	BALANCE Credit C Debit D
JAN27	BALANCE BROUGHT FORWARD			268.59 C
JAN28	SUNDRIES		100.00	368.59 C
JAN29	100019	111.70		
JAN29	100020	26.80		230.09 C
JAN30	AUTOBK STRATFORD	10.00		220.09 C
FEB 3	A N B S	75.00		145.09 C
FEB 5	AUTOBK TOTT CT RD1	15.00		130.09 C
FEB 7	100010	18.00		
FEB 7	AUTOBK 52 OX ST 1	10.00		102.09 C
FEB11	100022	8.60		93.49 C
FEB12	100023	7.37		
FEB12	AUTOBK TOTT CT RD2	10.00		
FEB12	AUTOBK NATW 600828	10.00		66.12 C
FEB13	AUTOBK TOTT CT RD2	5.00		61.12 C
FEB14	100026	18.97		
FEB14	SUNDRIES		12.13	54.28 C
FEB17	100021	18.00		
FEB17	AUTOBK STRATFORD	10.00		26.28 C
FEB19	BALANCE CARRIED FORWARD			26.28 C

Please file in the wallet provided

Most banks issue a statement of account at regular intervals, giving the serial numbers of drawn cheques, the amount of money paid out, including any standing orders and direct debits, and the money paid in. The customer can then check the serial numbers against the counterfoils in the cheque book to find out if cheques have been paid, and the balance remaining can be verified. (Instead of a counterfoil some cheque books have a grid at the front into which can be written the date, cheque number, the person receiving the cheque and the amount.) A customer wanting to know immediately how much money is in his or her account can request a notification of balance, and the bank clerk will tap out the account number on a computer terminal. Within seconds the information is transmitted from the computer, and the customer can be given the answer right away. Statements are usually sent to customers at regular intervals.

Deposit accounts

A deposit account is generally used to save up money or to hold spare funds temporarily, and interest is paid to the customer. The bank may ask for notice of withdrawal, as the money may be that which is loaned out in order to earn interest. No cheque book is issued with a deposit account, nor are the other current account payment methods available. There are various kinds of deposit schemes, and customers can enquire at their own bank to find out which would be the best scheme for their savings. Some deposit account holders may have a pass-book, instead of a cheque book, for making in-payments and withdrawals.

Budget accounts

A budget account helps the customer, who is also a current account holder, to spread out the payment of large expenses. These might include rates, holidays, gas and electric bills, and so on. Precise arrangements vary between banks, but one way is to draw up a list of regular bills and divide them by twelve. One-twelfth of the total is then transferred each month from the customer's current account to the budget account. If the bills payable in one month exceed the monthly amount transferred, they are still settled even if the budget account becomes overdrawn.

Standing orders

A standing order (or banker's order) is an instruction by the customer for the bank to pay to another person or business a fixed amount of money on a set day, monthly or annually, out of his or her current account until further notice or for a specified number of payments. The customer then knows that the payments will be made and does not have to remember to do anything more about them. A standing order is useful for many regular payments, for instance insurance premiums and hire purchase debts.

To **National Westminster Bank Limited** ♻

_____ Branch   **Standing Order Mandate**

Bank	Branch Title (not address)	Sorting Code Number
Please pay		— —

	Beneficiary's Name	Account Number
for the Credit of		

Amount in Figures	Amount in words	
the sum of £		

Date and amount of first payment		Due Date and Frequency
commencing	*now £	and thereafter every
	Date and amount of last payment	
*until	£	*until you receive further notice from me/us in writing
quoting the reference		and debit my/our account accordingly

This instruction cancels any previous order in favour of the beneficiary named above, under this reference

Special instructions

Account to be debited	Account Number

Signature(s) _____   Date _____

_____

* Delete if not applicable

Note: The Bank will not undertake to:
(i) make any reference to Value Added Tax or other indeterminate element
(ii) advise payers address to beneficiary
(iii) advise beneficiary of inability to pay
(iv) request beneficiary's banker to advise beneficiary of receipt

† If the amounts of the periodic payments vary they should be incorporated in a schedule overleaf

NWB1320 Rev Apr 78-1

Direct debits

A business or other organisation which is owed money can ask the debtor to sign a form authorising the debtor's bank to allow withdrawals to be made to the business against his or her current account balance. This is very similar to the standing order, but the difference is that the business which is owed money takes the necessary action to withdraw money from the debtor's account once approval has been given. This is more convenient than a standing order, if the sums to be withdrawn and the intervals may vary. There is no need for the debtor to keep changing the standing order, as the business receiving the payments will instruct the bank directly. The direct debit is therefore a very flexible method of payment, and is often used for domestic bills, such as those for gas and electricity.

Cash dispensers

These are automatic machines, found outside or sometimes inside banks or offices, which allow cash to be withdrawn by means of a plastic 'cash' card and a PIN (personal identification number) which is keyed in. The term 'cash dispensers' is becoming rapidly outdated, as these machines now also allow customers to order a new cheque book, ask for a statement of account or make a balance of account enquiry, and the range of services available will be extended further. They are more accurately described as computer-controlled automatic banks.

Safe deposits

Banks offer security and safe-keeping for documents and valuables which can be stored in the strong-rooms of the bank.

Investments

Banks can give investment advice and a stockbroking service for the purchase of stocks and shares, and they will deliver the share certificates of purchases, including purchases abroad, to the customer. They will also give advice on tax matters and provide an accountancy service for small businesses.

Travellers' cheques and foreign currency

Banks will change sterling into foreign currency for the traveller and issue travellers' cheques. These can be exchanged for cash when they are signed in other countries or in the UK. They are safer to carry than money, as they are valueless until they are countersigned by the person to whom they were issued. Banks will also arrange direct payments to persons with accounts in other countries.

Bureau de Change		
rates of exchange per £		
	we sell	we buy
AUSTRIA	25.30	27.05
BELGIUM	74.50	78.50
CANADA	1.8675	1.9275
DENMARK	12.95	13.50
FRANCE	10.25	10.71
W.GERMANY	3.63	3.83
GREECE	127.00	139.00
HOLLAND	4.02	4.23

Executors and trustees

Banks will act as executors of a will and trustees of an estate, and make sure that the wishes of a person who has died will be carried out.

References (status enquiries)

If customers wish to purchase goods on hire purchase, they sometimes have to give evidence that they are reliable people with a regular income. Banks will give references for both individuals and businesses who wish to engage in credit buying.

Personal loans

Banks may offer personal loans to customers who have a current account, and this service also covers clubs and societies. The loan is discussed with a senior bank official. If the official is satisfied that the customer has a regular and dependable income, the loan is granted. Loans are usually made for a wide range of purposes, such as for buying cars and for household repairs/improvements. The advantage of a personal loan from a bank is that the interest rate is often cheaper than that given by other financial institutions. The customer can then pay cash for goods or services required and take advantage of any discounts given for cash. The loan is repaid monthly, usually over two or three years, but longer in certain cases.

Business loans

In the same way business loans are often granted to small traders or self-employed professional people. A loan might be needed to modify present premises, buy new equipment or to give additional working capital. Collateral security is required for larger loans, and repayments may be monthly or by a single sum on the expiry date. Collateral security is the name given to items of value which the business agrees to give the bank, should it be unable to repay the loan, for example share certificates, jewellery or property deeds.

Leasing

Businesses which wish to expand need to find extra finance. One way in which banks can help is by providing leasing, which is finance in instalments.

Leasing is another word for renting and is used for virtually all equipment, plant and vehicles. There are several flexible payment plans available, and a business will choose the option which suits their requirements. Payment may be made at monthly, quarterly, half-yearly or annual intervals.

Rentals paid on a leasing agreement can, in most cases, be set against profits to reduce tax payable and the VAT charge can also be reclaimed.

Factoring

One difficulty which faces businesses is that of 'cash-flow', when they have to pay for raw materials and wages and then have to wait for money from the firms who buy the finished products. Some banks offer a factoring service to help with this problem. The supplier of goods sends an invoice to the customer and a copy invoice to the bank. The bank pay up to 80 per cent of the invoiced sales to the supplier, and then collect the money owed on the invoice from the customer.

The supplier does not get the full amount of money from the invoice, but saves the expense of sales ledger accounting, the risk of non-payment (which is taken by the bank) and the cost of any necessary legal action. The difference between the money paid to the supplier and collected from the customer provides the bank with its profit.

Bank giro credits

Customers can use bank giro credit forms to pay money to others who have accounts at their own bank or at another bank. Individuals without bank accounts can also use these forms by paying cash over the bank counter. Gas and electricity bills can be paid by this means. Some companies use bank giro credits to transfer employees' salaries from their own bank accounts into the individual bank accounts of their workers. They do this by making out a cheque for the total sum and giving to their bank a list of accounts and money to be paid into them, together with a bank giro credit form for each person. This avoids the need to sign individual cheques or give out cash in wage packets, and the cashier does not have to risk bringing large sums of money from the bank to the wages office. Businesses also use this multiple credit system for making monthly payments to their suppliers.

Date _____	**bank giro credit** ♺	£50 Notes	
Cashier's stamp and initials	Code No. [- -]	£20 Notes	
	Bank _____	£10 Notes	
	Branch _____	£5 Notes	
		£1 Note/Coin	
	Credit _____	S. & I. Notes	
		50p	
		20p	
		Silver	
	Account No. _____	Bronze	
Fee	Number of cheques	Paid in by _____	Total Cash
		Address _____ Ref. No. _____	Cheques, P.O.'s etc. see over
675-5			£

‖• 70

Night safes

Some traders receive a lot of money but are unable to take it into the bank because it is closed when the day's business is done. This causes a security problem, but they can solve this by using the night safe of their local branch. The bank can provide a trader with a wallet into which is put the cash and cheques taken during the day. The wallet is then locked and dropped into the night safe through a metal door in the outside wall of the bank. On the next working day, bank clerks open the wallet and pay the cash and cheques into the trader's account, or the trader can recollect the locked wallet from the bank.

NIGHT SAFE

Mortgages

Mortgage loans are now offered by banks to customers and others who wish to borrow money to buy their own homes. The borrower is expected to find part of the purchase price and the bank will arrange mortgages linked to life insurance (*endowment* mortgages) or to be repaid at regular intervals (*repayment* mortgages). As a rough guide, the bank will usually lend up to three and a half times the gross annual wage of the main income earner in the family plus a proportion of the gross annual wage of a second earner.

Credit cards

These are a facility completely separate from the current account and are issued by banks to customers and non-customers. They allow the holders to purchase goods and services from a wide range of shops, garages, restaurants, etc., up to an agreed limit. Cash can also be withdrawn at a charge from the related bank(s). The debt can either be paid off within a month, without any interest charge, on receipt of a statement, or in some cases be paid in monthly instalments with interest. Examples of credit cards are Barclaycard and Access.

Charge card or store cards

These are plastic cards which can be used to pay for purchases. Examples are American Express and Marks & Spencer store cards. The customer has to be over the age of 18, and the card is presented at the till point and the details, plus the account number of the card, are registered through the till and the transaction is recorded. A statement is sent to the customer once a month and if this is paid within 25 days, no interest is payable. The customer does, however, have to pay interest on any balance outstanding.

Bank drafts

A bank draft is a cheque drawn on the bank itself and not on the individual customer's account, and it is usually for a large sum of money. The money is taken out of the customer's account and put into the bank's account before the draft is issued. This is a safe way of receiving payment as the bank, already possessing the money, guarantees to pay the sum involved.

Opening a bank account

When young people begin work, they often find that they are to be paid by cheque or directly into an account by giro credit. When you go to work you may be asked whether you have a bank account (see Chapter 12 for National Girobank accounts). If you do not have an account, choose a bank near your work, so that you can go in your lunch hour. Alternatively, if you have a branch with 'late night opening' (usually a main branch) near your home, you may find it convenient to go there to draw your money out. Go to the bank of your choice, look for the 'Enquiries' desk and tell the clerk you want to open a current account. You will be asked to give the name and address of a responsible person (who also has a bank account) who can give you a reference. If one of your parents has a bank account and you go to his or her bank, you will be accepted on that basis. The bank will write to your referee to ask whether you are a suitable person to have a bank account. About a week or two later the bank will get in touch with you. You pay in some money to open your account, give a specimen signature, and you are then a customer of the bank, with access to services about which you have been reading!

If you open a current account, you will be given a paying-in book and a cheque book. Both of these will have counterfoils (or special front pages) which you can fill in for each cheque issued or in-payment made to make a record for future reference. If as a new customer you prove to be trustworthy and maintain the current account sensibly, the bank will after a few months agree to issue you with a *cheque guarantee card* which you must sign with a specimen signature (see above).

CHECK THIS OUT

Write out the following sentences, filling in the missing words:

1 Savings banks keep _____ safely until it is needed.

2 Well-known high-street banks owned by shareholders and working for profit are called _____ banks.

3 The Bank of _____ belongs to the State.

4 Your salary will probably be paid into a _____ bank account.

5 One way of spreading out large annual payments is to use a _____ account.

6 An instruction from a customer to the bank to pay a fixed amount of money on a set day is called a _____ _____ .

7 A _____ card can be used to pay for goods or services and if the account is settled monthly, no interest is due.

8 Private holders of a bank current account may be able to get a _____ loan from their bank.

9 Customers can use bank _____ _____ to pay money to others who have bank accounts.

10 A bank _____ is a cheque drawn on a bank.

How to write a cheque

There are three people involved with a cheque: the person who is drawing the money out of his account (the *drawer*); the person who is being paid (the *payee*); and the bank which is holding the money before paying it out of the account (the *drawee*).

The drawer will normally write four things on the cheque:

- the date;
- the payee's name;
- the amount of money in words and figures (so that there can be no mistake);
- his or her own signature (a specimen of which is held by the bank).

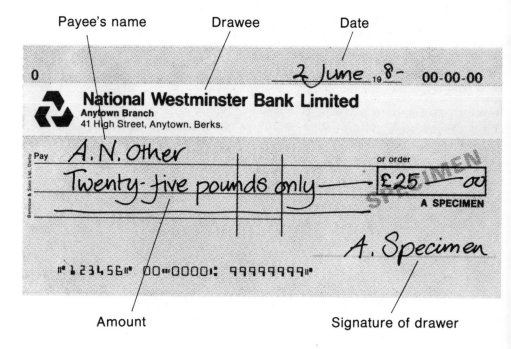

If two parallel lines are drawn down the cheque, it is a *crossed cheque* (crossed by two lines) and it can only be paid into a bank account and not exchanged for cash over the counter. The bank takes the money from the drawer's account (draws it out) and pays it into the payee's account, if with the same bank, or to the payee's bank if different, so that there is a record of the transaction in case the cheque is paid to the wrong payee.

If the cheque does not have parallel lines across it, it is an *open cheque* and can be taken to the branch of the bank on which it is drawn, and cashed. This type of cheque is therefore not so safe as the crossed cheque, as cash paid to the wrong person would be difficult or impossible to retrieve.

Apart from the *general* crossing of two parallel lines, various words can be inserted between the lines in order to make a cheque even less likely to be

paid to the wrong person. A cheque crossed 'A/c Payee' means that a bank will not pay it into any account other than that of the payee named on the face of the cheque. Adding 'Not Negotiable' is a further important safeguard. This does not prevent a cheque from being transferred to another person by the payee, but you should not cash such a cheque or accept it in payment unless you know the payee very well. Even if you unknowingly accept it from a person who has stolen it, then the drawer of the cheque can legally recover the value from you. If it has not been crossed in this way, then the drawer cannot recover the money from you and must attempt to trace the thief while at the same time having to pay another cheque to the original payee.

A further variation is the *special* crossing which has the name of the payee's branch inserted between the lines. This means that the cheque can only be paid into that branch and this obviously makes it much more easy to trace should it be stolen.

Most cheques these days have the general crossing *printed* on them. Only the drawer (the person who signs a cheque) can 'open' a crossing. If the payee (the person receiving the cheque) wants to use the cheque to obtain cash, he or she must ask the drawer to write 'Pay cash' on the cheque and include their full signature after the instruction. Banks,

however, dislike this procedure unless the drawer is taking out cash himself or herself, as it cancels the purpose of the crossing which is to prevent theft.

Another safeguard apart from crossing is that most cheques have the phrase 'or order' pre-printed on them following the space for the payee's name. This means that the cheque has no value to a person other than the payee unless the payee has *endorsed* it by signing on the reverse side, for instance by his/her 'order' allowing the cheque to be paid to another person. If it was a 'bearer' cheque, then it could be paid to anyone possessing it, without the payee's endorsement.

What not to do

Apart from safeguarding a cheque by means of crossing, one should also be careful when writing out a cheque. Here are some 'don'ts':

- don't issue blank cheques to anyone, for instance signed but the amount not filled in;
- don't sign a cheque before filling in the sum to be paid;
- don't leave a gap before or after the amount written in words – cancel any space with a line;
- don't leave a gap before, between or after the amount written in figures;
- don't leave out the name of the intended payee.

Why do you think each of these rules should be followed?

Advantages of cheques

The main advantages, depending on whether one is giving or receiving cheques, are:

- large sums of money need not be carried – cheques are safer and more convenient;
- large sums of money need not be kept in tills or used to pay wages;
- the clearing of cheques acts as proof of payment – a receipt is not needed;
- cheques can be sent through the post safely;
- when stolen, transfers can be more easily traced than cash;
- less time is spent in counting money and accounts can be more easily checked.

Disadvantages of cheques

Although they are a very important means of settling debts, they do have some disadvantages:

- they are not legal tender, as is cash, and do not have to be accepted in payment;
- they are valueless if the drawer has no money in his account;
- they need to be taken to and possibly paid into a bank;
- the clearing process (see over) means that several days may elapse before payment is received;

Don't give anybody a blank cheque – otherwise they might go out and spend your money

Large amounts of cash can be difficult to carry about!

- they are not practical for settling small debts in certain situations, for instance, a bus fare;

- not all persons have bank accounts and bank charges may be payable.

A referred cheque

A referred cheque is one on which the bank will, for some reason, not pay out of the drawer's account. If the bank knows that the drawer hasn't enough money in the account but is, for example, expecting some salary to be paid in to cover the cheque, the cheque will be marked RDPR (Refer to Drawer: Re-Present). The cheque then goes back to the drawer's bank and is sent through the system again (by which time the money to pay it is in the account. The technical reasons for refusing to pay a cheque could be:

- the drawer does not have enough money in his or her bank account;

- the signature does not match the specimen signature and might be forged;

- the cheque has on it a date later than the day of presentation;

- the cheque has been altered (and the drawer has not initialled the alteration, which could have been done without his/her knowledge);

- the cheque is over six months old (said to be stale);

- the drawer has for some reason asked the bank in writing to stop payment against the cheque.

If the bank is fairly certain that the cheque cannot be met, it has R/D (refer to drawer) written on it. Banks are very careful about returning cheques to payees, as this can damage the credit and reputation of their customers. They may be able to resolve some problems directly with customers, for example checking that a signature or alteration is genuine. If there is not enough money in a customer's account to meet a cheque and the bank is not willing to grant an overdraft, then the cheque will be returned to the payee and is said to have been 'dishonoured'. In this case, the payee will have to resolve the matter directly with the drawer in order to receive payment of the debt – the cheque is said to have 'bounced'.

CHECK THIS OUT

Write out the following sentences, filling in the missing words:

1 Three parties involved with a cheque are the drawer, the _____ and the _____ .

2 Four things normally inserted by the drawer of a cheque are _____ , _____ , _____ and _____ .

3 A crossed cheque can only be paid into a _____ _____ and not exchanged for cash.

4 A special crossing on a cheque will have the name of the payee's _____ written between two parallel lines.

5 When a payee _____ an order cheque, he gives the right to receive payment to the person to whom he transfers the cheque.

6 Never issue _____ cheques which are signed but with the amount of money left out.

7 A disadvantage of cheques is that they are not _____ tender.

8 The bank will not honour a cheque which was dated more than _____ months ago.

9 The bank will not pay out on a cheque if the _____ does not have enough money in the account.

10 Cheque cards should be kept separate from _____ books.

Bank clearing system

About four and a half million cheques are exchanged by the major banks every working day. At one time all the sorting and checking was done by people, who found the repetitive work very boring. The banks now use computerised sorting machines which can handle 2400 cheques every minute.

How it works

The page opposite shows the journey of a cheque through the general clearing system: Mr Brown pays the Music Shop for his music centre by cheque drawn on his bank, Homebank, Newtown.

As mentioned above, the cheques are quickly sorted by machine and the cheque normally goes through the system in three days. Each cheque has magnetic ink characters showing the branch code, the account number and the cheque number. While the written details on a cheque are keyed in, the computer can directly read in the character information. The computer keeps each customer's account on memory and it automatically adjusts the account as cheques are fed through.

The *general* clearing system, explained opposite, is used where there are two different banks involved and they are not both in the City of London. In other cases the clearing is different as follows:

- A *Town Clearing* occurs where the banks involved both are different clearing bank branches in the City of London. The cheque still passes through the Clearing House, but is specially cleared on the same day rather than taking three days.

- A *Branch Clearing* occurs where the cheque relates to two accounts held at the same bank branch. The cheque does not have to go to the bank's central Clearing Department, but is handled within the branch.

- An *Internal Clearing* occurs where the cheque relates to the *same* bank but to two different branches. The cheque is, in this case, transferred to the bank's central Clearing Department, but need not be sent to the London Clearing House as no other bank is involved.

The Music Shop Manager takes Mr Brown's cheque (among others) to his own bank, Townbank, Newtown.

Townbank, Newtown, collects all the cheques which come in that day (including Mr Brown's cheque) and sends them to Townbank Clearing Department in London.

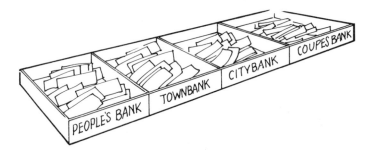

The cheques are sorted and put into trays according to the banks they belong to. Mr Brown's cheque goes into the Homebank trays.

All the trays for the various banks are then taken to the London Clearing House. All clearing banks do the same with the trays of cheques, drawn on other banks, which they have collected. The value of cheques in each tray is totalled, and each bank receives daily the trays of cheques which have been drawn on it.

Mr Brown's cheque is now in the Clearing Department of his own bank, Homebank, in London. It is next sent to his own branch in Newtown.

The cheque arrives in his own branch. A clerk checks his signature, date, and amount of money in words and figures. If all is correct and there is enough money in the account, the cheque is approved and Mr Brown's account is debited.

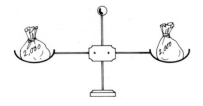

We have shown above how all the millions of cheques are cleared every day, but there still remains one problem. When the banks have exchanged cheques daily at the London Clearing House, there will be debts outstanding between them, as the value of cheques exchanged by each two banks is unlikely to balance. Even after 'setting off' debts between the banks, settlements will still need to be made, and this is arranged through the Bank of England.

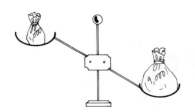

The Bank holds accounts for all the clearing banks (see page 105), so it is a simple matter of adjusting these accounts each working day. All the millions of pounds of debts paid daily by cheque are therefore settled by simple transfers on paper at the Bank of England.

SHORT QUESTIONS

1 What is the name given to a person who fills in and signs a cheque?

2 What is the name given to the person to whom a cheque is made out?

3 Give two instances when you might use a standing order.

4 Name four services offered by commercial banks, other than operating accounts.

5 What do we mean when we say a cheque has *bounced*?

6 What is a bank's night safe used for?

7 Give one difference between a current and a deposit account.

8 When should a cheque be endorsed?

9 What is a direct debit?

MULTIPLE CHOICE QUESTIONS

There are four possible answers to each of the following sentences. Study the introductory words, and then decide which of the alternatives correctly answers the question or completes the sentence. Write down the question number and follow it with (A) (B) (C) or (D), according to your choice.

1 Which statement is NOT true of the Bank of England?
(A) It belongs to the State
(B) There is one in almost every town
(C) It holds the country's reserves of gold
(D) Clearing banks have an account there

2 Which bank service is most useful to a person visiting another country?
(A) Safe deposits
(B) Travellers' cheques
(C) A budget account
(D) Bank giro credit

3 'Account payee only' written on a cheque means that the cheque must be
(A) exchanged for money over the counter
(B) paid into the account of the person presenting it
(C) passed from one person to another
(D) paid into the account of the named payee.

4 Which of the following is NOT one of the rules to be kept when writing a cheque?
(A) Always put in the name of the intended payee
(B) Sign your name but leave the amount blank
(C) Make sure the cheque is dated
(D) Check the words and figures before you sign

5 If a person decided to pay an insurance policy in equal instalments through the bank, the most appropriate service would be
(A) deposit account
(B) standing order
(C) credit card
(D) cheque.

6 Referring to a cheque drawn on an account, the term drawee means
(A) the bank at which the account is situated
(B) the person to whom the cheque is payable
(C) the person on whose account the cheque will be drawn
(D) the bank at which the cheque is presented.

7 Which banking service would you advise a person who wishes to pay in full for a car to use?
(A) A direct debit
(B) A bank draft
(C) A budget account
(D) A standing order

8 When regular payments such as those for a mortgage may vary, which of the following bank services would be most appropriate?
(A) An open cheque
(B) A standing order
(C) A direct debit
(D) A crossed cheque

9 Into which of the following accounts may cash and cheques be deposited *and* withdrawn without given any notice to the bank?
(A) A budget account
(B) An overdrawn account
(C) A current account
(D) A high interest savings account

10 Which of these items need NOT be filled in on a cheque?
(A) The payee and date
(B) The drawer's signature
(C) What the payment is for
(D) The amount in words and figures

11 An open cheque is one which
(A) can only be paid into another bank account
(B) has two parallel lines drawn across it
(C) can be cashed at the bank on which it is drawn
(D) has no amount written on it.

12 A current account holder wishes to borrow money for approximately three weeks and decides to approach his/her bank. You would advise him/her to ask for a/an
(A) personal loan
(B) bank draft
(C) overdraft
(D) budget account.

13 Which of the following enables the holder to buy items on instant credit?
(A) A banker's reference
(B) A credit card
(C) A cheque account
(D) A travellers' cheque

14 A person taking a new job where payment is by cheque would be advised to open a
(A) joint account
(B) current account
(C) budget account
(D) deposit account.

There are four possible answers to each of the following questions.

If you think (1) only is correct, write down A.
If you think (1) and (2) only are correct, write down B.
If you think (3) and (4) only are correct, write down C.
If you think (2), (3) and (4) only are correct, write down D.

15 Which of the following is a clearing bank?
(1) Rothschilds
(2) The Bank of England
(3) Barclays Bank
(4) National Westminster

16 A person can get money out of a bank account by
(1) writing a cheque drawn on his/her current account
(2) filling in a withdrawal slip for a deposit account and receiving cash over the counter
(3) asking for a personal loan
(4) using a night safe.

17 A cheque may be marked R/D (refer to drawer) because
(1) the cheque is more than two months old
(2) there is not enough money in the account to pay it
(3) the amount in words and figures is different
(4) there is something wrong with the signature.

STIMULUS RESPONSE QUESTIONS

The following questions carry a mark of 20. Each section of a question shows the marks for the correct response.

1 Read the following information carefully and then answer the questions which follow.
(See also Chapter 4 for additional information.)

On 1 August a manufacturer sold 100 cases of biscuits to a wholesaler at £8 per case less 15 per cent trade discount and an invoice was forwarded to the wholesaler together with the goods. A cash discount of 5 per cent is allowed if payment is made within 7 days. The wholesaler paid the manufacturer on 6 August by crossed cheque drawn on Barclays Bank PLC, Llandudno.

(a) What is trade discount?   (*3 marks*)

(b) Why does the manufacturer offer cash discount to the wholesaler?   (*2 marks*)

(c) What is the total amount due to the manufacturer as shown on the invoice?
                                                 (*2 marks*)

(d) How much did the wholesaler pay to settle the amount due on 6 August?   (*3 marks*)

(e) The wholesaler paid by crossed cheque. What is a 'crossing'? Why is it important?
                                                 (*4 marks*)

(f) On what type of banking account would the cheque have been drawn?   (*2 marks*)

(g) Suggest TWO other means of payment offered by a commercial bank.   (*4 marks*)

(Specimen question for the GCSE Commerce paper reproduced by permission of the Welsh Joint Education Committee.)

2 Read the following information carefully and then answer the questions which follow.

For many people the key service offered by a clearing bank is the current account. This account provides a convenient way of paying others and of receiving payment of a wage or salary by credit transfer. The current account, together with a number of other types of account, provides the banks with the funds to lend to industry and commerce. The traditional form of bank lending for business customers is the overdraft which is particularly suitable for meeting fluctuating working capital requirements. The clearing banks, through subsidiaries, also provide facilities such as leasing and factoring.

Adapted from *The Clearing Banks: Their Role and Activities* (Banking Information Service).

(a) (i)   Name the type of bank account referred to in the passage.   (*1 mark*)
     (ii) State TWO ways in which payment can be made from this type of account.
                                                 (*2 marks*)

(b) Name and describe the system, referred to in the passage, which is used for payments such as wages.   (*5 marks*)

(c) Name ONE type of bank account NOT mentioned in the passage.   (*1 mark*)

(d) (i)   Define working capital (line 11).
                                                 (*1 mark*)
     (ii) Why is the overdraft 'particularly suitable for meeting fluctuating working capital requirements' (lines 10 and 11)?
                                                 (*5 marks*)

(e) Show how business can benefit from the facilities provided by banks for:
     EITHER   leasing (line 13)
     OR   factoring (line 13).   (*5 marks*)

(Specimen question for the GCSE Commerce paper reproduced by permission of the Southern Regional Examination Board.)

3 Read the following and answer the questions about it.

Over 30 per cent of all adults in Britain own a credit card. It offers an easy way to spread payments over a period to suit the card holder, and if the outstanding debt is paid off in full each month, it is possible to get up to eight weeks' interest-free credit. Examples of bank credit cards are Barclaycard, Trustcard and Access.

A credit-card holder can pay for purchases at esablishments which have agreed to accept the scheme by showing the card. The trader makes a note of the card number and then claims the amount due from his or her bank. The card holder receives an account of the transactions from the bank and can settle the debit by cheque or by transferring the appropriate amount from his or her bank account.

Advantages include security – if people use a credit card, they need not carry cash with them. Credit cards do not have the £50 guarantee limit of cheques, cash can be drawn on a credit card if necessary, the number of cheques is reduced and so is the potential bank charge if a current account is overdrawn. Some credit cards offer free accident insurance if the traveller pays a total bill with a credit card. Disadvantages are that credit card interest rates are rather high and there is a personal limit on the amount a credit-card holder can keep outstanding.

(a) Give an example of a bank credit card.
(1 mark)

(b) Explain why bank customers may prefer to use credit cards. *(3 marks)*

(c) Describe how the card is used to make payments. *(4 marks)*

(d) Give two advantages and two disadvantages of using a credit card. *(4 marks)*

(e) What advantage can a traveller gain by using a credit card? *(4 marks)*

(f) A credit-card holder with a current account is paid on the last day of the month and has spent most of the salary in the first week of the new month. How can he/she get interest-free credit until his/her salary goes in the bank at the end of the month? *(4 marks)*

4 Read the following information and then answer the questions about it.

The Bank Giro system is a simple method of transferring money to the bank account of a customer of ANY bank by going into a branch of one of the banks and filling in a special form. It is also used to pay several bills by using only *one* cheque, and some firms use this method to pay their employees. A list is made of money to be paid and the name of the payees, together with details of their bank accounts, and a cheque to cover the total payments. Where employees are paid by this method, it cuts out the danger of withdrawing large amounts of cash from the bank to pay wages. The householder can use the system in order to settle gas, electricity and other accounts with a single cheque. The system was introduced in 1960.

(a) Do bank customers using the Bank Giro system have to belong to the same bank?
(2 marks)

(b) Give one instance of how a firm, and one instance of how a householder, can use the Bank Giro system. *(4 marks)*

(c) Explain how the system is used to pay several bills using a single cheque. *(6 marks)*

(d) Why might firms prefer using this system to using cash in order to pay their employees? *(4 marks)*

(e) Which other institution uses the Giro credit transfer system? *(2 marks)*

(f) When was the system introduced? *(2 marks)*

5 Read the following information and then answer the questions about it.

A standing order and a direct debit are very similar ways of ensuring that regular payments are made on time. A standing order instructs the bank to pay a fixed amount of money on a certain day, but a direct debit authorises the person or business to withdraw money from the debtor's account. It is used if the payments vary.

(a) What do standing orders and direct debits have in common? *(4 marks)*

(b) In what way are they different? *(4 marks)*

(c) From memory, give examples of items which are paid
   (i) by standing order *(3 marks)*
   (ii) by direct debit *(3 marks)*

(d) Which is the most flexible method of payment? *(4 marks)*

ESSAY QUESTIONS

1 Describe the bank services which you could use for the following.
   (a) Safety of cash received by a shop on Saturday afternoon. *(4 marks)*
   (b) (i) Safe-keeping of share certificates *(4 marks)*
       (ii) Obtaining money when the bank is closed. *(4 marks)*
   (c) Getting money while you are abroad on holiday. *(5 marks)*
   (d) Looking after money for the Badminton Club, of which you are the Treasurer. *(5 marks)*

2 (a) Describe a cheque, stating what important information should be on it, and why. *(6 marks)*
   (b) Explain *three* advantages of paying by cheque. *(6 marks)*
   (c) With the aid of an example, explain the effect of:
       (i) a general crossing of a cheque *(4 marks)*
       (ii) a special crossing of a cheque. *(4 marks)*

3 (a) What *two* main types of account can be opened by bank customers? *(4 marks)*
   (b) Explain the differences between these two types of account. *(8 marks)*
   (c) What are the benefits to a trader of opening each type of account in connection with his business? *(6 marks)*

4 (a) Describe a standing order and state the advantage of using this method of payment. *(5 marks)*

   (b) Identify and explain a similar bank service which could be used instead of a standing order. *(4 marks)*
   (c) Explain how payment is made by Banker's Draft and suggest an occasion on which this method of payment might be used. *(5 marks)*
   (d) Give *two* examples of credit cards and explain how they can be used for payment. *(6 marks)*

5 (a) Describe the use of a cheque guarantee card. *(2 marks)*
   (b) List *three* advantages of paying by cheque. *(6 marks)*
   (c) Describe *two* safeguards which should be used when writing out a cheque. *(4 marks)*
   (d) What four things must the drawer write on a cheque? *(4 marks)*
   (e) Explain the difference between a crossed cheque and an open cheque. *(4 marks)*

6 Two young people have just opened up a business. Name and describe which commercial bank services they should use in the following circumstances.
   (a) Making payments to several different creditors. *(4 marks)*
   (b) Raising money to buy new stock. *(4 marks)*
   (c) Obtaining credit from a wholesaler. *(4 marks)*
   (d) Paying regular insurance premiums. *(4 marks)*
   (e) Banking money taken at weekends after the bank is closed. *(4 marks)*

LEARN IT YOURSELF

1 Write to:

   Bank Information Service
   10 Lombard Street
   LONDON EC3V 9AS

   and ask for information about a speaker and choice of subjects for a talk. Make all the arrangements for choosing a talk and booking a speaker at a suitable time arranged with your teacher.

2 Make a wall display of bank services which you consider to be suitable for school leavers.

3 Find out what careers banks have to offer and make a display suitable for a Careers Convention using the information you have been able to find. You may link this with the bank speaker who may give you further information or answer a questionnaire which you have devised.

4 Make a poster demonstrating the correct way to fill in a cheque. Take five cheques (which may be obtained free from the Bank Information Service) and fill them in, each with a different mistake. Exchange your cheques with another person in your class and try to detect the deliberate errors.

5 Make a booklet or leaflet about the services which banks offer to people who own their own homes or who wish to buy a home. You may like to include services such as Budget Accounts and so on.

ASSIGNMENT – THE WORLD OF BANKING

Collect as many leaflets and information books as possible from several different commercial 'High Street' banks.

Compare the services they offer to:

(a) a person wishing to set up in business;
(b) an established small business;
(c) an ordinary customer who has had an account for some time;
(d) students on a grant.

Draw any conclusions you can about the services offered to each of these groups, including your opinion on the 'best bank' you have found for each group.

Give reasons for your opinion, backed up with the information which you have obtained from the bank.

Choose a bank about which you have gathered the maximum amount of information and write an account of the history, development and present-day ownership of the chosen bank.

TRANSPORT

Why we need transport

The purpose of transport is to make possible the transfer of people and goods from one place to another, whether locally or across the world. People use transport for both pleasure and work: as tourists they travel on holiday to distant parts, or visit friends or relatives who live far away. Many people also need to use transport in order to get to work; others, such as salespersons and journalists, have to travel long distances as part of their work.

Transport is necessary in order to allow the exchange of goods (freight) between different parts of a country, or between different countries. Goods have to be transferred from where they are produced to where they are needed. For example, raw materials need to be transported from where they are found to the processing plant or factory, and the finished product then needs to be transported to the consumer.

The differences between different parts of the world, in things such as available raw materials, climate, ease of communication and labour skills, have resulted in areas tending to specialise in what they can most easily and efficiently produce (see Chapter 1 on the Division of Labour and Chapter 15 on Foreign Trade). They can only do this, however, if they can exchange what they produce for what they need from other areas. In order to exchange over distances, the physical means of transport are necessary.

Therefore the availability of good transport facilities for people and goods brings the following benefits:

- because goods can be produced in the most suitable areas of the world, they can be provided more cheaply;

- because there is a larger market, businesses can produce on a much bigger scale and, therefore, at lower cost;

- consumers can have a much wider variety of goods available, for instance, tropical fruit and foreign cars in the United Kingdom, and those products which are out of season locally;

- people can enjoy the pleasure of visiting friends and relatives in far-away places, and they can visit other parts of their own country and go to other parts of the world;

- people have a wider choice of jobs and can perhaps earn more money because they can travel some distance from home;

- the more efficient the transport, the less is the cost to be added to the prices paid for goods by consumers;

- all of the benefits add up to a better living standard for people.

Methods of transport

In order to transfer people or goods from one place to another, more than one method of transport is usually available, and the following diagram shows the possibilities:

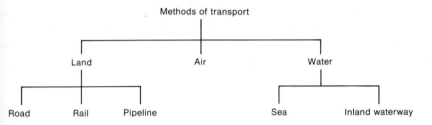

Each of these methods will be looked at in turn, and then finally the various considerations which can be taken into account in deciding which form of transport to use in a particular case.

Road transport

Road transport is by far the most important form of inland transport for both people and goods. The building and the maintenance of roads are largely the responsibility of central Government (Department of Transport) and local authorities. The Department of Transport deals with motorways and trunk roads (major national routes), while local authorities have responsibility for local roads and other main roads, although expenditure is supported partly by central Government funds.

People are carried by private vehicles (for example cars) and by licensed 'public' vehicles such as coaches and buses. Long-distance coach services are operated by the National Bus Company, while more local bus services may be controlled by Passenger Transport Executives, an example of which is London Regional Transport, and local authorities. However, the Government policy in recent years has been to encourage competition by licensing private operators to carry passengers and some authorities no longer operate a bus service.

A large proportion of road freight transport is carried by businesses using their own vehicles (see 'Own fleets' on page 132), but there are also many public carriers offering a variety of local and long-distance delivery services for other businesses. These carriers do not require any special licence, other than Road Fund, to operate vans and light lorries. However, those using heavy lorries, mainly for long distance work, need an *operator's* licence which is granted only where firms meet strict standards concerning the maintenance and operation of their vehicles. A large part of the road haulage industry was formerly owned by the Government through the National Freight Corporation, but this was returned to private ownership in 1982.

Road transport now provides a very wide range of general and specialist haulage facilities, for example, for oil and chemicals, and is responsible for nearly 60 per cent of all inland freight transport in the United Kingdom in terms of weight/distance carried. However, even though the United Kingdom is a group of islands, an increasing amount of imports/exports is being carried by road through the use of ferries with their roll-on/roll-off (RO-RO) facilities (see later).

Recent improvements

Both vehicles and roads have been improved greatly in recent years in order to make road transport more efficient and therefore more competitive and the work includes:

- the building of a national motorway network which is improving vehicle flows and delivery times;

- many major roads have been widened and straightened, reducing congestion and increasing vehicle speed;

- many town by-passes have been built, again reducing congestion and delays;
- new bridges and tunnels have been built to shorten journeys and take traffic away from other routes, for example the Humber and Severn bridges;
- vehicles with greater carrying capacity have been built and allowed on the roads, reducing the cost per unit of goods carried;
- vehicle design has been improved, thus reducing fuel costs and driver fatigue;
- computerised systems have been introduced for monitoring of vehicle movements and the arrangement of return loads.

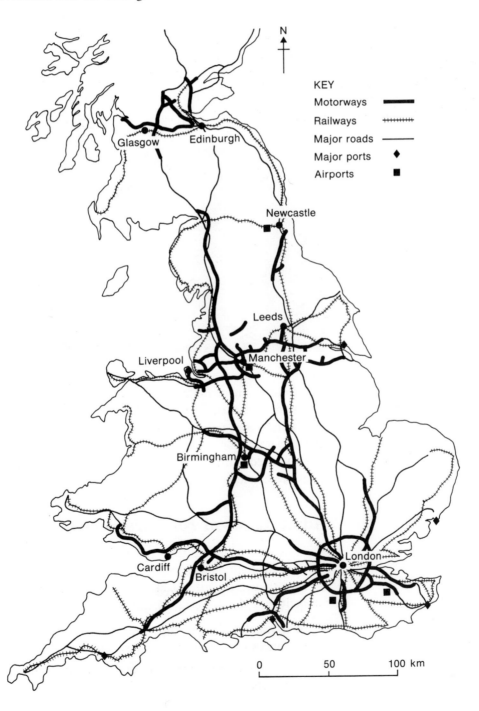

Own fleets

Many businesses arrange their own deliveries using their own vehicles because there are certain advantages in doing this:

- it *can* be cheaper if there are regular and sufficient loads to be carried;
- it gives direct contact with customers and problems can be sorted out more quickly;
- a business is handling its own goods and is therefore more likely to look after them;
- a business can respond more quickly to customers' urgent needs;
- deliveries can be arranged more flexibly concerning routes and times – delivery schedules can be changed;
- the fleet provides free advertising for the business wherever the vehicles travel.

However, these advantages have to be compared with the high cost of operating an own fleet. Vehicles have to be purchased, licensed, maintained, fuelled and insured. Drivers have to be paid regularly and a transport manager will be needed. All these costs can mean that the operation is dearer than hiring the service of haulage firms when needed, unless frequent use is made of the fleet and adequate loads are carried.

Advantages of road transport

- It is much quicker than rail over short distances, as there is no intermediate handling;
- door-to-door delivery reduces the chance of damage or theft and is generally more convenient;
- it is usually cheaper than rail for smaller loads and over shorter distances – lower operating costs and less handling;
- roads are more widespread and reach most parts of the United Kingdom;

- delivery times and routes are more flexible compared with other forms of transport;
- roads such as motorways are more suitable for difficult loads, especially in terms of width and height;
- many of the benefits of own fleets cannot be obtained by rail.

Disadvantages of road transport

- It is much less suited for carrying large quantities of bulk goods, such as coal and iron ore – many loads are needed compared with one train;
- it can be slower than rail over long distances, because of traffic congestion;
- the social costs of road transport may be higher in terms of air pollution, noise and damage to roads/buildings;
- road vehicles can carry only a certain maximum weight;
- road transport is more likely to be disrupted in bad weather conditions compared with rail;
- the direct vehicle operating costs are high compared with the load carried, especially the driver's wages and fuel which is heavily taxed.

Rail transport

Railways are used extensively by passengers and freight, but as road transport has developed their importance has declined steadily during the twentieth century. Railways in the United Kingdom now account only for approximately 15 per cent of inland freight carried, in terms of distance and weight.

All the main railway routes in the United Kingdom are operated by British Rail, which is a public corporation. It came into existence when the private railway companies were nationalised in 1948. Since then the railways have generally operated at a loss, and the taxpayer's money has provided government subsidies. Over the years various measures have been taken to improve British Rail's financial position, the most famous being the 'Beeching' Plan in 1963. As a result of this plan, a large number of uneconomic stations and lines were closed down, and since then the emphasis has been on improving the service on major routes. However, certain uneconomic lines have been kept open in the public interest where they are of special importance to local communities.

In order for rail to provide better competition with road transport, the following improvements have been made in recent years:

- the development of fast 'inter-city' passenger services, especially the High Speed Train;

- the development of fast mainline services for the delivery of goods – the 'Freightliner' services;

- as part of the Freightliner system, the rolling stock has been modified to provide door-to-door container services (see later);

- in order to improve speed and safety, automatic signalling and continuously welded track have been introduced;

- rolling stock has been modernised and special forms developed for various goods, for example car transporters and demountable tanks for liquids;

- more efficient and powerful diesel engines and the electrification of some routes;

- the introduction of an express parcel delivery service by passenger train – called Red Star (same-day delivery – station to station) and Night Star (overnight delivery – door-to-door);

- the development of computer-controlled marshalling yards to speed up the rearrangement of wagons;

- the introduction of a national computerised database, giving information on the movement and location of all rail wagons (called TOPS).

Advantages of rail transport

- Bulk consignments of goods, such as coal and iron, can be handled more cheaply than by road transport, where a large number of vehicles would be needed to transport the same quantity carried by one train;

- over longer distances, say 200 miles, rail can be faster than road between main centres of population;

- rail routes go direct to the centre of cities and avoid road traffic congestion;

- there is less damage to the environment, for instance, from air pollution, and it is safer to carry dangerous goods by rail;

- very bad weather conditions are less likely to halt rail transport than road.

Disadvantages of rail transport

- Rail transport itself cannot generally deliver door-to-door, and the need to transfer from and to road makes the process slower, especially over short distances;

- the need to transfer goods increases the risk of theft and damage (but containerisation has helped here – see page 142);

- rail has very high fixed costs because of the need to operate and maintain its own permanent way and stations, whereas roads are used by the public in general;

- because of the costs of transfer and operation, rail tends to be more expensive than road, especially over short distances;

- rail transport has to run to fairly rigid timetables, whereas road transport is more flexible, especially where firms have their own fleets (see page 132).

CHECK THIS OUT

Write out the following sentences, filling in the missing words:

1 The development of transport has allowed countries and regions to _____ in what they can produce most easily and efficiently.

2 Methods of transport are by land, by _____ and by water.

3 Road transport is very convenient, as it offers a _____ _____ _____ delivery service which avoids intermediate handling.

4 Road transport can now provide a much faster service over long distances because of the building of _____ and the improvement of trunk roads.

5 Road transport is responsible for nearly _____ per cent of all inland freight transport in the United Kingdom.

6 Railways account for approximately _____ of inland freight carried, in terms of distance and weight.

7 All the main railway routes in the United Kingdom are operated by British Rail, which is a _____ _____.

8 Railways are especially suitable for carrying _____ loads over long distances.

9 The introduction of _____ engines and the electrification of some routes has improved the efficiency of rail transport.

10 Rail transport runs to fairly rigid timetables, but road transport is more _____.

Sea transport

Shipping is the main method of transport for carrying freight between continents and to or from islands, but the development of air transport has reduced its importance for carrying passengers. The island position of the United Kingdom means that sea transport is essential for carrying the majority of the vast quantity of imports and exports, as the only alternative is air transport.

Sea transport can be divided in the following ways:

Liners and tramp vessels

There are both passenger and cargo liners, but passenger liners will usually carry some freight, for example mail, and cargo liners may carry a few passengers. Liners are so-called because they operate on specified routes, such as Southampton to New York, at scheduled times and dates. Transportation can therefore be planned ahead and space booked, while charges are made according to the published tariffs, although there may be special rates for frequent users. Charges on many routes are fixed jointly by the various liner companies operating a particular route, through organisations called *shipping conferences*.

Tramp vessels do *not* operate on regular routes or at fixed times, but sail wherever and whenever shippers require their cargo to be taken. Bulk commodities such as coal or timber are usually carried; there are normally no passengers. Businesses which want commodities to be transported *charter* a tramp vessel, that is, they hire the use of it either for a period of time or for a voyage. *Time charters* can be for very long periods, perhaps ten years, or for short periods of six months, and the vessel has to be paid for whether or not it is being used. *Voyage charters* involve the hiring of the vessel for the carriage of freight between two or more ports. Vessels can be chartered through organised freight markets such as the Baltic Exchange in London.

General cargo and specialised vessels

This distinction relates to the type of cargo carried. Some vessels are built to carry a wide range of different goods, usually in smaller quantities, but others are built specially to carry a particular type of commodity or to have a particular role, for example:

- container ships – to carry large standard-size metal boxes (see later);

- bulk carriers – to carry large quantities of one commodity, such as coal or timber;

- tankers – a special type of bulk carrier to carry particular liquids or gases, for instance an oil tanker;

- ferries – to allow vehicles, including lorries and trains, to drive on for a sea crossing and then drive off – sometimes called RO–RO vessels (short for roll-on/roll-off).

Ocean and coastal vessels

Ocean vessels are those which travel long distances across the oceans of the world such as the Atlantic and the Pacific Oceans, and are often very far from land. The term 'coastal vessels' can be used to include all those ships which operate fairly close to land and generally undertake shorter journeys than ocean vessels. They tend to be smaller than ocean vessels and can use smaller ports. Examples are those which operate along coasts between ports in one country, such as London to Hull, or between two countries such as Calais to Rotterdam. They may make short sea crossings, for instance, Liverpool to Dublin or Hull to Oslo.

It is important to realise that the above sections refer to three *different* ways of dividing sea transport into categories and that various cross combinations are possible. For example, a tramp vessel could be an oil tanker which is operating on short routes in the North Sea, or a liner could be a container ship which has its regular route across the Atlantic Ocean. See what other variations exist.

Lloyd's Register

This is issued yearly and is a Register of ocean-going ships. After a ship has been surveyed, it is classified according to the soundness of its design, structure and maintenance, and the survey is repeated regularly to ensure that the required standards for its classification are being maintained. This Register is important to those who are insuring or chartering ships.

The Register should not be confused with *Lloyd's List and Shipping Gazette* which is published by Lloyd's Corporation (see Chapter 11) and shows the daily movements of vessels.

Advantages of sea transport

- Very large bulk loads can be carried by one ship;
- ships offer a relatively cheap form of transportation compared with air;
- no permanent way needs to be built or maintained (except access to docks);
- it is the most suitable form of transport for carrying large, heavy items.

Disadvantages of sea transport

- It is a relatively slow form of transport and is unsuitable for urgent goods;
- it cannot deliver goods directly to inland destinations and costly transfers may be needed (but see 'Containerisation' later);
- goods can be easily lost or damaged (but see 'Containerisation' again);
- bad weather can cause delays and losses at sea.

Ports and docks

If sea transport is to work efficiently there must also be good ports and docks, so that cargo can be handled quickly and cheaply. Ports therefore need:

- good transport connections inland;
- mechanised handling facilities;
- experienced and trained staff, such as dockers;
- sheltered docking and deep-water access;
- adequate pilotage and berthing facilities;
- fuelling, provisioning and maintenance facilities;
- warehouse and office buildings.

Ports have often been criticised for not providing a good service, with goods and ships being delayed, goods being lost or damaged and charges being high. In recent years, however, there have been major investments and improvements in the main ports, especially in mechanised handling and the use of containers (see later), so that the transfer of goods is speedier and the costs of importing/exporting have been reduced.

Air transport

Air transport is the most recent method to be developed and it is now the most important method for carrying passengers over long distances between continents. However, it still carries only a very small proportion of freight in terms of weight, although the distance that can be covered compensates substantially, and its importance is growing only very slowly.

Most countries have their own national airlines which are controlled
by each government. In the case of the United Kingdom, this used
to be British Airways, which was privatised in 1987. There are also
many other private airlines which carry passengers and/or freight.
Airlines operate many scheduled flights between most countries in
the world, that is flights leaving and arriving on set days and at set
times, but there are also chartered flights where an aircraft is
specially hired by a business to carry a group of passengers, for
instance on a skiing holiday, or a large quantity of freight. This is
similar to the arrangements for using ships, and the Baltic Exchange
is the main charter market for aircraft as well as for ships.

Advantages of air transport

- A high travelling speed which makes air transport a very quick
  method over long distances;
- both land and sea can be crossed in one journey without the
  need to transfer people or cargo;
- the speed of air transport over long distances makes it especially
  important for transporting perishable goods or live animals, and
  urgent medical supplies or spare parts;

- light valuable goods such as diamonds can be transferred with less fear of theft, and therefore insurance rates are low;

- the speed of air means that stocks of light valuable goods can be kept low, saving space and tied-up capital, as they can be renewed quickly when necessary;

- expensive delicate equipment such as computers can be carried with less fear of damage, and less packing is needed;

- people can reach destinations very quickly, thus saving time and energy.

Disadvantages of air transport

- Air is an expensive means of transport, especially for heavy, bulky goods such as cement and coal;

- the carrying capacity of aircraft is limited in terms of weight and volume;

- air transport is less convenient for many people because the location of the relevant airport may mean that considerable distances have to be travelled before the air journey can begin;

- over short distances, the aircraft speed cannot make up the time lost getting to and from an airport, and the longer checking-in time;

- bad weather conditions are more likely to delay or halt air transport compared with land or sea transport.

Improvements

In order to overcome these disadvantages, there have been many improvements in air transport in recent years, making it much more competitive. Among the improvements are:

- the size of aircraft has increased so that they are more economic to run when compared to the load carried;

- improved design, for instance of the fuselage and engine, has increased fuel efficiency, which has helped to reduce costs;

- aircraft are now much faster and more reliable;

- improved loading through larger doors, for example at the nose and tail, has speeded the process and raised the maximum size of load;

- the number of airports has increased and handling facilities improved, so that less time is wasted at each end of a journey;

- special lightweight containers have been developed for aircraft;

- adverse weather causes fewer delays because of the development of improved landing and navigation systems such as 'auto-pilots'.

Inland waterways

These waterways consist of canals, rivers and lakes. In the United Kingdom people now use them mostly for pleasure and they carry a very small proportion of all goods transported. In other parts of the world, however, they are of much greater importance, for example the Panama Canal, the Great Lakes of North America and the River Rhine in Europe.

In the United Kingdom, there are nevertheless some inland waterways which have limited commercial importance, for example the Manchester Ship Canal, the Aire and Calder navigation in the North-East and the Caledonian Canal in Scotland. Most canals are the responsibility of the British Waterways Board (a public corporation), which maintains them, has its own fleets of barges for hire and charges tolls for the use of the canals by private barges.

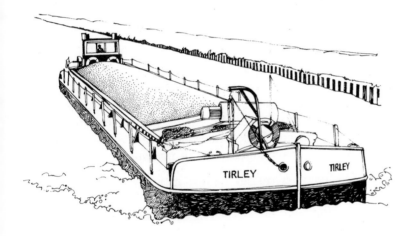

Inland waterways are unlikely to regain the importance to the United Kingdom's transport system they had in the late eighteenth and early nineteenth centuries, as they have been superseded firstly by rail transport and then by road transport. The advantages of inland waterways compared with these alternative forms of transport are generally outweighed by their substantial disadvantages.

Advantages of inland waterways

- Barges can carry large loads of bulky goods such as coal, cement and clay;
- fuel and other barge operating costs are quite low;
- the smoothness of the journey makes them suitable for carrying fragile goods.

Disadvantages of inland waterways

- Inland waterways reach only a limited number of locations and there is no national network in the United Kingdom;
- the method of transport is extremely slow, because of the restricted speed of barges and many locks on the routes;

- many waterways, especially canals, are very narrow and cannot take wide barges;
- labour costs are high in relation to the short distance which can be covered daily;
- very cold weather prevents their use because of freezing over;
- canals are very expensive to maintain – banks, dredging, locks and aquaducts need regular attention.

Pipeline transport

Pipelines have been widely used since the nineteenth century for supplying gas and water to local areas, but in recent times their use in transferring gas and liquids over long distances has increased dramatically. In the United Kingdom, crude oil is transported by pipeline both overland and under the sea, and there is also a national pipeline grid for the supply of natural gas.

An important advantage of pipelines is that once built they cost very little to use. Maintenance costs are low (so very little labour is needed), and fuel costs are very small compared with the use of vehicles. A continuous flow of the product is more guaranteed, as pipelines are not normally affected by the weather or labour strikes. There is less pollution of the atmosphere, compared with vehicles, and there is greater safety, especially for flammables.

Pipelines are, however, rather limited in use when considering the type of product which can be carried, and once built they can be used only for one type. Installation costs are high as they are usually placed underground, and long-term use must therefore be guaranteed if they are to be financially worthwhile.

Containerisation

Containers are not a separate method of transport, as they are carried by several of the methods of transport which we have looked at previously. They are very large 'boxes', usually with steel frames and aluminium panels, into which goods are packed for transportation. Each container can then be quickly and easily loaded onto the carrying vehicle or ship by mechanical means, and can similarly be unloaded at destination. Individual cartons of goods do not have to be handled.

More importantly many of these containers are of standard sizes and can be transferred between different forms of transport, especially between road, rail and sea, as lorries, rail wagons and ships have been specially designed to hold standard containers. In this way, an *integrated transport system* has developed, so that goods can be carried by more than one form of transport in order to reach their destination, but without the need for slow and expensive transfer of individual items. A lorry could, for example, pick up a container from a town without a rail connection and take it to the nearest railway station. A train could then take the container to a port where it could be unloaded at the dockside directly onto a ship for transfer by sea to another port, where the same arrangement could apply in reverse.

The use of containers has benefited the distribution of goods within countries and abroad because:

- the transfer of goods is much quicker because of the speedy handling;
- vehicles and ships can be used more fully as they do not have to wait long to be loaded/unloaded and there is a faster turn-around for the next journey;
- distribution costs are reduced because of faster, mechanised handling and the need to employ less labour;
- there is less chance of theft because containers are locked on departure;
- there is less chance of damage because the containers are sealed and there is less handling;
- less warehousing is needed as the containers can be stored outside;
- once they have been checked and sealed by Customs, the containers can be taken across national frontiers without further checking until they reach their destination (the TIR system).

Containers cannot, however, improve transport facilities in all cases. This is because:

- not all vehicles and ships are standardised to carry containers;
- not all departure or destination points have the mechanised handling facilities: large capital investment is needed for these;
- they are not economic for carrying very small loads, as there would be wasted space;
- many goods are unsuitable for containerisation, or there is no advantage in using containers as, for example, when transporting bulk coal supplies or motor vehicles;
- some forms of transport, such as narrow barges and aircraft, are unsuitable for standard containers (but note that special smaller and/or lightweight containers are used).

CHECK THIS OUT

Write out the following sentences, filling in the missing words:

1 The island position of the United Kingdom means that _____ _____ is essential for carrying most imports and exports.

2 Ships can be classified as _____ and tramp vessels.

3 Businesses which want commodities to be transported by sea _____ a tramp vessel either for a period of time or for a voyage.

4 Coastal vessels may operate along coasts between ports in one country, or between two _____ or they may make short sea crossings.

5 The Register of ocean-going ships which is issued yearly is called _____ _____.

6 Air transport carries a _____ proportion of freight in terms of weight.

7 Air transport is particularly suited to the carrying of _____ valuable goods such as _____.

8 Air transport may be inconvenient for people who live _____ distances from the nearest airport.

9 _____ allow goods to be transferred easily from one form of transport to another.

10 Most canals in the United Kingdom carry only a very small proportion of goods, and people use them largely for _____.

Which transport to use

The advantages and disadvantages of the different forms of transport have been examined, but how does a business decide which form to use for moving a certain quantity of goods from point A to point B? Some or all of the following general points will need to be considered:

- *Cost* – the cheapest form of transport will be chosen, provided that it satisfies other needs. Cost is more important in the transfer of cheap, bulky goods than light, valuable ones.

- *Time* – speed of delivery is more important in some cases than in others. Perishables and goods required urgently need fast transportation, even if the cost is higher.

- *Availability* – some means of transport will not be available for transferring goods or sending people to all destinations. For example, many places do not have a railway station, and choice is more restricted when sending goods abroad.

- *Distance* – the time saved by a faster means of transport on a short journey is less significant than on a long journey.

- *Safety* – the chances of damage or theft are greater in the case of some methods of transport. This point is more important for fragile and valuable goods (note the use of containers).

Apart from these general points, there may also be special considerations in particular cases:

- the buyer may give instructions about the method of transport required;

- return loads may be available if a particular method of transport is used;
- it may be impossible to send certain types of goods by some types of transport because of weight, height, width, etc.;
- a particular carrier may be known to give a reliable service.

All these many different points have to be considered and each one has to be balanced against the others where they are important. For example, the fastest and cheapest method of transport might not be used because the safety of the goods could be better guaranteed by another method.

The points above have been considered in relation to goods, but mostly apply also to the transport of passengers. For example, what decides which form of transport you use when you go on holiday?

SHORT QUESTIONS

1 Name the two main methods of inland freight transport available for use in the United Kingdom.

2 What is the TIR system?

3 What is a tramp ship?

4 Give one reason why road transport is so popular.

5 What is Lloyd's Register?

6 What is meant by *chartering* a ship?

7 What type of transport would you use for taking diamonds from London to Singapore? Give one reason for your answer.

8 Give two points which a business will consider when deciding on suitable transport.

9 Give an example of a specialised cargo ship.

10 Give one reason why transport is needed.

MULTIPLE CHOICE QUESTIONS

There are four possible answers to each of the following questions. Study the introductory sentence, and then decide which of the alternatives answers correctly the question or completes the sentence. Write down the question number and follow it with (A) (B) (C) or (D), according to your choice.

1 We need transport because
  (A) nowadays everyone lives close to their work
  (B) we have to send goods in containers
  (C) areas tend to specialise
  (D) holidays abroad are becoming more common.

2 Which of the following institutions helps shipowners?
  (A) Lloyd's of London
  (B) The Baltic Exchange

  (C) The London Commodity Exchange
  (D) travel agency

3 The cheapest and quickest way of sending newspapers from Manchester to Edinburgh to catch the morning delivery will be
  (A) tramp steamer up the coast
  (B) by air
  (C) by post
  (D) by rail.

4 A benefit of road transport has been
  (A) the fact that vehicles can only carry a maximum weight
  (B) direct vehicle operating costs are low
  (C) the motorway network has improved road delivery times
  (D) road transport is always cheaper than rail transport.

5 Which of the following is an *advantage* of road transport?
(A) It eliminates the risk of pilfering
(B) It can operate to a flexible schedule
(C) It is a cheap way to transport heavy loads over long distances
(D) It is the quickest way to transport bulky loads over long distances

6 Liners are those ships which
(A) can carry passengers but not cargo
(B) can carry passengers *and* cargo
(C) only operate between foreign ports
(D) have no regular schedule.

7 Containerisation is a transport system which involves
(A) packaging goods in equal quantities to fit a container
(B) transporting units of standard sizes for trains and lorries
(C) breaking down large units of goods to fit into boxes
(D) keeping goods in standard size packets.

8 A large bakery distributing bread would normally transport it by
(A) rail
(B) car
(C) container unit
(D) van.

9 Which of the following statements is true of canals?
(A) Canals are very economical for transporting goods.
(B) Old stretches of canals are being reclaimed and used for leisure.
(C) All canals are now closed to barges.
(D) Anglers on canals are trying to have boating banned.

10 A disadvantage of rail travel is that
(A) it is expensive to move heavy freight
(B) goods wagons are not being used all the time
(C) only passengers can be carried on fast inter-city routes
(D) special cheap rates can be quoted only for a whole train-load of goods.

11 When road transport is chosen, it is because
(A) it is important to maintain use of motorways
(B) goods can be delivered from door to door
(C) it is usually the cheapest way of carrying goods long distances
(D) people are always available to accept deliveries.

12 Air transport is unlikely to be suitable for transporting
(A) light, expensive, perishable goods
(B) medicines to a disaster area
(C) goods such as diamonds which need to be secure
(D) non-urgent spare parts for machinery.

13 Goods exported from the United Kingdom to the Common Market (the EEC) would NOT go by
(A) rail
(B) air
(C) tramp ship
(D) car ferry.

14 A disadvantage of pipeline transport is that
(A) maintenance costs are low
(B) it is affected by the weather
(C) the cost of installation is high
(D) fuel costs do not compare favourably with road transport.

There are four possible answers to each of the following questions.

If you think (1) only is correct, write down A.
If you think (1) and (2) only are correct, write down B.
If you think (3) and (4) only are correct, write down C.
If you think (2), (3) and (4) only are correct, write down D.

15 Which of the following types of transport is/are suitable for the United Kingdom for international trade?
(1) Hot air balloon
(2) Aeroplane
(3) Tramp steamer
(4) Cargo liner.

16 Which of the following statements is/are correct?
(1) Air transport is used only for very light goods
(2) Sea transport is used only for international trade
(3) Motorways have reduced the time taken for long journeys by road
(4) Freightliner is NOT a fast mainline service for delivery of goods

17 Disadvantage(s) of canal transport is/are that
(1) extremes of weather prevent its use
(2) it is a slow method of transport
(3) operating costs are very high
(4) barges cannot carry large loads of bulky goods.

18 Ports which are to handle cargo efficiently need
   (1) access to an airport
   (2) mechanised handling facilities
   (3) fuelling facilities
   (4) experienced staff.

19 Air travel has the advantage(s) of

   (1) getting urgent supplies quickly to where they are needed
   (2) being a quick way to go abroad from the United Kingdom
   (3) having no delays which cuts down time taken for a journey
   (4) being a cheap way to transport people on holiday.

STIMULUS RESPONSE QUESTIONS

The following questions carry a mark of 20. Each section of a question shows the marks for the correct response.

1 Read the following information carefully, and then answer the questions on it.

New premises for Phillips Contract Hire are situated conveniently in the centre of the country and in easy reach of the northern industrial areas.

Phillips offer one of the finest truck rental services in the area, with 135 vehicles ranging in size from 20 cwt to 40 tons and specialised refrigerated lorries mean that they can cater for most requirements. The fleet is renewed every two years so that there are few breakdowns.

Trucks are serviced in Phillips' own workshops with every facility, and the rental fee includes a maintenance package and 24-hour breakdown service. Long-term rentals are very competitive and customers are beginning to appreciate the savings to be made by renting transport.

(a) Why are the new premises said to be convenient? *(2 marks)*

(b) How can the firm cater for most requirements? *(3 marks)*

(c) What steps does the firm take to counter truck breakdown? *(3 marks)*

(d) What does the truck rental customer get for his/her money? *(4 marks)*

(e) Suggest *two* savings a customer might make by renting transport. *(4 marks)*

(f) State *two* disadvantages to a firm of not buying outright its own fleet of vehicles for delivering goods. *(4 marks)*

2 Read the following information and then answer the questions on it.

Computex is a United Kingdom manufacturer of home computers. Most deliveries within the United Kingdom are made using Computex's own fleet of vehicles while deliveries abroad are usually made by air.

(a) (i) Give *four* reasons why Computex uses road transport for most deliveries in the United Kingdom. *(4 marks)*

    (ii) What might be the *advantages* and *disadvantages* to Computex of having its own fleet of vehicles for such deliveries? *(8 marks)*

(b) Why does Computex normally use air transport for deliveries overseas? *(4 marks)*

(c) (i) Name *two* telecommunication services. *(2 marks)*

    (ii) Briefly show how *each* of these services might be used by Computex to meet customer's orders more quickly. *(2 marks)*

(See Chapter 12 on Telecommunications to assist with the answers for (c).)

(This question appears by kind permission of the Southern Regional Examinations Board for the GCSE Commerce paper.)

ESSAY QUESTIONS

1 (a) What are the reasons for the increase in the commercial use of air transport during recent years? *(12 marks)*

   (b) Why is it likely that other types of transport will continue to carry a larger volume of goods than air transport? *(8 marks)*

   (This question appears by kind permission of the London & East Anglian Group for the GCSE Commerce paper.)

2 (a) Describe the use of containers in goods transport. *(10 marks)*

   (b) Explain the advantages of containers in the distribution of goods. *(10 marks)*

3 (a) Why is the total amount of freight carried annually by air transport still relatively small? *(8 marks)*

   (b) Give *three* different examples of goods which are often transported by air, indicating the reason in each case. *(12 marks)*

4 (a) What are the main points to be considered when deciding which form of transport should be used to move goods to customers? *(15 marks)*

   (b) Explain the work of the Baltic Exchange in connection with the transporting of goods. *(5 marks)*

5 (a) What advantages are to be gained by sending goods by road transport? *(10 marks)*

   (b) What are the disadvantages of road transport compared to rail transport? *(10 marks)*

6 Air freight has the advantage of speed, but it has some disadvantages. Explain these disadvantages, distinguishing between
   (a) goods to be distributed within the United Kingdom; *(10 marks)*
   (b) goods to be sent abroad. *(10 marks)*

7 In view of the increasing congestion on the roads in the United Kingdom, the Government could pass laws which restrict goods carried by road, and have them transported by rail. Indicate
   (a) the advantages (i) to road users and (ii) to customers, and *(10 marks)*
   (b) the disadvantages (i) to road haulage firms and (ii) to customers, *(10 marks)*
   which could arise as a result of such an action.

8 (a) Describe *two* major developments in transport which have taken place in recent years. *(8 marks)*

   (b) Explain *three* factors which could influence a manufacturer's choice of transport, giving examples. *(12 marks)*

NOW TRY THIS

Choose from the following words and use them to fill in the blanks in the following sentences. Write out the sentences together with the words you have chosen.

containers   flexible   sea   choice   railway   passengers

1 When goods are transported from other areas, we have a wider _____.

2 Manufacturers can send goods by land using pipeline, road or _____ transport.

3 Rail transport has been greatly improved by the use of _____.

4 Road transport is the most important form of transport in the United Kingdom for both freight and _____.

5 The United Kingdom depends mainly on _____ transport to carry its imports and exports.

6 Transport by road is the most _____ kind of transport.

LEARN IT YOURSELF

1 Prepare a topic folder on the Baltic Exchange.

2 Make a study of how people in the area reach their place of work, and how people in business who have to travel in the course of their work do their travelling. You may use a tape recorder and personal interview to record this assignment. Ask friends and neighbours, fellow students and teachers to put you in touch with a variety of people they know who use various forms of travel.

3 Find out the location of your nearest airport and the purposes for which it is used. (There may be a Freight Manager there who will be able to give you information.) Find out the main types of goods which go by air, and anything else of interest on the topic of air travel.

4 For one week collect any newspaper or magazine references to freight transport, especially any local news. Present the cuttings in a folder, and add a short report about any developments or problems which these cuttings show.

5 Considering our ever-increasing problems of expense, pollution, congestion and noise caused by our existing transport systems, design a method of transport that may be used in 200 years' time. Include plans, sketches and explanations.

ASSIGNMENTS – THE WORLD OF TRANSPORT

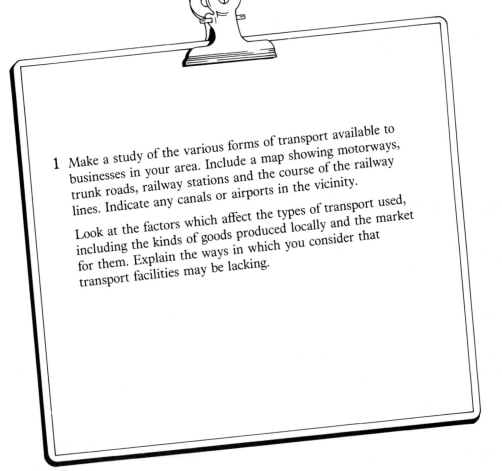

1 Make a study of the various forms of transport available to businesses in your area. Include a map showing motorways, trunk roads, railway stations and the course of the railway lines. Indicate any canals or airports in the vicinity.

Look at the factors which affect the types of transport used, including the kinds of goods produced locally and the market for them. Explain the ways in which you consider that transport facilities may be lacking.

2 Find out if your local authority has information for tourists to your area and if so, how do tourists reach your locality? What transport is available for them to visit places of interest? Could there be any improvement made to transport facilities? If so, what?

Present a report of your findings, with maps and illustrations.

CHAPTER 10

INSURANCE

Introduction

Insurance is a means whereby individuals and organisations can protect themselves from possible losses caused by many everyday and less frequent risks. These risks are continually present in our lives, for example cooking on a stove could result in fire damage and injury, and driving a car could result in a collision and injury to yourself or others. Risks *do* result in some losses, but usually they do not. However, no one knows beforehand what will happen so we insure particular risks just in case, although as we shall see later, not all risks can be insured.

Pooling of risks

The first insurance in the United Kingdom was provided in the fourteenth century. The owners of ships, setting out on sea voyages to other parts of the world, suffered so many losses through sinking and piracy that a group of owners got together in London to help one another. Each owner paid a sum of money into a central fund or 'pool' and owners who were unlucky enough to lose their ships were compensated out of this pool.

The operation of insurance today still rests on the idea of pooling risks. Individuals or organisations wishing to 'cover' a certain risk (for example fire damage to property) regularly pay a sum of money, called a *premium*, into a 'pool' of money and are called the *insured*. Those who actually suffer fire loss are then compensated from this pool out of all the premiums paid, while the majority who do not suffer loss receive nothing. In this way the risk is spread among all the insured.

These various 'pools' are organised by insurance companies, friendly societies and Lloyd's underwriters (see later) who are called the *insurers* and who collect the premiums and arrange to pay out claims. The size of premiums to cover particular risks is fixed so that the total money received is enough to cover all the claims and expenses involved in running the pool, as well as making a profit for the insurers. How premiums are fixed will be discussed later, but if an insurance company gets its figures wrong, then it may be unable to pay all the claims and it will go out of business.

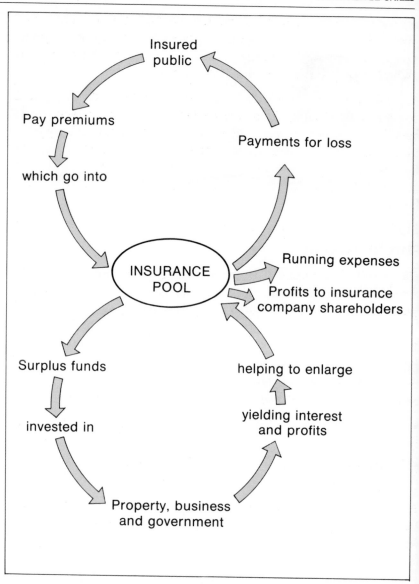

As you can imagine, the total value of premiums paid to insurers is very high and the 'pools' are very large. Most of this money will not be needed immediately to pay out on claims from the insured persons. This is especially true in the case of life assurance which often runs for many years. This means that the insurers continually have spare funds which they lend to individuals, businesses and the Government in return for profits and interest. These sums are in turn paid into the pools, thus making them more secure and, in the case of endowment assurance (see later), some of these profits may be paid out to insured persons in addition to their basic claims.

Importance of insurance

Insurance is extremely important to both individuals and businesses. If individuals and their families are unfortunate enough to suffer a loss, for example their home burning down, then insurance helps them to rebuild their lives more quickly. Similarly, insurance helps businesses to overcome unfortunate events, such as a factory explosion, which might otherwise force them into bankruptcy and closure. Insurance thus encourages businesses to invest and expand, which increases their efficiency and their profits, and in turn helps to improve the community's living standards.

As shown above, insurance also directly helps individuals and businesses by lending them funds which the insurance companies have built up over the years. Individuals can, for example, buy their own houses, and businesses can expand and improve. The following figures, based on British Insurance Association calculations, give an idea of the ways in which insurance companies use each £1 of their funds:

34p is invested in shares in industry and commerce, at home and abroad;

29p is lent out to businesses and families, for example for property purchase;

26p is lent out to the British Government and local councils;

11p is kept in reserve to pay claims by the public.

Insurance is of special importance to the United Kingdom because of the help which it gives to the country's balance of payments by earning foreign currency abroad. It does this in two ways:

• Many insurance policies are sold abroad and the profits from these are returned to the United Kingdom.

• Funds are invested abroad in businesses and governments, and dividends/interest are similarly returned to the United Kingdom.

All this helps to boost the country's so-called 'invisible earnings' (see Chapter 15) from abroad, which helps to pay for essential and other imports.

CHECK THIS OUT

Write out the following sentences, filling in the missing words:

1 Insurance is a means whereby individuals and organisations can protect themselves from _____ _____ which may result from many risks.

2 The operation of insurance today rests on the idea of the _____ of _____.

3 The insured public make regular payments called premiums, which go into _____ _____

and pay running expenses and all insurance claims.

4 Insurers have spare funds which they lend to individuals, _____ and the Government in return for profit and interest.

5 Insurers will lend money to _____ to buy their own homes.

6 Insurance earns _____ currency by selling insurance policies abroad.

Life assurance

This can be subdivided into four types, each designed to meet the needs of different individuals.

Whole life

This form of assurance guarantees a sum of money to the dependants of the assured when that person dies. The person decides on the value of the policy required, and the assurance company then calculates how much the person will have to pay each year for the whole of his or her life. Alternatively, a close relative can take out life assurance on the other person and pay the premiums instead. Later in the chapter (see pages 161–2), we shall see how premiums are fixed in general, but in this case, age and health are the main considerations. As you grow older the chance of dying becomes greater. For example, more people die at the age of 60 than do at 30. This is why older people have to pay higher premiums, as do those who have a personal record of ill-health or a family history of a particular illness. A person's occupation may also give rise to a higher premium, as some occupations have a record of more accidents or more disease. These considerations also affect the premiums charged for the other types of life assurance explained below. These are not automatically for a person's entire life, therefore the policy duration will also affect the figures.

Term

Term assurance is similar to whole life, except that a person is covered for a fixed period of time only, for example 20 years, and not for the whole of his or her life. This type of cover is cheaper, as the insurance company will not have to pay for the person if they die after the period covered has ended. This is often used to give temporary cover when a person's children are growing up, or during the period of a large loan or mortgage, so that an individual's dependants are not left with large debts if the insured person dies. The disadvantage is, however, that the policy has no value at the end of its full period.

Life endowment

A popular way of saving for the future and taking out life assurance is by having *life endowment assurance*. The person who is insured can agree to pay a fixed monthly or yearly sum for a fixed period of time and in return can get an agreed sum of money at a fixed date in the future. The agreed date of payment is called the maturity date. If the insured person dies before the maturity date, his or her dependents receive the lump sum originally agreed and need make no more payments. This type of assurance is quite expensive as it allows a person to save and have life cover. Some insurance companies offer a *with-profits* endowment assurance. This means that the insurance company adds bonuses to the sum the person is insured for each year. These are paid from the profits the company makes by investing money from the assurance pool. A with-profits assurance costs more than *without-profits* cover because of this extra benefit.

If a person prefers to receive regular payments rather than one lump sum, they may choose an *annuity assurance*. In return for the insured person's regular payments (or single large payment) to the assurance fund, the company guarantees to make regular payments from a fixed date in the future until the person dies. Most people arrange for the fixed date to coincide with the day when they retire from work. In some ways, annuity insurance is like a pension fund as it guarantees an individual regular payments until they die, in return for small regular instalments beforehand. This is very popular with self-employed people who have no pension from an employer.

MOSSTOWN ASSURANCE CO.

Your Tax Free Benefits
(amount of guaranteed life cover payable on death)

Net monthly payment	£6	£8	£10	£12	£15
Male age* next birthday	£	£	£	£	£
25–30	38 300	49 149			
35	27 200	34 021	41 353		
37	25 100	32 365	37 842	50 282	
40	17 400	21 823	25 058	33 324	41 661
46	10 500	15 012	15 169	20 291	24 118
50	6600	8326	9639	12 978	15 031
55	4700	6230	7974	8326	9382
60+	2800	4731	5891	6307	7661

*For women, take 3 years off the male age

An example of an advertisement for life endowment assurance

Fire insurance

This was a very early form of insurance which developed very rapidly after the Great Fire of London in 1666. Under a fire policy, insurance companies will compensate for damage to buildings and contents, unless the fire was started deliberately by the insured. Lightning damage is usually included, and fire policies are often extended to cover damage by natural events, such as wind, flood and earthquake. Where special precautions are taken, for example the installation of a sprinkler system, lower premiums are charged.

Fire can happen to anybody

Business interruption

Normal fire insurance covers a business for any damage to premises or contents, but it does not cover for the losses which occur when a business has to close down temporarily or restrict production because of a fire. Profits may be lost because goods cannot be produced and sold, and some costs may still have to be paid, for example rates and the wages of some staff. These losses arise as a consequence of fire, and such cover is sometimes referred to as consequential loss insurance.

It can also be extended to losses arising as a consequence of other perils which are covered by fire insurance, for example flooding, but beyond this there are other examples such as losses arising from the breakdown of machinery or computers, accidental damage by vehicles, power failure or the inability of other firms to supply essentials because of fire or similar problems.

Goods in transit

Goods run the risk of being damaged or stolen when they are in transit (that is, being transported) from point to point. A goods-in-transit insurance policy will give protection against loss.

Cash in transit

You may have seen films which show all the precautions taken by security firms when cash is transferred between banks and businesses, but even then armed hold-ups and other thefts still happen. Firms can take out insurance against the loss of cash as a result of hold-ups or other misfortunes when cash is being transported.

Plate glass

The glass used in the windows of shops and in the doors of many commercial premises is specially strengthened and very tough. This makes it very expensive and, if it is broken, it is costly to replace. Businesses are therefore wise to insure for damage caused by accident or by vandalism.

Employer's liability

The law requires all businesses to have employer's liability insurance. This means that if any of the firm's employees are killed or injured and the firm is at fault, there is money available to compensate them or their dependants. The law requires that each firm displays its insurance certificate at its place of business.

Although not legally required, larger businesses also take out *public liability* policies, which covers them for claims made by the general public who have suffered loss through the fault of the business. An example might be an injury caused through tripping over a loose tile on a shop floor.

Commercial Union Assurance
Certificate of Employers' Liability Insurance

C U
ASSURANCE

(A copy or copies of this certificate must be displayed at each place of business at which the policyholder employs persons covered by the policy)

POLICY NUMBER

UQ923830040   D

NAME OF POLICYHOLDER

STANLEY THORNES PUBLISHER

DATE OF COMMENCEMENT OF INSURANCE

31 DECEMBER 1986

DATE OF EXPIRY OF INSURANCE

31 DECEMBER 1987

We hereby certify that the policy to which this certificate relates satisfies the requirements of the relevant law applicable in Great Britain, Northern Ireland, the Isle of Man, the Island of Jersey, the Island of Guernsey and the Island of Alderney, or to offshore installations in territorial waters around Great Britain and its Continental Shelf.

B. R. West
Signed on behalf of Commercial Union Assurance Company plc

Theft

Apart from the special 'transit' insurances explained above, businesses and individuals also need to cover for possible losses through thefts from premises and homes. Thefts are not always caused by 'break-ins' and losses can occur through the dishonesty of a business's own employees. To cover such losses, a business can take out a *fidelity guarantee* policy, which is especially important where employees are handling large sums of cash or small, valuable goods.

Marine insurance

This type of insurance is concerned with sea transport, although it also covers some aircraft insurance. It can be divided into four types:

Cargo   This type covers goods which are being carried by the ship for damage or loss. Insurance can be taken to cover a valuable cargo on a particular voyage, say from London to New York, but *open* (or *floating*) policies are often arranged for overseas traders. An open policy may be taken out if it is not certain how many voyages will be made or how long cover will be needed. An open policy gives cover for a fixed amount of money, and as each voyage is made, the value of the goods moved is deducted from the total insurance cover, until it is used up.

Freight   This refers to the actual charge for carrying cargo and not to the cargo itself. Where the freight charge has been prepaid to the shipping company, then it forms part of the cargo's value and risk. The shipping company will take out a separate policy if this is not the case, because if cargoes are not delivered through, for example, loss at sea, they will otherwise be unable to claim the charge.

Hull   This covers the value of the ship itself, in case of damage or total loss, and liability for damage to other ships. Usually, such cover is now issued on a 'time' basis, for example, one year, rather than a voyage basis.

Liability   This is required because shipowners may become liable for the injury or death of passengers travelling on ships or for damage to or loss of their property. Damage could also be caused to harbours and docks.

Household insurance

All the forms of insurance discussed above are concerned with individual risks, but there are also 'composite' forms of insurance available which cover a number of different risks in one policy. Household, holiday and motor vehicle insurance are three common examples. For instance, a person on holiday may be able to claim for loss as a result of illness *and* theft if they have holiday insurance.

Household insurance is divided into two main parts: contents and buildings.

Contents Insurance covers the moveable items in your home (for example, furniture, carpets, sports equipment, records, televisions and videos, etc.) so long as they are in the house – or, in most cases, being used by you away from home. Loss as a result of theft, fire, flooding, lightning and other dangers, such as accidental damage, will be covered. Even if you are sharing a house or flat, it is a good idea to take out contents insurance.

Most contents insurance takes account of wear and tear of the goods damaged or stolen, so the money which the insurance company gives to the insured is equal in value to the condition of the goods when they were lost or damaged. If your five-year-old stereo was stolen, the money you would receive would cover the cost of buying a five-year-old second-hand model, but not enough to buy a brand new replacement. This is called the indemnity principle. However, the insurer *can* take out a more expensive *new-for-old* contents policy, which guarantees the full replacement cost of new goods in place of old ones which are damaged beyond repair, or have been stolen.

Buildings Insurance gives protection if anything should happen to your house and garage. If the building is damaged or destroyed as a result of a fire or explosion, the insurance company will compensate the insured person up to the amount of rebuilding costs, provided that the value of the policy is sufficient (see later under 'Making a Claim'.) Other risks usually covered include damage by vehicles or

aircraft, flood, lightning and subsidence. Apart from contents and buildings, household policies often cover also for personal accident and liability for claims arising from accidents caused to others. As you can see, this form of policy offers a wide range of insurance in one package for the householder.

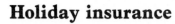

Holiday insurance

Holiday insurance is used by many people. Anyone who is injured or taken ill on holiday, especially when abroad, may have expensive medical fees to pay. Depending on how much the insured person pays for it, holiday insurance will cover bills up to an agreed limit of at least £5000. Protection against the possibility of luggage or money being stolen is also given, and if a person is too ill to take a holiday which has already been booked or paid for, the insurance company will pay any cancellation charges. In addition, it is now possible to insure against a holiday being cancelled as a result of a strike, bad weather or transport breakdown, and additional expenses may be claimed if any of these cause a lengthy delay.

Motor insurance

Motor insurance affects more and more people as the number of drivers on the roads increases. The Road Traffic Acts make it illegal for anyone to drive a motorised vehicle on the roads without sufficient insurance to compensate for the death or injury of other persons. The cover which provides such compensation is called *third-party motor vehicle insurance*. The insurance company and the insured person are the first and second 'parties', and anyone else is a *third party*. This includes, for example, pedestrians, cyclists, passengers in the insured's own vehicle and the drivers or passengers in other

motor vehicles. This is the minimum legal requirement. *Third party, fire and theft* is another popular policy, covering the insured person's vehicle for loss by fire and theft as well. The most secure but expensive form of motor insurance is called *fully comprehensive*. This includes third party, fire and theft, but also covers damage to the insured person's own vehicle, injury to, or death of the insured driver and loss of belongings in the vehicle. An example would be the loss of car rugs or coats, but the cost is usually limited. If a driver has an accident which is someone else's fault, the other person's insurance will pay because the driver is then the third party, but with comprehensive cover the insured person's car will be repaired or replaced by his or her insurance company where the accident was the fault of the insured person, as well as paying compensation to any third parties involved.

CHECK THIS OUT

Write out the following sentences, filling in the missing words:

1 Life assurance can be subdivided into four types, which are _____, _____, _____ and _____.

2 Insurance can be divided into four main types: life, accident, marine and _____.

3 Businesses need insurance cover for risks such as fire, the possible theft of cash and goods in transit, and the breaking of _____ _____ windows.

4 Marine insurance covers freight (which refers to the charge for carrying cargo), hull, the cargo itself and _____.

5 'Composite' forms of insurance, such as household insurance, cover a number of different _____ in one policy.

6 Buildings Insurance gives protection if a building is damaged or _____.

7 Holiday Insurance protects people against being _____ or taken ill on holiday, and against the possibility of their _____ being stolen.

8 Three types of motor vehicle insurance are third party, _____ _____ _____ _____ _____ and _____ _____.

9 If the driver of a motor vehicle has an accident which is someone else's fault, the other person's _____ _____ will pay compensation.

Calculating risks and premiums

As explained under the 'pooling of risks' earlier, insurance companies need to fix the premiums charged for insurance cover so that there is enough money in the pools to meet all the claims for compensation and the operating expenses/profits. How are these premiums fixed?

The work is carried out by *actuaries* who look at past statistics about the value of losses produced every year by particular risks. Over a period of years a good average value of losses can be calculated and this gives a probable value for future years, taking into account any anticipated changes or trends. The actuaries can then fix premiums to cover this loss, allowing a margin for error. However, the future can never be certain, and if claims in one year are higher than expected, insurance companies have to dig into their invested reserves to pay them and possibly raise premiums for the following year, when perhaps there are fewer claims and reserves can be built up again.

Premiums are thus decided by the value of losses expected, which in turn indicates the level of risk. Some activities are more risky than others and therefore higher premiums are charged, but the premiums can also vary according to individual circumstances. Let us look at motor car insurance, where the risk of loss is affected by:

- The age and experience of the driver(s). Statistics show that young inexperienced drivers have more accidents and their premiums are therefore higher.

- The type and value of car. Certain cars are more prone to accidents than others, for example sports cars, and a Rolls Royce will be more costly to repair or replace than a Citröen 2CV, so the premiums will be higher.

- The area where the car will be mainly used. The rate of accidents and thefts in the London area is much higher than in rural Devon.

- Where the car is kept. Cars in garages are less likely to be stolen than those left parked on roads.

- The purpose for which the car will be used. A car for business is likely on average to be driven more than one used for 'social and domestic' purposes, and the risk of an accident is greater as a result.

- The previous accident record of the driver(s). A driver who has had, say, three accidents in a two-year period is considered to be a high risk compared with one who has had no accidents for, say, five years. In fact, low risk drivers often receive a 'no-claims bonus', that is, a reduced premium charge. This could be, for example, a 60 per cent reduction for four or five years of claim-free driving.

A 50-year-old driver of a medium-sized family saloon car with a clean 30-year driving record who lives in a rural area of Hampshire and only uses the vehicle for non-business purposes will be charged a very low premium. On the other hand, an 18-year old who has less than one year's driving experience and has had two accidents already, and who wants to drive a Ferrari in London, would be regarded as such a high risk as to be refused insurance by many companies!

Sometimes a motorist may agree to pay for the first part of any accidental damage claim, up to a fixed amount, as long as the insurance company pays off the amount outstanding when this payment has been made. This is called *paying the excess*. Young drivers or drivers who have had several accidents may have to agree to a *compulsory excess*, which means they *have* to pay the first part of any claim as part of their insurance agreement. If motorists agree to have a *voluntary excess*, the insurance company will charge them less for their insurance because they will not have to meet the claim in full. The amount of excess differs between insurance companies.

Uninsurable risks

A person can only obtain insurance cover for possible loss if he or she has an insurable interest in whatever or whoever is being insured. However, even when such interest exists, there are still many risks for which insurance companies will not give cover. These are called uninsurable risks, and examples are:

- Business losses arising from difficult trading conditions or bad management. There are so many uncertainties in business that insurance companies consider past experience of losses to be no clear guide to the future, so that they cannot accurately calculate the premiums to be charged. Another point is that business people might not take too much trouble to avoid a loss of profit if they knew they were going to be compensated for it.

- Injury or death caused by exposure to nuclear radiation. Insurance companies consider that they do not have sufficient experience of possible losses to be able to calculate how much they might become liable for in these cases. If you look at the policy covering your own house or contents, you will find this as one of the 'exceptions'.

- Activities where the risk of loss or injury is very high. An example would be a young inexperienced driver with a high accident record who wanted to obtain insurance cover for a fast sports car. The premium would be too high to pay, because the chances of an insurance company having to pay out are too great.

An uninsurable risk is a risk for which the chance and level of possible loss cannot be calculated, or for which the insurance company is almost certain to have to pay compensation.

Taking out insurance

As explained at the start of the chapter, the main insurers are the insurance companies and Lloyd's underwriters. If you wish to obtain information about insurance cover and perhaps take out a policy, then most insurance companies can be approached directly by post or telephone. However, many people obtain their insurances by approaching a local insurance broker who sells insurance on behalf of the companies in return for a commission based on premiums collected. In the case of Lloyd's underwriters, you cannot contact them directly and *must* go through a specially designated Lloyd's broker. The advantage of buying insurance through a broker is that advice should be available as to the most suitable and best value policy for your particular needs.

Before you can insure anything or anyone, one of the principles of insurance is that you must have an *insurable interest*. This means that if a loss arises, then you must be the one who will suffer from it. For example, you cannot insure the life of a friend because his or her death would not be considered as affecting you significantly, but you can insure your parents. In the same way, you cannot insure for fire in the house owned by your neighbour, because if it burned down, it would not cause you any personal loss.

Applying and paying

To obtain insurance cover, you must always fill in a *proposal form*. All questions on the form must be answered and you must sign it, stating that you have been truthful and have given all relevant information. The insurance company must also be truthful with you about the insurance cover which you are buying. This is referred to as having the *utmost good faith* when entering into an insurance contract, and it is another vital principle of insurance. The premium to be charged can only be accurately fixed if full and truthful information is given. If you are found later to have broken this principle, then the insurance company may refuse to pay if you claim for a loss, and the contract may be considered as void. An example would be if you want car insurance and do not tell the company that you have 'souped up' the engine of your car, or if a person whose life is to be insured has had a serious illness, but does not state this fact.

If the company agrees to give insurance, the proposer (customer) will be told how much the *premium* for insurance is and, when pain, cover begins and a *policy* is issued. The policy is the written agreement between the proposer and insurance company about exactly what is to be insured and any special conditions which are to be made, for example excess payments. In the cases of motor insurance and employer's liability insurance, a *certificate of insurance* is issued also. Sometimes when the certificate of insurance and policy are being prepared, temporary cover can be given by the insurance company issuing a *cover note* which has the same effect as a certificate, but only for a limited period until the certificate is issued.

When it is time for the insurance to be renewed, the insurance company will issue a *renewal notice* which reminds the insured that the insurance cover is running out and should be renewed by payment of a further *premium*.

aldermary insurance company

motor car insurance proposal form

THE PROPOSER (the person seeking the insurance)

Name and Address _____

_____

Address where the car is usually kept _____

Occupation or business _____ Proposer's Age _____

THE CAR

Make and Model _____ Year _____

Estimated value
(including accessories) _____ Registration Number _____

Has the engine been
altered to increase performance? _____ Is the car normally
kept in a garage? _____

OTHER INFORMATION

Type of policy required
(Comprehensive/Third Party
Fire and Theft/Third Party) _____

Use of Car
(Pleasure/Business/
Commercial Travelling) _____

Have you passed your
driving test? _____

Will the vehicle be
driven by any other _____
person under 25?

Have you had any accidents
in the last 4 years? _____

Have you or any other
driver had any driving _____
convictions in the last 10 years?

IMPORTANT: You are breaking the law if you make any false statements on this form. If you fail to disclose all information the insurance policy may not operate.

The insurance policy will not cover you until a Cover Note (evidence that you are insured) has been issued to you.

DECLARATION
I declare that to the best of my knowledge and belief, the above answers are true and that all material information* has been given.

Date _____ Signature _____

*Material information is information which the insurance company must be given to help them decide how to treat the risk you are proposing

A specimen insurance proposal form

Making a claim

A person who suffers a loss and wishes to claim money from an insurance company will need to fill in a *claim form*. This gives the insurance company the details of the loss and how/when it happened. Documentary evidence may be needed – for example a death certificate when life assurance is being claimed on a deceased person, or one or more quotations from garages for the cost of repairing a damaged car. In the case of large or doubtful claims, the insurance company will usually send an *assessor* or *loss adjuster* to investigate the circumstances and estimate the cost of damage or replacement.

The aim of the insurance company, in the case of a claim, is to *indemnify* the insured person, that is to put him/her back in the same financial position after the accident as before. Indemnity is another important principle of insurance. This is the rule by which an insured person should not profit from an insurance policy, but should only be compensated for the value lost. This, however, assumes that the damaged property is fully insured. If a person has insured his house, for example for £50 000, and £60 000 is claimed if it burns down, because the price of houses has risen, then the insurance company will only pay the £50 000 maximum. The person is said to be *under-insured*. On the other hand, a person could have *over-insured*, in which case only the value lost can be obtained, otherwise a profit would be made which is against the principle or rule of indemnity.

The application of the indemnity principle also means that:

- Once the insured person has been fully compensated, the insurance company takes over the right to any remaining value. They own the scrap of the car which has been 'written-off' and have the right to any sum which can be recovered from a third-party, such as the insurance company of another vehicle in an accident. This is called *subrogation*.

- If the insured person is covered for a particular risk by two companies, then full compensation cannot be claimed from both companies, as the insured person would make a profit out of a loss. Instead, each company will pay a proportion of the loss, for example fifty per cent each. This is called *contribution*.

Some funny claims

Having an accident and claiming on your insurance can be a very serious affair. Sometimes, though, the claims forms make interesting reading, as the following examples from real claims forms show:

- 'I thought the window was down but it was up, as I found when I put my head through it . . .'

- 'I collided with a stationary bus coming in the opposite direction . . .'

- 'I knocked the man over. He admitted it was his fault, as he'd been knocked down before ...'
- 'To avoid a collision, I ran into a lorry ...'
- 'Coming home, I drove into the wrong drive, colliding with a tree I haven't got ...'

CHECK THIS OUT

Write out the following sentences, filling in the missing words:

1 To obtain insurance, you must show that you have an _____ interest, and that you will be affected by the loss of the insured item or person.

2 Uninsurable risks are those such as goods not selling. The risk cannot be accurately _____ and so it cannot be insured.

3 If you wish to be insured, you must first fill in a _____ form.

4 The principle of _____ _____ _____ requires that both the insurance company and the customer (the proposer) tell the truth.

5 Indemnity is the rule which says that the person claiming should only be _____ for the value lost.

6 Once compensation has been paid, the insurance company has the right to any remaining value, such as the scrap of a car which has been 'written off'. This is called _____.

7 The written agreement between the insurance company and the proposer is called a _____.

8 In the case of motor insurance, a _____ of insurance is issued.

9 A person who suffers a loss and wishes to obtain money from the insurance company must fill in a _____ form.

10 The aim of the insurance company is to _____ the insured person, which puts him or her back in the same financial position as before the loss happened.

Lloyd's

Insurance cover can be obtained from Lloyd's underwriters as well as from insurance companies. Lloyd's is best known for its shipping insurance, but in practice, most types of insurance (apart from life assurance) are dealt with by the underwriters. The organisation of Lloyd's is very different from that of the insurance companies and therefore requires a special mention. Like the Stock Exchange, Lloyd's developed in a London coffee house. This coffee house was run by Edward Lloyd from 1688 and was very popular with merchants, who would insure ships and cargoes as a sideline to their everyday business. Even after Lloyd died in 1713, the coffee house carried on under his name, doing the same business. Eventually it became so well known and well used that it was obliged, in 1774, to move into the Royal Exchange to conduct its business.

The name of Lloyd has remained and the organisation is now controlled by the Lloyd's Corporation. The Corporation itself does

The Lutine Bell. This is rung whenever Lloyd's hear that a ship has been lost at sea

not, however, issue insurance policies, but provides the facilities for *underwriters* who take the actual risks. To be allowed to operate at Lloyd's these underwriters must have substantial personal wealth and be of good reputation, because they have to accept unlimited financial liability for any valid claims made under the policies which they have issued. Many of these underwriters are people, often well-known, from different walks of life. They do not actually transact insurance business themselves but deal through professional underwriters and underwriting agents who operate at Lloyd's. Several underwriting members may operate within *syndicates*, because many of the risks covered are so large. An example is insuring huge oil tankers and passenger liners. Syndicates allow underwriters to share a risk. Very large risks may be spread between several syndicates, or part of the risk is *reinsured* with other syndicates. Individual members are said to 'underwrite' policies by having their names under the details of the risks being covered, on the 'slips' used at Lloyd's.

The Corporation has a central compensation fund into which all syndicates must pay, as the reputation of Lloyd's is very important in maintaining the confidence of businesses seeking insurance cover. Should a syndicate's members get into financial difficulties and be unable to pay valid claims, then the debts are met out of this fund. However, this is fortunately only necessary on rare occasions.

A view of the new Lloyd's building in the City of London

SHORT QUESTIONS

1 Name one risk which cannot be insured.

2 What is the purpose of insurance?

3 With whom could a company insure a ship?

4 What does 'insurable interest' mean?

5 What is the name of the form used when applying for insurance cover?

6 What is the meaning of *utmost good faith*?

7 What is the sum of money paid for insurance cover?

8 What is life endowment insurance?

9 Give an example of *subrogation* being applied in insurance.

10 In what way is *new-for-old* household contents cover different from the standard cover?

MULTIPLE CHOICE QUESTIONS

There are four possible answers to each of the following questions. Study the introductory words, and then decide which of the alternatives answers correctly the question or completes the sentence. Write down the question number and follow it with (A) (B) (C) or (D), according to your choice.

1 If a person wishes to insure a car, the name given to the document which first has to be filled in is a/an
   (A) proposal form
   (B) insurance form
   (C) fidelity guarantee
   (D) cover note.

2 'Third party' in insurance refers to
   (A) the underwriter
   (B) the person taking out the policy
   (C) the person making a claim against the policy holder
   (D) the person working in an insurance office.

3 The principle of indemnity in insurance means that
   (A) insurance cannot be taken out for costly risks
   (B) the insured person is restored to the same position as before the loss
   (C) the premium paid is the same for all policy-holders
   (D) compensation paid will be in excess of the loss suffered.

4 Which is NOT a way in which insurance companies use their funds?
   (A) They lend to industry and commerce
   (B) They lend to people who wish to purchase property
   (C) They lend to Lloyd's
   (D) They lend to local councils.

5 An insured person cannot make a profit out of a loss. This is called
   (A) insurable interest
   (B) indemnity
   (C) utmost good faith
   (D) underwriting a loss.

6 An annuity insurance is
   (A) a lump sum paid when a person reaches statutory retirement age
   (B) assurance which allows a person to save and to have life cover
   (C) a guaranteed regular payment from a fixed date until a person dies
   (D) payment to which the insurance company adds a bonus annually.

7 A fidelity guarantee covers
   (A) losses due to changes in fashion
   (B) compensation for loss in motor vehicle accidents
   (C) compensation for loss through an employee telling lies
   (D) compensation for loss through an employee stealing.

8 Whole life assurance is paid to
   (A) a person suffering as a result of an accident
   (B) a person reaching the age of 60
   (C) the dependants of the person named in the policy if he/she dies
   (D) only to persons who die before the age of 60.

9 Lloyd's of London is
   (A) a commodity exchange
   (B) a corporation whose members offer insurance
   (C) the place where an insurance contract is signed by the insurance company and the insured person
   (D) an agency for chartering cargo space in ships.

There are four possible answers to each of the following questions.

If you think (1) only is correct, write down A.
If you think (1) and (2) only are correct, write down B.
If you think (3) and (4) only are correct, write down C.
If you think (2), (3) and (4) only are correct, write down D.

10 Marine insurance covers
   (1) life assurance for a ship's passengers
   (2) accidental damage to a ship
   (3) damage to a ship's cargo
   (4) accidents to a ship's crew.

11 A businessman can insure against the risks of
   (1) bankruptcy
   (2) fire
   (3) theft by employees
   (4) accidents to a plate-glass window.

12 Which of the following factors is NOT taken into account when insuring a private car?
   (1) The area where the driver lives
   (2) The age of the driver
   (3) Whether the driver has a mortgage
   (4) The driver's family commitments

13 Insurance is concerned with
   (1) keeping property safe
   (2) compensating for something which is certain to happen
   (3) the pooling of risk
   (4) compensating any insured person who then has a loss.

14 All motorists are required to have
   (1) at least third party insurance
   (2) insurance against third party, fire and theft
   (3) fully comprehensive insurance
   (4) a second named driver on the insurance policy.

STIMULUS RESPONSE QUESTIONS

The following questions carry a mark out of 20. Each section of the question carries marks.

1 Look at the proposal on the opposite page filled in by Judith Richmond, who is applying for car insurance, and answer the questions which follow.

   (a) Judith wishes to have comprehensive cover for her car. What is the cheapest form of cover she could have? *(1 mark)*

   (b) Explain why there is a declaration at the bottom of the form. *(4 marks)*

   (c) (i) What excess is Judith prepared to pay? *(1 mark)*
       (ii) In what situation would Judith have to pay this excess and why is she prepared to pay it? *(2 marks)*

   (d) In 12(b) on the proposal form Judith says that she was involved in a car accident. How important is the fact that the other car ran into the back of her? *(4 marks)*

   (e) How will the details given on this form affect the amount (premium) that Judith will have to pay to insure her car? *(8 marks)*

(This question appears by kind permission of the Northern Examining Association from specimen questions for the GCSE Commerce paper).

WHERE NECESSARY DELETE — THAT WHICH IS NOT APPLICABLE

PRIVATE CAR PROPOSAL FORM

YOU SHOULD TELL US OF ALL FACTS LIKELY TO INFLUENCE THE ACCEPTANCE AND ASSESSMENT OF THIS PROPOSAL. IF YOU FAIL TO DO SO, YOUR POLICY MAY EITHER NOT OPERATE OR NOT OPERATE FULLY. SHOULD YOU HAVE ANY DOUBTS ABOUT WHAT YOU SHOULD TELL US CONTACT YOUR INSURANCE ADVISER OR LOCAL N.E.M. OFFICE.

NAME OF PROPOSER in full ..... MISS JUDITH RICHMOND ..... PLEASE USE BLOCK LETTERS
Mr./Mrs./Miss/Ms

PERMANENT ADDRESS ..... 24 OLDGATE STREET, ... NEWCASTLE.

TELEPHONE No

Garage address (if different from above) ..... AS ABOVE

1. PERIOD OF INSURANCE FROM 19TH JUNE 1986 TO 19TH JUNE 1987

2. FULL OCCUPATION (Including any spare time or secondary occupation) ..... DOOR-TO-DOOR SALESPERSON
(Indicate type of business) e.g. Clerk — Builders, Mechanic — Factory etc.

3. DETAILS OF CAR/S TO BE INSURED

FOR BROKER USE PREMIUM QUOTED £

Tick appropriate boxes

Index Mark and Registration No.	Make, Model/Model No. and Type of Body: e.g. Saloon	c.c. Rating	Year of Make	Date Car Purchased	Proposer's Estimate of present value incl. accessories	Comprehensive	Third Party Fire & Theft	Third Party	C	A	B	£50	£100
C625 HYM	FORD ESCORT L	1·6	1985	1/10/85	£4,500	✓				✓	✓		
	SALOON												

(Cover: Comprehensive / Third Party Fire & Theft / Third Party; Class of Use: C A B; Excess: £50 £100)

4. Is/are the vehicle(s) (a) OWNED by you? YES/NO (b) Registered in your name? YES/NO If NO to either give details .....

5. Have any of the above vehicles been specially tuned, modified or adapted? YES NO If YES give details

6. Have you OWNED any vehicles in the past three years? YES/NO If YES state total number OWNED at any one time during the last THREE years:
19 83 Total number owned ..1.. 19 84 Total number owned ..1.. 1985 Total number owned ..1..

7. Do you own or have the use of any other vehicle or have the use of a company vehicle? YES/NO If YES give details .....

8. Do you require driving to be restricted to yourself? YES/NO or yourself and your spouse only? YES/NO

9. Are you now or have you been insured in respect of any motor vehicle? YES/NO If YES state Company and Policy No. CARFAX 728/6111/925

10. Will any person (other than yourself) who will drive the vehicle be under 25 years of age? YES/NO hold a provisional licence? YES/NO have had less than one year's driving experience since passing the driving test? YES/NO If YES to (a) (b) or (c) show details in the Drivers Schedule below.

11. Show particulars below of YOURSELF and your SPOUSE (whether expected to drive or not) and any driver mentioned in question 10 above.
If proposal is in the name of a company show particulars below of main users

DRIVERS	NAME	Date of Birth	Type of Licence held (Full U.K., International or Provisional)	Date First Issued	FULL OCCUPATION (including any spare time or secondary occupation)
YOURSELF	As above	2/3/61	FULL	1/4/80	As above
YOUR SPOUSE (whether expected to drive or not)			If licence not held state NONE	✱	
OTHERS				✱	

✱ Indicate type of business, e.g. Clerk — Builders, Mechanic — Factory etc.

12. Have YOU or ANY PERSON who will drive the vehicle ever suffered from:
(a) any physical or mental DISABILITY or infirmity, e.g. heart condition, diabetes, loss of a limb, or normal movement of a limb, defective vision (unless corrected by glasses) or defective hearing? YES/NO If YES give details

(b) been involved in any ACCIDENT or LOSSES in connection with any vehicle over the last three years? YES/NO If YES give date, cost and brief details of circumstances
23/9/84 £300 , CAR RAN INTO BACK OF ME AT TRAFFIC LIGHTS.

(c) been CONVICTED of any offence in connection with the driving of any motor vehicle during the past ten years, or is any PROSECUTION PENDING YES/NO If YES state date(s), offence code, fine, period of disqualification, if any.

13. In respect of YOURSELF or ANY PERSON who will drive the vehicle has any Company or Underwriter
(a) DECLINED your/their proposal? (a) YES/NO If YES to any part give details
(b) Required you/them to carry the FIRST PORTION of any LOSS? (b) YES/NO
(c) Required an INCREASED PREMIUM or imposed SPECIAL CONDITIONS? (c) YES/NO
(d) REFUSED to RENEW your/their policy? (d) YES/NO
(e) CANCELLED your/their policy? (e) YES/NO

DECLARATION I/We wish to effect an insurance with and apply to become Members of the Association. I/We declare that the above statements and particulars are to the best of my/our knowledge and belief true and complete, and no material fact has been mis-represented, mis-stated or withheld. I/We agree that this proposal shall form the basis of the contract between me/us and the Association and will be deemed as incorporated in the Policy to be issued. If this Proposal has been written by anyone else that person is my agent for this purpose and not the agent of the Association.

● IF YOU HAVE NOT PERSONALLY COMPLETED THE ANSWERS TO THE QUESTIONS, YOU SHOULD CHECK THEM CAREFULLY BEFORE SIGNING THIS DECLARATION.

Date 3rd June 1986. ● Proposer's Signature Judith Richmond.
State status of signatory when signing on behalf of company or firm

If the space(s) provided above for your answer(s) is inadequate please give details on a separate sheet of paper.

2 Look carefully at the information below before answering the questions below.

Western Assurance PLC has prepared the following data for those wishing to take out a 20-year with-profits endowment policy.

Figure 1

Age of insured person	Annual premium per £1000 assured
below 25 years	£30
between 25 and 30 years	£35
between 31 and 35 years	£40
between 36 and 40 years	£45
over 40 years	on request

John Adams, who is 28 years of age and married, wishes to take out a 20-year with-profits endowment policy for the sum assured of £5000. He has been sent the following graph by Western Assurance to illustrate the likely returns on this type of policy.

Figure 2

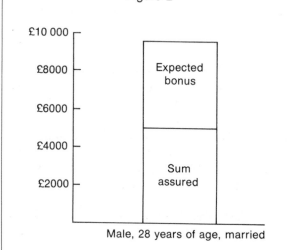

Male, 28 years of age, married

(a) What is the name, given in the data, for
   (i) a payment to an assurance company *(1 mark)*
   (ii) a contract of assurance? *(1 mark)*
(b) Why does the table in Figure 1 contain different rates of premium? *(2 marks)*
(c) Calculate, showing workings, the total annual premium which John would have to pay to Western Assurance for the policy required. *(2 marks)*

(d) How do assurance companies decide rates of premium such as those shown in Figure 1? *(4 marks)*
(e) Give details of the benefits which John and his family might obtain by taking out the endowment policy. *(6 marks)*
(f) John decides he cannot afford the endowment policy quoted but he still wants to obtain £5000 life cover for his family. Name and briefly describe the other types of life assurance policy which could give him the cover he requires. *(4 marks)*

(This question appears by kind permission of the Southern Regional Examinations Board from specimen questions for the GCSE Commerce paper.)

3 Read the information below carefully, and then answer the questions on it.

If you have a disposable income (that is, the income which is left after various allowances of money to live on are taken into account) of more than £2225 and your savings are at least £3000, you will be expected to contribute to any legal aid you may need.

As a result of this ruling, legal expenses insurance is fast proving to be an up-and-coming market. Companies in this field offer plans which will pay an insured person's legal fees in legal arguments over faulty services, personal injuries or industrial disagreements.

If you consider insuring yourself through a Legal Protection Scheme, it is a good idea to get quotations from different firms, as the cost varies greatly.

(a) What is disposable income? *(3 marks)*
(b) How much income and savings are people allowed to have and still be able to apply for legal aid? *(3 marks)*
(c) What can people do to avoid expense if ever they need legal aid? *(3 marks)*
(d) What kinds of legal action can be insured against *(6 marks)*
(e) If a person decides to insure himself/herself against any legal expenses which may occur, what is he/she advised to do before deciding which plan to adopt? *(5 marks)*

4 Read the following passage and answer the questions on it:

Motor vehicle insurers are blaming the rapidly rising cost of insuring vehicles on increasing claims, which are being made by 25 per cent of all drivers. The average cost of repairing vehicles is £700 and poor maintenance of roads, cheaper petrol and increasing numbers of car thefts contribute to more claims.

The premium you are charged is affected by your driving record, your age, where you live and the amount of driving you do. Drivers who do not make insurance claims qualify for a low risk 'no claims discount' which keeps the cost of the premium down. Other ways of reducing the premium are: restricting the number of drivers, agreeing to pay the first £100 of any claim, or only covering the car for accidents to a third party, or fire and theft. Shop around for premiums and drive carefully: after two years of trouble-free driving you may get a 40 per cent discount.

(a) Why is the cost of insuring motor vehicles rising rapidly? *(4 marks)*

(b) Different factors affect the premium which a driver will be charged. Explain which drivers will be offered a low premium and which a high premium when these factors are taken into account. *(10 marks)*

(c) Cars can be insured against accidents to a third party, or also against fire and theft. What other insurance for cars is also available? *(2 marks)*

(d) How can a driver qualify for a 'no claims discount'? *(2 marks)*

(e) A motorist who has not made a claim on his/her car insurance for over two years is required to pay £300 premium, less discount. How much discount could the driver expect, and how much would he/she have to pay for the cover? *(2 marks)*

ESSAY QUESTIONS

1 (a) Why is insurance based on statistics? *(10 marks)*

(b) Compare the risks which are likely to be insured against by (i) a department store, and (ii) an exporter of machine tools, and explain which risks are common and which are specific to each business. *(10 marks)*

(This question appears by kind permission of the London and East Anglican Group from specimen questions for the GCSE Commerce paper.)

2 A furniture shop has two sales assistants and a van for delivery work.
(a) Describe *four* risks which the owner should insure against. *(12 marks)*
(b) Describe *one* risk which could not be insured, giving reasons. *(8 marks)*

3 (a) Explain with examples the statement: 'The three main principles of insurance are *utmost good faith*, *insurable interest* and *indemnity*.' *(12 marks)*

(b) Explain why each principle is important in any insurance contract. *(8 marks)*

4 (a) Explain why *hull*, *cargo* and *freight* insurance are important in sea transport. *(9 marks)*
(b) Who would you expect to take out each of these three types of policy, and why? *(9 marks)*
(c) What is an *underwriter*, and where could one be contacted? *(2 marks)*

5 A friend of yours is buying an older car. Explain to this friend
(a) why it must be insured *(4 marks)*
(b) what cover is available *(9 marks)*
(c) how to go about taking out a policy. *(7 marks)*

(Include the following terms: insurance broker, policy, proposal form, premium, third party, and add any other terms which you think are important.)

LEARN IT YOURSELF

1 Imagine you are going to buy or rent a house which you will be sharing with another person. Find out what sort of insurance cover you will need, and why. Information can be obtained from insurance companies, banks, and building societies.

2 Using the *Yellow Pages*, find out the number of insurance companies in your area. Construct a short questionnaire and ask friends, neighbours and relatives if they will tell you which, if any, of the local insurance companies they use. Construct a bar-chart to show the most popular down to the least popular of local insurance companies.

3 Contact an insurance company or insurance broker and ask them to let you have a motor insurance proposal form and any information about insuring a vehicle. Prepare a wall-chart using the material to illustrate the steps a vehicle owner would have to take to insure the vehicle. If possible, groups can do this using different insurance companies and then compare costs, bonuses allowed, and how claims are made and paid out.

4 From information available from insurance companies and brokers, and advertisements, compare charges between different companies for assurance (life cover). Try to obtain information about life endowment, whole life and term assurance. You may like to present your findings in a table or as a bar chart.

5 Prepare a wall-chart to illustrate the type of insurance cover which you or your fellow-students might need if you decide to start your own business. Assume that you need transport and that you have passed your driving test. Information on starting your own business is available from: Careers Information Office, your local library, your local authority and many of the commercial banks. This information also includes ideas on insurance cover.

NOW TRY THIS

Prepare a series of small cards with the following words, each on one card only:

Life assurance
Fire insurance
Employer's liability insurance
Household insurance
Travel insurance
Motor insurance
Insurable interest

Premium
Policy
Utmost good faith
Marine insurance
Insurance broker
Proposal form
Indemnity

and any other terms which you think might be useful.

The class divides into groups of two or three people. A card is given to each group, face down so that the wording cannot be read.

The groups are now insurance clerks who have had a letter asking them to explain to a member of the public the term on their particular card.

On the word 'Go' the cards are turned over, the clerks find the word in their textbook (or from their memory) and, working together, write a quick explanation. They are allowed five minutes to do this, and then they must stop work.

A spokesperson is chosen (the eldest member of the group perhaps, or the one whose name comes last in the alphabet, or the tallest person, etc.).

The spokesperson reads out the group explanation and other groups listen, making a note of anything which has been missed out. The explanation scores ten if perfect, nine if one fact is missing and so on.

Each group has a turn and the groups record their score.

The game can go on if the cards are re-shuffled and given out again, but this time the explanation must be given from memory.

The winner is the group scoring the highest marks.

AIDS TO MEMORY

Learn the following to help you remember what can
be insured.

A person can insure his life,
His house for fire and theft,
On holidays, for accidents
Or luggage being left.

Employers insure businesses
For accidents to all,
In case of fire or stolen goods
Insurance men will call.

We may insure our motor car
Third party, fire and theft
Or fully comprehensive
If we have some money left!

You can't insure for fashion clothes
The fashion may not last
Or young and silly drivers
Who speed along too fast!

ASSIGNMENT – PLANNING INSURANCE

Imagine a young person of 18, who has passed a driving test and who is
thinking of setting up in some kind of business. In an interview with the
bank, the business plan has been approved.

(a) Decide what the business is to be.
(b) Decide what insurance cover will be needed.
(c) Use the *Yellow Pages* or a business directory from your school/
    college or public library, to find the names and addresses of local
    insurance companies. Telephone or visit, explaining your project,
    and ask for any leaflets, brochures or other information. If
    necessary, include the cost of insuring a motor vehicle the young
    person will drive.
(d) Compare the information which you have received from the various
    companies.
(e) Select which company is best for each of the types of insurance
    which the business will require.
(f) Give reasons for the choices of insurance company which you have
    made, and back up your reasons with the facts which you have
    discovered.
(g) Present your findings neatly.
(h) Draw any conclusions you have made about the cost of insurance to
    a business.

THE POST OFFICE

CHAPTER 11

Introduction

In 1635, Charles I introduced a postal service for the people. The further a letter travelled, the higher the cost of postage, which had to be paid by the person *receiving* the letter. The General Post Office was established in 1660, but it was not until 1840 that the person *sending* the letter paid for the postage. To prove that this postage had been paid the world's first stick-on postage stamp was introduced. In 1919, a regular international airmail service was started and letters could be sent between London and Paris by air.

In 1969 the General Post Office (known as the GPO) changed from being a government department to a public corporation. It is now known simply as the Post Office. Every working day, the Post Office delivers many thousands of letters and parcels, using sea, road, rail and air transport, ranging from the bicycle to Concorde.

The Post Office now offers a very wide range of services, using a network of main and sub-post offices in every town and all larger villages. Its work can be divided as follows:

- postal services;
- National Girobank;
- postal order service;
- other services.

Information on the services offered by the Post Office, including the charges currently made, details of inland and overseas post, and savings and National Girobank services can be obtained from *The Post Office Guide*, on sale at post offices. Another publication which can be purchased from the Post Office and which may be useful to businesses is the *Postal Addresses and Index to Postcode Directories*.

The Post Office was separated from the telecommunications side of the business in 1981. The telecommunications services, including the telephone and telex, are now operated by British Telecom (see Chapter 12).

Postal services

The most frequently used Post Office service is the mail. Letters, postcards and parcels should bear the postcode as the last line of the address. This postcode is then tapped out on a keyboard which puts a pattern of phosphorescent dots on each envelope, so that it can then be sorted electronically very quickly. Around 90 per cent of mail is now sorted using the postcode system and every address in the United Kingdom has a postcode. The address should be on the bottom half of the envelope, like this:

The stamp goes in the top right-hand corner and postmark printed across the top of the envelope to cancel out the stamp. The use of postcodes and the mechanisation of sorting are now very important for the fast delivery of mail.

First-class post

Letters posted by the first-class service, by the recommended daily posting times, are usually delivered on the first working day after collection. The service costs more than second-class mail. Special contracts can give discounts for large quantities of mail.

Second-class post

These letters are usually delivered within three working days of collection and this service is used for less urgent or perhaps heavier mail. Bulk rebates are available on large prepaid quantities of second-class mail.

Parcel post

This provides a relatively cheap, but slower, service for sending larger or heavier items. Second-class postal items must be sent by parcel post if they weigh over 750 grams, although there is no weight limit for the more expensive first-class post. However, both the first- and second-class post have a smaller maximum *size* limit than the parcel post, although there is still a size limit for the latter as well.

Business reply service

If a firm wants replies from its customers without asking them to pay postage, a reply card, label or envelope, printed first or second class, can be sent to them or included in an advertisement. The firm using the service (known as the *addressee*) obtains a licence from the Head Postmaster and pays postage for all the replies received, plus a small additional charge. The equivalent service for parcels is called the Postage Forward Parcel Service.

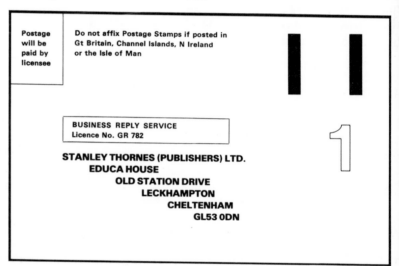

Freepost

A special licence is also needed for FREEPOST, where second-class letters and cards can be sent to a special address which must include the word 'FREEPOST' under the addressee's name. The addressee then pays postage on all the replies received, plus a small additional charge. These licences are usually used by businesses which are advertising goods and services, perhaps in pamphlets and magazines, so that anybody who is interested is encouraged to reply because no stamp is needed.

Household delivery service

Unaddressed mail will be delivered by the Post Office to *every* address in a specified area or areas. This reduces postage costs and allows direct mail businesses to reach all prospective customers cheaply in a required area or even countrywide.

Nightrider

This service offers delivery on the next working day for parcels and packets posted within the London Postal Region.

Special delivery

Letters (only first class) sent by this service are delivered on the day after posting, even if they arrive at the delivery office too late for normal delivery. A special messenger is used to take the letter to its destination. There is a refund available to the sender if the letters cannot be delivered next day.

Railway letters

If railway stations are staffed, arrangements can be made for certain stations to accept first-class letters and packets for transmission to another station. The letters or packets can either be called for or transferred to the post. By this method, urgent letters can be sent quickly between firms with easy access to a staffed railway station. Airway letters can also be sent by British Airways on certain inland routes.

Certificates of posting

A certificate of posting can be obtained for an unregistered letter or a parcel. This can be produced as evidence to the addressee that an item has been sent and also as evidence to the post office if the item is lost and compensation claimed. Such compensation is, however, very small and is unsuitable for valuable items.

Registered letters and packets

Valuable items and money can be sent through the post using first-class registered letters or packets. The envelope or packet is marked with a blue cross on all sides, and it must be handed in to a post office, where a copy of the certificate of posting is handed to the customer. There is a system of compensation up to a specified maximum if a registered letter or packet goes astray. For items sent by parcel post, there is a separate Compensation Fee (CF) Parcels service.

Recorded delivery

Recorded delivery provides a record of posting and delivery. The addressee or a representative signs a form to say that the letter or parcel has been received, and a small compensation fee is possible in the event of loss or damage in the post. When the letter is taken to the Post Office, a special receipt form is filled in and given to the sender as proof of posting. Letters sent by recorded delivery must be handed in at the counter and not dropped in the letter box.

A special delivery label

A receipt label for recorded delivery

Important documents and papers such as examination papers are often sent by this method, but there is no compensation for any valuables enclosed, such as jewellery or money. The sender can also receive an advice of delivery for an additional fee.

Cash on delivery

Under this Post Office service, firms can send letters (first-class registered) or parcels to customers and ask the postman to collect payment when he delivers the items. The sum is then remitted to the sender by the Post Office.

Poste restante

This service is useful for a person who is visiting a town and does not know where he or she will be staying, or for how long, and who wishes mail to be received. Letters, cards and parcels marked 'poste restant' or 'to be called for' can be addressed with the name of the person to whom they are sent and the address of a main post office in the town. The addressee then calls at the Post Office to collect the mail.

Private boxes

Some firms receive a large amount of mail every day, and so they may have a private posting box. A private box has its own number to which items can be addressed, and this allows businesses to collect mail from the delivery office rather than waiting for the next normal delivery to their premises. Businesses may also have their own private posting boxes from which the Post Office will collect mail. Registered letters or parcels, however, must be taken to the local post office in the usual way, as the private box service is only for ordinary letters and parcels.

A private box

Franking machines

When permission has been obtained from the local head post office, a business may lease or purchase a franking machine from an approved company. The business pays the Post Office lump sums of postage in advance, and the machine then stamps the value of the necessary stamps (first- or second-class) and the postmark on each letter or card sent. A control card has to be submitted to the local post office at the end of each week as a check on the accuracy of the machine. Main post offices will also accept unstamped mail in large quantities for franking by the Post Office itself.

A franking machine

Selectapost

The Post Office will divide up an addressee's mail before it is delivered, for example into the different departments of a business, as long as the various divisions required appear clearly in the address. This saves businesses the time needed to sort large mail deliveries.

Overseas mail

Letters, packets and parcels may be sent abroad by surface or air mail. For European destinations, letters are automatically sent by air if this is the quickest method and no special envelopes or markings are needed. Outside Europe, mail is sent by surface (sea or land) unless additional postage is paid and items are marked 'Par Avion'. Special lightweight (blue) envelopes, paper and pre paid letter forms can be bought in order to keep down the cost of postage.

Swiftair

This is a high-speed letter post available to all countries. Airmail letters and printed papers sent by this service receive priority treatment and are delivered by a special messenger where this will provide the quickest service. Items should have a Swiftair label on the top left-hand corner and normally be handed over a post office counter. It costs more to send items in this way, but the delivery time is usually one day earlier than by ordinary mail. For overseas surface mail, Express Delivery provides a similar service.

Datapost

This is a special courier service which offers high speed and reliable delivery. Items travel separately from ordinary mail and if delivery is not on time as guaranteed, payment is refunded. There are two variations on the service. Datapost Sameday guarantees that items can be handed in and delivered on the same day within local areas and between main cities in the United Kingdom. Datapost Overnight guarantees delivery on the next day on a nationwide basis.

International Datapost

Business papers and other items can now be sent by courier-style delivery to certain countries which offer the Datapost service. This provides security and reliability, and in some cases items can be delivered within 24 hours. EMS stands for Express Mail Services including Swiftair for mail sent abroad and Datapost Inland and International.

Electronic post

Where a business wants to mail a large quantity of standard letters to different addresses, it can supply the letter content and the names/addresses on computer tape to the Post Office. The quantity of letters and envelopes needed is then produced at one of the Post Office's Electronic Post Centres by means of advanced computing and laser printing technology, and the letters are sent out by first-class delivery. If necessary, the whole process can be carried out in one day under the Priority Service. Individual names and addresses are printed in each letter, and each can also be personalised within the text of the letter if required. A business's own letterhead can be used and enclosures such as a leaflet can be sent with each letter. The service saves businesses much time and cost, and it can be used for a variety of purposes such as circulating existing or prospective customers, company shareholders or employees.

Intelpost

Sometimes businesses need to send exact copies of items like drawings or plans very quickly. Intelpost is a Royal Mail service available from the Post Office offering a high-speed facsimile transmission between many towns and cities in the United Kingdom and to/from some countries overseas. It gives an exact copy of original documents and drawings up to A4 size by electronic means over long distances. This service is available from many head post offices on normal weekdays, and the local post office will be able to tell enquirers where the nearest Intelpost transmission office is. Businesses with their own special equipment can also electronically send facsimiles directly to Intelpost offices or even directly to other businesses or branches having the same facility.

CHECK THIS OUT

Write out the following sentences, filling in the missing words:

1 Letters posted by the first-class service are usually delivered on the _____ _____ day after collection.

2 A firm may obtain a licence from the Head Postmaster for customers to reply in pre-paid envelopes using the _____ _____ service.

3 A _____ of posting can be used as proof of posting, and is used for parcels containing goods of low value.

4 Articles of high value can be sent through the post using first-class _____ letters or packets.

5 People may call at a main post office in a town where they are staying in order to collect mail sent to them there. This service is called _____ _____.

6 A _____ machine prints envelopes with a stamp and a postmark.

7 A high-speed postal courier service available in the United Kingdom and certain other countries is called _____.

8 Exact copies of drawings and plans can be sent from many head post offices using the _____ service.

National Girobank

This is a separately managed business within the Post Office Corporation, and its services are available at post office counters and/or directly by post to the Girobank Centre at Bootle. All transactions are in fact passed through a centralised computer system at Bootle, where all Girobank accounts are held.

The National Girobank now provides most of the services available through the commercial banks (see Chapter 8). Both current and deposit accounts can be opened, and a range of services is available depending on the type of account held, including Girocheques, cheque guarantee cards, Giro transfers (national and international), standing orders, direct debits, travellers' cheques, foreign currencies and loans. Many of these services are available to businesses as well as individuals, but a special service for businesses is Cashcheques. These are open cheques which can be paid to individuals who can then cash them at a named post office.

A service which can be used by people who are not Girobank account holders is Transcash. By filling in a payment slip and handing it in with cash (or in some cases a cheque) at a post office, a person can pay bills or send money for other reasons. Within the United Kingdom, however, this service can only be used to make payments to persons with Girobank accounts. To send money abroad the receiver need not have such an account, and payment can be by cash or cheque depending on the country of destination. A business having a Girobank account can provide its customers with a Freepay number, so that they can use Transcash to pay bills without any transfer charge.

FREE BANKING WITH GIROBANK

CHANGE YOUR MONEY AND GO AS YOU PLEASE

TRAVELLERS CHEQUES FOREIGN CURRENCY

Girobank
TRAVEL SERVICES
A simply more convenient way to go as you please.

Trans Trans Trans Trans
cash cash cash cash

NATIONAL

Girobank

Bootle Merseyside GIR 0AA

Trans Trans Trans Trans
cash cash cash cash

Credit
Girobank account number

Amount
Standard fee payable at the counter

19

14D

Credit
Girobank account number

Amount
Standard fee payable at the counter

Name
of payee

Name and
address
of payer
BLOCK
CAPITALS
PLEASE

Signature

Date

19

...e do not write in the space below Please do not write in the space below Please do not write in the space below Please do not write in the s...

Businesses now use the National Girobank facilities for many different purposes, for example:

- paying salaries or pensions to staff by Girocheque or Giro transfers;

- receiving instalment payments from customers through standing orders/direct debits;

- receiving single payments by Giro transfer/Transcash by attaching a slip to customers' bills, for example gas, electricity, telephone charges and mail order debts;

- making payments by Cashcheques to persons not having Giro or bank accounts;

- paying in cash/cheques at post offices.

A special advantage which the National Girobank has over the commercial banks is that its post office counter facilities are available daily for much longer hours than the banks, and also on Saturday mornings, unlike most banks at present. In addition, post offices are often found in more remote areas of the country than banks. The National Girobank is likely to become increasingly competitive with the commercial banks.

National Savings

Various types of savings facilities are offered by the Department for National Savings through the Post Office:

National Savings Bank

This bank offers interest on money invested, and money can be deposited and withdrawn at any savings bank post office. For an *ordinary account*, no withdrawal notice is required for a small sum, but there is a low limit on the amount of cash which can be withdrawn on any one day. An *investment account* gives a much higher rate of interest, but withdrawals are subject to one month's notice from the day the application is received at the National Savings Bank.

NATIONAL
SAVINGS

Premium Savings Bonds

These are sold in units of £1 but the minimum purchase is £10. Above £10, bonds are sold in multiples of £5. Each unit has a separate chance in the weekly and monthly prize draws, and the winners can receive £50 or larger prizes of up to £250 000. However, no interest is payable on these bonds. Bonds can be cashed by completing a withdrawal form at any post office.

National Savings Bonds

These bonds are for people who wish to invest lump sums at higher rates of interest. Three months' notice has to be given for a withdrawal, and if this is required in the first year, there is a loss of interest. Two types of bonds are available: deposit and income. In the case of deposit bonds, interest is added yearly to the investment, whereas for income bonds, interest is paid monthly to the investor.

National Savings Certificates

These can be bought at Post Offices currently at £25.00 per unit in certain multiples, for example, 1, 2, 10, 80. They can be held for five years, but this period is normally extended. Fixed interest is paid on some issues of certificates, while others are 'index-linked' and repaid in line with the increase in the General Index of Retail Prices (sometimes with supplements). Interest is paid at an increasing rate annually, and bonuses are sometimes paid at the end of five years or more, so that it is advantageous not to cash in the certificates at an early stage.

Postal order service

A specimen postal order

Small sums of money can be sent through the post using postal orders. The sender fills in the payee's name (in ink) and the name of the post office or town where the order will be presented. Then the counterfoil is filled in and detached, and the sender keeps it. The payee, on receiving the postal order, takes it to the named post office, or any post office in the named town, and receives cash on signing the order. Alternatively a post office or town need not be named, but instead the order is crossed, in which case it must be paid into a bank account before cash can be received. British postal orders can also be cashed and issued in certain other countries.

All other post office payment services are now operated through the National Girobank Service.

Other services

On behalf of the Government, the Post Office provides the following services for the general public:

- issuing various licences, especially TV, motor vehicle and dog;
- providing a wide range of application forms for sending elsewhere, for example driving licences, full passports and certain tax payments;
- selling stamps (other than postage), for example for contract notes and national insurance payments;
- issuing British Visitor's Passports;
- paying out retirement pensions and various Government allowances, such as child and invalidity benefits.

CHECK THIS OUT

Write out the following sentences, filling in the missing words.

1 The National _____ provides many services which are also available through the commercial banks.

2 People who are not Girobank account holders can use a service called _____ at a post office.

3 The National Savings Bank has two types of account: _____ and _____.

4 Premium _____ _____ go into a prize draw each week and month, and winners can receive £50 or more.

5 National Savings Certificates can be held for at least _____ years.

6 One way of sending a small sum of money through the post is to use a _____ _____.

7 Two kinds of licence available through the Post Office are _____ and _____.

8 You may obtain a British Visitor's _____ from most main post offices.

SHORT QUESTIONS

1 Why is it important to use the postcode in addresses?

2 What is the difference between first- and second-class post?

3 What kinds of item might be sent by recorded delivery?

4 What is a certificate of posting?

5 What is the difference between the business reply service and Freepost?

6 Explain poste restante.

7 How would you send cash through the post?

8 Give *five* Government services provided through the Post Office.

9 Mention *three* items of information you would be able to get from the *Post Office Guide*.

10 What are private boxes?

MULTIPLE CHOICE QUESTIONS

There are four possible answers to each of the following questions. Study the introductory sentence, and then decide which of the alternatives correctly answers the question or comples the sentence. Write down the question number and follow it with (A) B) (C) or (D), according to your choice.

1 Which of the following is NOT a Post Office service?
   (A) Letter delivery
   (B) Telephone repairs
   (C) Paying out pensions
   (D) Savings and payment facilities.

2 Letters, postcards and parcels should
   (A) be handed in at the Post Office
   (B) be sorted by hand
   (C) be weighed and stamped only at the Post Office
   (D) be addressed with a postcode.

3 Which of the following information is NOT available from the *Post Office Guide*?
   (A) Details of National Giro services
   (B) Current charges for parcels
   (C) The times when post offices are open
   (D) Details of inland and overseas postal services.

4 A business stamping a post-mark and the value of necessary stamps would be using
   (A) Freepost
   (B) a franking machine
   (C) the Business Reply service
   (D) a certificate of posting.

5 The service where important documents and papers can be sent through the Post Office by completing a special receipt form is called
   (A) registered delivery
   (B) poste restante
   (C) parcel post
   (D) recorded delivery.

6 A firm wishing to receive *first-class post* replies from customers without asking them to pay postage, would use the
   (A) Freepost service
   (B) household delivery service
   (C) Business Reply service
   (D) Nightrider service.

7 The service where the addressee can call at a main post office and collect his/her mail is called
   (A) special delivery service
   (B) private boxes
   (C) Selectapost
   (D) box number service.

8 Letters which arrive at the delivery office too late for normal delivery will arrive next day if sent by
   (A) first-class post
   (B) second-class post
   (C) Freepost
   (D) special delivery.

9 Premium Savings Bonds are those which
   (A) are for people who wish to invest lump
       sums at higher rates of interest
   (B) offer prizes in a weekly or monthly draw
   (C) pay interest at an increasing annual rate,
       usually for five years
   (D) offer high interest on money regularly
       invested.

10 Unaddressed mail delivered for a firm to *every*
   address in an area is called
   (A) Business Reply service
   (B) special delivery
   (C) registered packets
   (D) household delivery service.

11 An urgent letter should be sent by
   (A) first-class post
   (B) registered post
   (C) recorded delivery
   (D) Business Reply service.

12 Evidence that an item which has been sent
   through the post has been lost is provided by
   (A) a registered letter envelope
   (B) a poste restante information slip
   (C) a certificate of posting
   (D) a cash on delivery receipt.

13 The National Girobank does NOT provide
   (A) cash dispensers
   (B) standing orders
   (C) cheque guarantee cards
   (D) travellers' cheques.

14 A service offering high-speed facsimile
   transmission between some towns in the United
   Kingdom by electronic means is called
   (A) electronic post
   (B) special delivery
   (C) Intelpost
   (D) Swiftair.

15 Post can be sorted into different departments of
   a business, before it is delivered by the Post
   Office, by using
   (A) private boxes
   (B) recorded delivery
   (C) first-class post
   (D) Selectapost.

There are four possible answers to each of the
following questions.

If you think (1) only is correct, write down A.
If you think (1) and (2) only are correct, write down B.
If you think (3) and (4) only are correct, write down C.
If you think (2), (3) and (4) only are correct, write down D.

16 All Post Office payment services are now
   operated through the National Girobank Service
   except for the
   (1) postal order service
   (2) paying out of child benefits
   (3) Transcash service
   (4) direct debit service.

17 Firms which have a large amount of mail every
   day may collect mail from the delivery office
   using
   (1) private boxes
   (2) Selectapost
   (3) poste restante
   (4) recorded delivery.

18 An advantage of National Girobank not found
   in other banks is that
   (1) it is open during the Post Office business
       hours
   (2) salaries can be paid through this bank
   (3) standing orders can be paid through this
       bank
   (4) it offers both current and deposit accounts.

19 A business which wishes to use Electronic Post
   would supply
   (1) the letter content and the names and
       addresses on computer tape
   (2) leaflets which are to be enclosed
   (3) a courier to deliver Datapost
   (4) their own laser printing machine.

20 Which of the following service(s) is/are provided
   by the Post Office on behalf of the Government?
   (1) Issuing television licences
   (2) Issuing British Visitor's passports
   (3) Payment by Cashcheques
   (4) The National Girobank

STIMULUS RESPONSE QUESTIONS

The following questions carry a mark of 20. Each section of a question shows the marks for the correct response.

1 Read the following passage and then answer the questions on it.

Ann is our new office junior, so show her how to work the franking machine and then tell her that tomorrow she has to collect the case with the mail from Uptown Post Office. Oh – take the case with you on the way home and show her where to go, will you? Then you can hand in this letter: it must go by Datapost Overnight. Mark the letter to America PAR AVION and make sure *that* goes tonight. Take this computer tape with you to the Post Office together with this packet of leaflets and a box of letter headings. We want to circulate existing customers and prospective customers with details of our latest offer. Send the share certificates by recorded delivery, and put all these letters for Mr Ford in a packet and send them Poste Restante to Downtown Head Post Office. We found Mrs Anderton's missing ring after she had gone home, so send that by Registered Post. Ask if the leaflets, including postcards to be returned to us, can be delivered to every house on Bardon Estate as quickly as possible.

(a) How is the postage for franked letters paid to the Post Office? *(2 marks)*

(b) What Post Office service will Ann use when she collects the mail in the morning? *(2 marks)*

(c) Explain briefly what will happen to the letter which goes by Datapost Overnight. *(2 marks)*

(d) What does PAR AVION mean? *(1 mark)*

(e) What Post Office service will mail the leaflets and letters to different addresses? *(1 mark)*

(f) Why is Ann asked to take leaflets and letter headings with the computer tape? *(2 marks)*

(g) How will Mr Ford get his packet of mail? *(2 marks)*

(h) What would happen if the package containing Mrs Anderton's ring went astray after it had been posted? *(2 marks)*

(i) What service is the firm using for the postcards which it wants prospective customers to return? *(2 marks)*

(j) Where do these prospective customers live? *(1 mark)*

(k) What service ensures that every household in the area receives a copy of the firm's leaflets? *(1 mark)*

(l) What kind of firm might Ann be working for? Give a reason for your answer. *(2 marks)*

2 Read the following passage and then answer the questions about it.

I want to put some money in the bank, but they're all closed by the time I get home from school. My Mum says she'll save up for a summer holiday every month from now until next May, and she's not sure what the best way is. She works, you know, so she can only go late in the afternoon or on Saturday morning to the bank, and our little sub-branch is closed then. Dad says he thinks he'll invest his Christmas bonus this year and put it towards the new house we're getting in three years.

(a) Advise the speaker about a National Savings service which he/she can use. *(6 marks)*

(b) Suggest the type of National Savings account which would yield the best possible interest for the speaker's mother. *(6 marks)*

(c) Assuming that the speaker's father cannot go to a bank during working hours, suggest the type of National Savings account in which he might invest his money. Give reasons for your answer. *(8 marks)*

ESSAY QUESTIONS

1 Describe the ways in which businesses can send mail and parcels quickly, using Post Office services
   (a) in this country;   *(10 marks)*
   (b) abroad.   *(10 marks)*

2 (a) What are the main services offered by the National Girobank?   *(10 marks)*
   (b) Compared with the commercial banks, and from the customer's point of view, what are the National Girobank's
       (i) advantages;   *(5 marks)*
       (ii) disadvantages?   *(5 marks)*

3 (a) Describe briefly four services provided by the Post Office which might be used by business firms.   *(12 marks)*
   (b) Give a situation in which each service might be appropriate.   *(8 marks)*

4 Look at Chapter 2 (The Retailer) and Chapter 5 (Business Ownership) when answering the following question.

   (a) Outline the main features of mail order trading.   *(5 marks)*

   (b) Why are the prices charged by mail order firms often higher than the prices of similar goods in shops?   *(2 marks)*
   (c) Name and briefly describe THREE Post Office services which allow payment to be made by mail order customers who do not possess bank accounts.   *(6 marks)*
   (d) (i) Distinguish between gross profit and net profit.   *(2 marks)*
       (ii) Show that a mail order firm's advertising campaign could result in a lower level of net profit for the firm.
                                              (5 marks)

(This question is reproduced from specimen questions for the GCSE Commerce paper by permission of the Southern Regional Examinations Board.)

5 Explain what arrangements the Post Office makes to carry:

   (a) valuables or important documents;   *(5 marks)*
   (b) goods which need proof of posting; *(5 marks)*
   (c) goods which must be paid for by the customer when the postman delivers them;
                                              (5 marks)
   (d) goods which need proof of delivery.
                                              (5 marks)

LEARN IT YOURSELF

1 Go to your local Post Office and collect as many leaflets as you can about the different Post Office services available. In pairs or in a group, make a wall-chart or display for your classroom.

2 Contact the Public Relations Officer at your nearest Head Post Office and arrange a visit to see how the mail is received, sorted and distributed. Make a brief report on the visit and on any specially interesting features, such as Intelpost, which you may see.

3 Using the *Post Office Guide* and a pair of scales, make up several different parcels, weigh them and work out how much it would cost you to send

them (a) somewhere in the United Kingdom;
     (b) somewhere abroad chosen by you.

4 Make a survey of streets in your own area or of the locality of your school, and on a map, mark the Post Offices and at least *three* post boxes. Include a key which shows the times of collection from the post boxes.

5 Write to the Post Office, and also write to or visit your Careers Office, Job Centre or Library and find out what careers are possible in the Post Office. Make a report on at least three careers, giving details of the responsibilities, salary and prospects for each.

NOW TRY THIS

Pair up the following words with their definitions and then write them out as full sentences:

(a) The postcode

(b) The Business Reply Service

(c) Registered letters and packets

(d) Recorded delivery

(e) Poste restante

(i) is a service provided for visitors to a town, who can call at a main Post Office to collect mail addressed to them there.

(ii) is used for items such as legal documents where proof of posting is required.

(iii) is the last item of an address.

(iv) allows businesses to issue reply cards or envelopes on which the postage need not be paid by the sender.

(v) are marked with a blue cross on all sides and used for sending valuable items through the post.

ASSIGNMENT – THE POST OFFICE

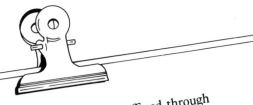

Carry out a survey of the financial services offered through

(a) the Post Office
(b) the commercial banks

and explain which services offered by each are alike, and which services are different. Look particularly at services which offer alternatives to paying in cash for goods and services received.

Make a report on your findings, illustrating with leaflets, documents and other illustrations.

OR

Devise a questionnaire and arrange to interview a bank official who will answer your questions. (You may arrange this through the Bank Information Service.) Ask the same questions of a Post Office Official. (You may arrange this through the Public Relations Officer at your Head Post Office.)

It may be possible to use a tape recording as a report for this assignment instead of a written report. Ask the official's permission before you make a taped interview.

CHAPTER 12 TELECOMMUNICATIONS

Introduction

The means of communication provided by the Post Office (covered in Chapter 11) rely on various forms of transport to carry messages physically from point A to point B. In addition, there are communication systems which do not require transport, but in which information is carried electronically by cable or by wave signals through the atmosphere. The term 'telecommunications' is used to cover these methods.

The national telecommunications cable network in the United Kingdom is controlled by British Telecom, which became a public corporation separate from the Post Office in 1981 and which was 'privatised' (sold by the State) in 1984. Although British Telecom still has a monopoly because it controls this national network, which provides telephone, telex and other facilities, it is facing an increasing amount of competition. People and businesses no longer have to rent telephone handsets or other equipment from British Telecom, as they can now be purchased outright from British Telecom or from other manufacturers and shops. All these appliances must, however, be approved by British Telecom if they are to be connected to the national network. Other companies, for example Mercury, are now allowed to provide competing network services. OFTEL is the independent body which has been set up as a 'watchdog' over the different telephone systems. It stands for Office of Telecommunications and deals with complaints about British Telecom and other systems that have not been satisfactorily dealt with.

In addition to cable communications, there are also those which are transmitted through the atmosphere, such as the television and radio services. Television programmes are transmitted by the British Broadcasting Corporation and various independent companies, such as Thames Television, while national radio is operated by the BBC together with local radio services provided again by the BBC but also by many independent companies such as Capital Radio in London or Piccadilly Radio in Manchester.

The national telecommunications systems in the United Kingdom are also connected to most other countries in the world to provide an international network. The links were for many years by radio and cable, but the development of satellites has brought a new

limension to long-distance telecommunications. Many radio, TV and
elephone connections are now achieved via satellites which transmit
signals between earth stations. British Telecom is involved internationally in providing these facilities (see later).

An Edwardian telephone exchange

A telephone exchange today

British Telecom services

British Telecom provides a very wide range of telecommunications
services, which has been expanding rapidly in recent years.

Telephone services

As a means of voice communication, the telephone dates back to the
nineteenth century, but it is still of very great importance for both
personal and business use. It offers rapid connection and
communication, and allows the interchange of large amounts of
information and ideas in a short space of time. A major disadvantage
is that there is no automatic record of the call, as in the case of
posted messages (for example business orders) but, as you will see
below, there are now telephone services which can provide 'hard
copy' – a printed record.

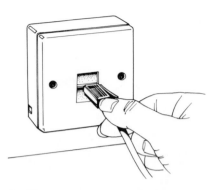

Handsets can now be easily plugged into the British Telecom network using a standard socket

If you are connected to the British Telecom network, then you can make calls to others similarly connected or to networks in other countries. These calls can be local, national or international. Originally, all calls went through an operator, but direct dialling has gradually been extended from local to long-distance national calls (Subscriber Trunk Dialling – STD), and now even to many international calls (International Direct Dialling – IDD). This has speeded up and extended the connections and has greatly reduced the cost of telephone calls.

Telephone subscribers have to pay an installation charge, quarterly rentals on hired telephone handsets, and charges for each call made with additions for special services used. However, handsets can now be purchased outright from British Telecom or other companies, so that hire charges can be avoided, although you still have to pay rental for connection to the network. All subscribers are entitled to an entry in area telephone directories and 'Directory Enquiries' can be used for other areas. There are also special directories produced by British Telecom, for example *Yellow Pages* and classified business directories, as well as competing private directories, such as *Thomson's Local Directory*.

Many businesses have their own internal telephone systems purely for internal use or with a switchboard which is connected to the national network. These systems can be provided by British Telecom or by other competing companies. Where connections cannot be made by means of the cable network, for example to ships and cars, then radio links are used. Satellites are now used for bouncing off transmissions to/from distant parts of the world.

The use of satellites is one of the main developments in telecommunications in recent years, and the importance of satellites to international links is rapidly overtaking that of submarine and land cables which have been used for many years. The satellites operate in conjunction with giant dish aerials at earth stations, such as those at Goonhilly Downs in Cornwall and Madley near Hereford. Signals between earth stations can be bounced off a satellite, enabling clear telephone connections to be achieved around the world, as well as providing for international TV transmissions (see later). British Telecom is a main partner in Intelsat, an international organisation which controls the launching and operation of many telecommunication satellites. Some businesses are now also being provided with their own small dish aerials for direct satellite communication.

Within the United Kingdom, two of the most important recent developments in the telephone network are electronic, digital telephone exchanges and optical fibre cables. The electronic exchanges, called System X, will provide much faster connections by phone, thus allowing more calls to be handled at busy times, as well as being more reliable. The main trunk network is to be completed by 1988, but it will probably take a further ten years to complete all the local links to people's homes. Optical fibre cables are gradually replacing the copper cabling, because they can carry many more calls simultaneously, as well as TV transmissions, they are cheaper to instal and maintain, and there is less sound interference. Transmissions are carried along the fibres by pulses of light.

As part of the telephone system, British Telecom provides a very wide range of services, some of which are explained below. You should find out about the many others.

Fax

This service allows businesses to send facsimiles (exact copies) of documents to distant places, nationally and internationally, via the telephone network. The document is reproduced immediately at the receiving end and the service is therefore much faster than the post. If the sending or receiving business does not have the necessary equipment, then British Telecom has Bureaufax offices in major British cities, where documents can be received or accepted (see Chapter 11 for the Post Office Intelpost service).

A fax machine

Telecom Gold

This provides an electronic mail service which allows computers and suitable word processors to pass immediate printed messages between one another using the telephone network. Because of its high operating speed, a large amount of information can be sent very cheaply, especially over long distances.

Voicemail

This is the 'voice' equivalent of the electronic mail service. A message can be given on the phone without the need to be connected to the recipient. Instead it is stored digitally and can be retrieved later by phone by the person/business to whom it has been 'sent'. For example, a travelling representative could 'send' orders when the central office is closed or lines are engaged by using an ordinary public callbox.

Prestel

This is British Telecom's Viewdata service, which links central computers to home and business TV sets (specially adapted) or computer VDUs using the telephone lines. The computers store a vast amount of information, which is continually being updated, for example on share prices, sports results and holiday vacancies. Unlike teletext services (see later), it provides two way communication, allowing subscribers to make bookings, place orders, access their bank accounts and send messages. For messages there is a Mailbox service which sorts messages electronically and allows addresses to access them on the TV screen or VDU. Individual businesses can have their own private Viewdata service, allowing them to link their various branches and offices using the Prestel computers. Charges are based on telephone time/distance, computer time and frame charges for the information given (sometimes free).

Radiopaging

Radiopager

This service covers most of the United Kingdom. Originally, it was a 'bleeper' system which warned people that they were required, for example to return to base or to their phone. It has now been developed to provide a visual display on the pager of up to 70 characters (called Message Master).

Radiophones

This is a more recent development which provides mobile telephones. These can be hand-held, installed in a car or fixed payphones on trains and express coaches. These services are still being extended to cover the whole country. Cellnet is a completely mobile system, being developed by British Telecom and Securicor, which is planned to cover 90 per cent of the country by 1989. Vodaphone is a competing network developed by another company, Racal.

Tele-conferencing

Through the Audio-conferencing service, two groups of people can be linked by phone so that a joint meeting can be held at a distance. British Telecom also offers expertise in organising such conferences to best effect. The Slow Scan service allows visual communication in addition. A related service is the facility for linking up to 18 individuals by phone simultaneously for discussion and consultation. In addition, there is a sound and vision *Videoconferencing* service operating to Europe, the USA and Canada.

Telemessages

These are printed messages which can be given to British Telecom by telephone (or telex – see later) up to 10 p.m. (7 p.m. on Sundays) for delivery to the addressee on the next working day. A message can be sent to an individual or to multiple addresses, and it arrives in a distinctive yellow envelope. An *international telegram* service is available for messages to/from other countries.

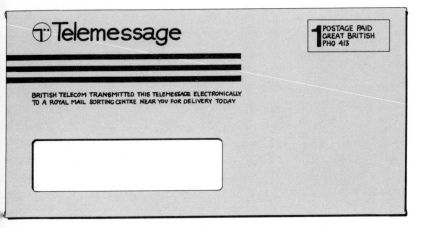

Datel

Through the use of modems attached to the telephone network, this service allows the transmission of data between computers within the United Kingdom or in many countries around the world. Data can be transmitted at various speeds up to 2400 bits per second on the standard systems, but higher speeds are available with special facilities. The service allows computers in the offices of large companies spread over a wide area to communicate with one another, for example to transfer information on daily sales to be added together at head office.

X-Stream services

These provide for the digital transmission of data between computers. There are public services for use by different businesses, and also private services which link different sections of a business in various locations. *Packet Switch Stream* (*PSS*) is the public service, which for example, is used by the banks for their automated clearing of credits. *Kilostream* and *Megastream* offer private circuits, the latter providing a higher capacity. *Satstream* provides links by using satellites and small-dish earth terminals installed for individual businesses. Some of these services are available internationally for connection to countries having similar facilities, and some can provide for the digital transmission of speech, video and facsimile as well as data.

Interstream

These services are being developed to allow for links with the telex and telephone networks.

Freefone

A business can encourage customers to call it by publicising a Freefone number (or name) which allows people to ring without charge. *Linkline 0800* is a special Freefone service which allows the normal telephone number of a subscribing business to be called without charge by prefixing it with 0800. *Linkline 0345* does not provide free calls, but charges the user only at local rate for long-distance calls.

Phonecards

These can now be used in many public telephone booths instead of cash. They are small, green plastic cards which can be bought in 20, 40, 100 and 200 unit denominations from post offices and other shops. When the card is inserted into the slot provided in the booth, calls can be made, and units are erased on the card according to time/distance used. *Creditcalls* can similarly be made using credit cards such as Access and Visa, but the card account is debited instead.

Information services

By calling on the telephone, a variety of information, often right up to date, can be obtained. Examples are the weather forecast, cricket scores and business news. In addition, one can call for a particular record to be played, for a daily cooking recipe or for a children's story. A list of these services is given in your local telephone directory.

Telex

The British Telecom telex service is the printed equivalent of the telephone service. A telex subscriber can send a message by dialling another subscriber's telex number, and it will be immediately printed out at the receiver's end. The system has the advantage of being fully automatic, so that it can be used 24 hours a day without the receiver having to be there personally. The message is printed out and waits for the user to arrive. Compared with the telephone, telex also has the merit of giving a permanent record, so that there is less chance of messages being forgotten, misunderstood or denied.

The service is available not only in the United Kingdom, but also to and from many countries abroad. A telex directory gives numbers for subscribers in the same way as a telephone directory. Calls are charged on the basis of time and distance, as for the telephone.

Modern telex terminals operate electronically and incorporate microprocessors, so that together with the telephone, they are rapidly becoming a part of a totally integrated computer-based office system for receiving, processing, storing and retrieving information. The communication revolution has begun and while there is much progress to take place, rapid development is likely to occur for the rest of this century.

CHECK THIS OUT

Write out the following sentences, filling in the missing words:

1 British Telecom separated from the _____ _____ in 1981.

2 British Telecom became a _____ _____ in 1984.

3 STD stands for _____ _____ _____ and IDD stands for _____ _____ _____.

4 The service which allows one to dial a telephone number without charge to the caller is _____.

5 The _____ service allows complete documents to be transmitted and reproduced at the receiving end.

6 Datel provides for the transmission of data via the telephone network by the use of _____.

7 The _____ service provides for the delivery of messages on the following day to individuals and businesses.

8 Phone calls from public kiosks without the use of cash can be made by the use of _____ or _____ _____.

9 Viewdata services allow two-way communication, but _____ services operate only one-way.

10 The _____ _____ service enables speech to be stored digitally and then retrieved by the receiver.

Radio communication

In addition to British Telecom services, there is also radio and television communication. Much of this is in the form of *broadcasting*, which is one-way only and transmitted so that it can be received by the general public, provided people have the necessary equipment – a radio or a television set. Radio is also used, however, for a variety of purposes in two-way communication, for example for ship-to-shore links and for contacting vehicles such as police cars and taxi-cabs.

The radio broadcasting services, both local and national, are used mainly for entertainment purposes, but information can also be transmitted quickly to a large number of people at one time, for instance details of road conditions and football results. Business can use radio for advertising purposes on commercial stations and business news such as changes in the stock market prices is given.

Television

In the United Kingdom, there are four channels available for television broadcasting, operated by the BBC and independent companies. Millions of people can be reached at the same time with both sound and vision, but the communication is one-way only. Again, advertising on commercial television is important to businesses (see Chapter 7) and there are sometimes also special programmes of interest to business people, for example on computing.

A more recent service provided through television communication is Teletext, which provides a wide range of information for households and businesses via special television sets. There are two competing services: BBC's Ceefax, and IBA's Oracle on ITV. Information is continually being updated, for example stock exchange prices and foreign exchange rates. These Teletext services are distinct from Viewdata services such as Prestel (see earlier) because they offer one-way communication only. Although Prestel is received by a television set, it is transmitted via the telephone network and not received aerially, and a two-way link therefore exists.

Cable television

While the national television programmes are transmitted through the atmosphere, in more recent years cable television has developed and is now available in many areas. Cables are laid under pavements and roads, and houses are then linked to the circuit after payment of a fee. Cable television will enable users to receive additional local programmes which will give them a wider choice, and there will be better reception. The Government is selling franchises to businesses which allows them the sole right to provide cable television in given local areas. British Telecom already provides cable television in some areas, and it is involved in developing others. The new optical fibre cabling (mentioned earlier in the chapter) can carry not only speech and computer data, but also these local television programmes.

Satellite television

The use of satellites in connection with international telephone links was mentioned earlier, but these satellites and their earth stations are also essential for the transmission of television programmes around the world. Television cannot be transmitted long distances along the earth's surface, and the use of satellites allows events thousands of miles away (for instance, sporting fixtures and political meetings) to be seen clearly and instantaneously. British Telecom, often in conjunction with other nations, has an important role in providing the satellites and stations.

SHORT QUESTIONS

1 What are subscriber trunk dialling and international direct dialling?

2 What is the main advantage of the telex service compared with the telephone?

3 How does System X improve the telephone network services?

4 How does British Telecom help in the transmission of television programmes?

5 What are X-Stream services provided by British Telecom?

6 Give *three* kinds of information which can be obtained by dialling special British Telecom telephone numbers.

7 Briefly describe the Prestel service.

8 How is the use of optical fibre cables improving telephone connections?

9 How can businesses benefit from the use of Radiophone services?

10 What is the cable television service?

MULTIPLE CHOICE QUESTIONS

There are four possible answers to each of the following questions. Study the introductory sentence, and then decide which of the alternatives correctly answers the question or completes the sentence. Write down the question number and follow it with (A) (B) (C) or (D), according to your choice.

1 The term 'telecommunications' covers
   (A) messages carried by Post Office couriers
   (B) communications by telephone only
   (C) communications by cable only
   (D) communication carried by cable or wave systems.

2 British Telecom separated from the Post Office in
   (A) 1984
   (B) 1981
   (C) 1980
   (D) 1986.

3 British Telecom has a monopoly because it
   (A) is the only organisation which can rent out telephones
   (B) controls the national telecommunications cable network
   (C) controls television and radio services
   (D) rents out local radio stations.

4 An advantage of a telephone call is
   (A) instant communication
   (B) all calls are recorded
   (C) most calls go through the operator
   (D) telephone handsets can be hired, thus saving money.

5 System X is a development involving
   (A) a dish aerial for satellite communication
   (B) overseas television transmissions to the United Kingdom
   (C) new electronic telephone exchanges
   (D) telecommunications satellites.

6 An electronic mail service allowing computers to pass immediate printed messages between one another is called
   (A) telex
   (B) Telecom Gold
   (C) cable communications
   (D) Fax.

7 Messages can be given on the telephone, stored digitally and retrieved later by using
   (A) recorded message tape
   (B) Fax
   (C) Voicemail
   (D) Radiopaging.

8 Prestel is
   (A) one-way television viewing
   (B) a Viewdata service
   (C) the name of a computer system
   (D) a Teletext service.

9 Cellnet is
   (A) a bleeper system
   (B) an audio-conferencing system
   (C) a mobile telephone system
   (D) an electronic message sorter.

10 Freefone is a
   (A) telephone call using a credit card
   (B) telephone/computer link
   (C) link between a telex and a telephone
   (D) number which people can ring without charge.

11 Radio is NOT used for
   (A) entertainment
   (B) giving information
   (C) Viewdata
   (D) advertising.

12 The Teletext service provides
   (A) information for individuals and businesses
   (B) two-way communication using screen and telephone
   (C) a choice of four channels for the user
   (D) a printed-out message for the user.

13 Cable television is available when
   (A) every household in the United Kingdom is linked to a cable
   (B) the Government decides to provide the service to everyone
   (C) households have cable laid underground and are linked free of charge
   (D) households pay a fee to be linked to the underground cable system.

14 Television can be transmitted round the world using
(A) cables under the sea
(B) special optical fibre cable
(C) satellites and earth stations
(D) equipment provided only by British Telecom.

15 British Telecom faces competition because
(A) other manufacturers can now sell telephones and other equipment
(B) the BBC operates television programmes
(C) local radio is operated by independent companies
(D) 'Oftel' watches over the industry.

There are four possible answers to each of the following questions.

If you think (1) only is correct, write down A.
If you think (1) and (2) only are correct, write down B.
If you think (3) and (4) only are correct, write down C.
If you think (2), (3) and (4) only are correct, write down D.

16 The national telecommunications system in the United Kingdom is linked to other countries in the world by
(1) couriers
(2) satellite
(3) radio
(4) cable.

17 Special directories produced by British Telecom include
(1) *Yellow pages*
(2) *The Phone Book*
(3) *Kelly's Business Directory*
(4) *Thomson's Local Directory*.

18 Bureaufax is
(1) a service for sending facsimiles from special British Telecom offices
(2) a telex service
(3) a system of optical fibre cables
(4) an international telephone service.

19 Telemessages are
(1) messages transferred by computer
(2) messages transmitted by telephone and visual communication
(3) the successor to telegram messages
(4) printed messages to be delivered on the next working day.

20 Telex is available
(1) only at certain times of the day
(2) as an automatic system which does not need an operator
(3) internationally
(4) in the United Kingdom.

STIMULUS RESPONSE QUESTIONS

The following questions carry a mark of 20. Each section of a question shows the marks for the correct response.

1 Read the following passage, and then answer the questions on it.

A survey, showing that a business person makes an average of two and a half thousand telephone calls every year, calculated that in one year, he or she can spend up to a whole week hanging on to the telephone waiting to speak to a particular individual.

British Telecom Voicebank, which carried out the survey, says that the waiting time is caused because four out of five business people find the telephone often engaged, or that the person to whom they wish to speak is not available. It also discovered that 20 per cent of telephone messages left are either forgotten or misinterpreted.

(a) On average, how many calls does a business person make? *(2 marks)*

(b) Give *two* reasons why they are often kept waiting on the telephone. *(6 marks)*

(c) What *two* things happen to twenty per cent of telephone messages? *(2 marks)*

(d) Who carried out this survey? *(2 marks)*

(e) How does Voicebank help to reduce the amount of time wasted in using the telephone? Give an example of the way in which it can be used. *(8 marks)*

ESSAY QUESTIONS

1 (a) Explain why British Telecom services are becoming increasingly important for computer communications.   (*10 marks*)

   (b) Describe the various technical developments which are improving the telephone service both nationally and internationally.   (*10 marks*)

2 (a) Describe the main services which British Telecom now provides for businesses.   (*8 marks*)

   (b) Describe the various ways in which
      (i)   radio services   (*6 marks*)
      (ii) television services   (*6 marks*)
      can assist businesses.

3 (a) Describe *two* ways in which a person can obtain the telephone and telex numbers of subscribers.   (*8 marks*)

   (b) Explain *four* different methods by which telephone calls can be paid for by callers and receivers.   (*12 marks*)

LEARN IT YOURSELF

1 Write to your local Public Relations Office of British Telecom (see your local Phone Book) and ask for information and leaflets about telex. Use this information to write a brief account IN YOUR OWN WORDS about the use of telex in business.

2 The Office of Fair Trading (310c Field House, Bream's Buildings, London EC4A 1PR) gives guidelines about the use of the telephone for selling. Write to them and obtain a copy of the guidelines. Look in the press or Job Centres for details of a job as a tele-sales person. Imagine that you were going to be interviewed for such a job, and that you would be asked questions about the guidelines. Prepare some possible questions and answers. Together with a fellow-student, role-play an interview.

3 Look under 'local information' in the front of the Phone Book for services which may interest you. Dial 100 and ask for Freefone . . . (here you give the appropriate service) and ask for information to be sent to you. Produce a leaflet giving information about your chosen service.

4 Telephone technique is an important aspect of business life. Find information from office practice or other relevant books, such as *Office Skills*, on how to answer the telephone and produce a pamphlet or notice with the most important points highlighted. List any reference books at the end of your work.

NOW TRY THIS

The following diagram is a matrix containing services provided by

(a) the Post Office
(b) British Telecom.

Pick out the services provided by the Post Office and list them under that heading.

Then pick out the services provided by British Telecom and list them under that heading.

Give the line number and the letter of the column in each case.

There are ten Post Office services, and ten British Telecom services.

	A	B	C	D	E
Line 1	Radiopaging	Bureaufax	Datapost	Linkline	International telegrams
Line 2	Postal orders	Recorded delivery	Telex	Business reply service	Prestel
Line 3	National Girobank	Audio-conferencing	Special delivery	Datel	Intelpost
Line 4	National Savings	Yellow Pages	Transcash	Payment of allowances and pensions	Cellphones

ASSIGNMENT – THE HISTORY OF TELECOMMUNICATIONS

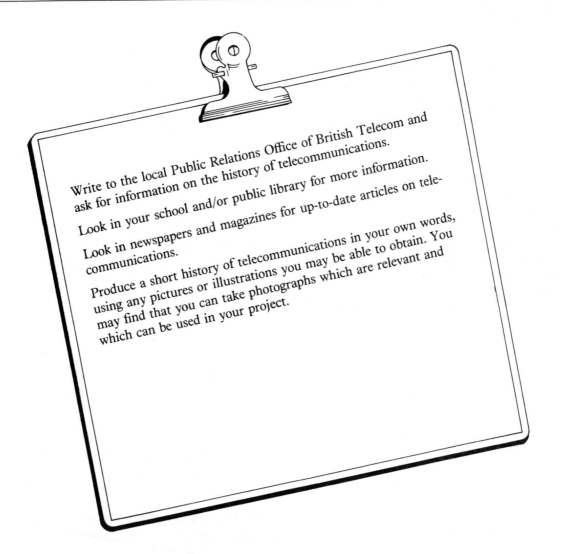

Write to the local Public Relations Office of British Telecom and ask for information on the history of telecommunications.

Look in your school and/or public library for more information.

Look in newspapers and magazines for up-to-date articles on telecommunications.

Produce a short history of telecommunications in your own words, using any pictures or illustrations you may be able to obtain. You may find that you can take photographs which are relevant and which can be used in your project.

CHAPTER 13 — BUILDING SOCIETIES

House purchase

In the United Kingdom houses are usually bought by means of a mortgage loan, which in many cases is arranged by a building society. The society lends money for the purchase of a house but holds the deeds to the property, and if the borrower fails to keep up with the repayments, the society is entitled to sell the house in order to regain its money. In other words, people who borrow money in this way to buy a house risk the possibility of having the house taken from them if they repeatedly fail to pay the monthly loan instalments.

As building societies have developed over the last 200 years, they have become the biggest lenders for house purchase. They now lend many billions of pounds annually and account for over 80 per cent of all money lent for house purchase.

The following table shows the amount of money lent for house loans during 1984:

Institution	£ million
Building societies	14 271
Commercial banks and Trustee Savings Bank	2 314
Insurance companies and pension funds	208
Total	16 793

Source: *Building Societies' Association Bulletin*, July 1985.

More than half the houses in this country are owned by the people who live in them, so quite clearly building societies play an important part in our lives as a way for saving for and purchasing a home, as well as an important way of saving up for other things.

How building societies grew

Up to 200 years ago, only the very wealthy owned their own homes. Most ordinary people rented houses, or were allowed to live in them as part of their job. During the Industrial Revolution, more and more people crowded into towns and cities to find work, and accommodation became difficult to find. The few houses available were built as cheaply as possible and were often crowded and unhealthy. Many workers soon realised that if they wanted to live in reasonable, uncrowded homes, they could not always rely on landlords to provide them.

Societies were formed where each member paid a small amount each week until the society could afford to build a house. The house was then ballotted or auctioned off, and the process would begin again until all the members were housed. When all the members had a house, the society ceased to operate. These societies were therefore called *terminating* societies. The first one was started in Birmingham in 1775. The *permanent* societies we have today soon became more popular because they kept going, but it was not until the early twentieth century that the last terminating society was wound up.

In the nineteenth century owning a house came to mean much more than just having somewhere decent to live, although this was very important in itself. It also allowed people to play a full part in society by giving them the right to vote and sit on juries. The Government passed several laws trying to ensure that the building societies were run properly but it was not until the Building Societies Act 1874 that building societies were put on a secure footing. All societies are required to be registered with the Registrar of Friendly Societies whose office has responsibility for making sure that they are run according to their rules.

During the twentieth century, building societies have continued to grow rapidly in importance, but their number has fallen as a result of the merger of many small societies. There are now less than 200 societies, including a small number of very large societies, such as the Halifax and the Woolwich, each of which has assets running into billions of pounds. Investing in such societies is very secure, but some smaller societies occasionally have difficulties.

How building societies operate

Building societies have shareholders, although they operate in a very different way from the shareholders of companies. Each shareholder has only one vote in electing directors so no one person or group can control a society by holding a large number of shares. The profits made by a society are ploughed back and shareholders receive only the agreed rate of interest on their investments, whereas in a company the share dividend would vary with the profits made. Furthermore, the shares cannot be sold to another person.

Societies lend out their investors' money for house purchases, and the interest received on the loans pays for the interest on the investors' savings. However, the societies need to keep a reserve for emergencies and only about 85 per cent of money received is lent for house purchase. Some of the remainder is kept as cash in order to meet withdrawals, while the rest is invested in low risk securities, such as government bonds, on which interest is received. Building societies are not allowed to make more risky investments, company shares for example.

How to arrange a mortgage

Assume you are thinking of buying a house. The largest lump sum you will have to pay is a deposit. For first-time buyers, 5 per cent or 10 per cent of the final house price will usually be required, although 100 per cent mortgages are possible. It helps if the deposit is saved up with the building society from whom the purchaser wishes to receive a mortgage. When you have found a house, you should ask to see the building society manager to arrange a mortgage. The basic information the manager wants is:

* how much has been saved up;
* how much is earned;
* how much the house costs;
* how much money you wish to borrow.

These points are always considered whether a buyer is arranging a loan through a bank, insurance company or building society. The lender will then assess the purchaser's ability to make repayments. Anyone who is considering buying a house should also take into account all additional costs such as solicitor's fees, estate agent's fees, Government stamp duty and removal expenses.

Once the purchaser has satisfied the building society about his or her ability to pay, the loan will probably amount to about two and a half or three times the gross yearly earnings. In the case of 'joint ownership', a proportion of a partner's earnings will probably be included.

Types of mortgage

Mortgages on property are usually arranged for periods of up to 25 years and tax relief can be obtained on the monthly interest payments on the first £30 000 of any mortgage loan for buying a house. The interest is paid net of tax, so for every £100 due, only £75 is paid (if the basic tax rate is 25%) and the building society claims the other £25 from the Inland Revenue. This is called the MIRAS scheme (Mortgage Interest Relief At Source). If you earn enough to be paying a higher rate of tax than 25 per cent, then you can obtain additional tax relief directly from the Inland Revenue, for example 40 per cent tax payers get an extra £10 per £100 allowed off their monthly interest payments.

BUILDING SOCIETIES

There are two main types of mortgage loan, and anyone deciding to arrange a mortgage will find it best to get advice in choosing the one which is the more suitable for them.

PLEASE COMPLETE THIS PAGE (Delete alternative which does not apply in answers with YES/NO printed)

PROPERTY AND LOAN DETAILS

B1 Type of property Bungalow/House/Maisonette/Flat etc | Detached semi detached or terraced

B2 State type of construction IF NOT brick or stone with tile or slate roof | Age of property

B3 If the property is a flat or maisonette on which floor is the unit situated . . . .

B4 State if property is freehold leasehold or feudal | Chief/Ground Rent – Feuduty | £ pa

B5 Unexpired lease still to run . . . . years | Service/Maintenance Charge | £ pa

B6 If a rising ground rent give details of reviews

ONLY COMPLETE QUESTIONS B7 TO B9 IF THE PROPERTY IS BEING BUILT OR NEWLY BUILT

B7 Name and address of Builder. . . . .

B8 Cost of basic building including land . . . . £ | Will the property have an N.H.B.C. Certificate | YES/NO

B9 Cost of any extras (eg garage, central heating) £ | Does the builder require stage payments | YES/NO

B10 State name of Vendor and how the Society's Valuer can gain access to the property in business hours. If the property is vacant please enclose the key | Tel. No.

B11 State name and telephone number of selling agent, enclose a copy of sale particulars if available | Tel. No.

B12 If you already own the property is it charged as security for a loan or overdraft | YES/NO

B13 Purchase price . . . . £ | Year of original purchase if already owned by you

B14 Total advance required . . . . £ | Repayment period . . . . years

B15 How do you wish to repay the mortgage By an endowment linked scheme . . . . | YES/NO | or by capital & interest payments | YES/NO

NB. Interest rates on large loans and endowment mortgages may be higher than the normal basic interest rate

B16 If the capital and interest payment method is chosen you are recommended to arrange some form of mortgage protection assurance. Please confirm that Anglia should supply information from this form to an approved Insurance Company so that you can be given details of available life assurance. | YES/NO

B17 Mortgage payments will be made (Please tick method required)

BY BANK STANDING ORDER | TO AN ANGLIA OFFICE | BY BANK CREDIT TRANSFER | BY POST OFFICE GIRO

B18 Will you occupy all the property as a private residence immediately on completion of the mortgage | YES/NO

B19 Give details if any part of the property is a) let or will be let, or b) used or will be used for business purposes

B20 Give details of any repairs or improvements that you intend to make to the property

B21 In the last three years have you applied to any source for a loan on this or any other property . . . . | YES/NO

If YES to whom and with what result . . . .

B22 If you are a first time buyer and intend to apply for assistance under the Homeloan Scheme give your account number and name of the savings body

Part of a mortgage application form

1   Repayment mortgage

In this case, the agreed monthly payment is made up of an amount for interest charged on the loan and also an amount for paying off some of the sum borrowed. In the early stages of the loan the amount of the loan repaid is small and the amount paid in interest very high, but, as the loan is paid off, the interest falls and the proportion of each monthly payment going towards paying off the loan increases. This continues until the loan is repaid after the agreed number of years.

2   Endowment mortgage

In this case, a life endowment insurance policy (see Chapter 10) is taken out with an insurance company, such as Sun Life or the Norwich Union. A premium is paid monthly to the company and the *interest only* on the mortgage loan is paid monthly to the building society. None of the loan is repaid during the period of the mortgage, so that interest payments remain the same (unless interest rates change). When the endowment policy matures the sum received will pay off the building society loan and there will also normally be a surplus, which is a bonus to the house owner. Tax relief is received on the interest for the duration of the loan and the MIRAS system usually applies again. An advantage of this method is that, if the borrower dies, the loan is automatically paid off at once by the life assurance company.

The *low cost start endowment loan* is a similar scheme to the one described above, but is particularly useful to first-time buyers who expect their salaries to increase over the years. Premiums in the first year can be as little as half the normal rate and increase gradually until the full amount is reached after five years.

Most mortgages are taken out for a period of 25 to 30 years, but the average life of a mortgage is less than ten years, because people who move house usually pay off the mortgage and take out a new one on their new home.

The home-loan scheme for first-time buyers

This Government scheme helps people who wish to become first-time buyers by helping them to raise the initial deposit on a house.

Once the home-buyer's savings, which must be placed with an institution such as a building society, the Trustee Savings Bank, National Girobank or the National Savings Bank, have reached £300 and have been kept in the account for one year, the saver qualifies for a free cash bonus. It is paid to the saver on completion of the house purchase.

If the saver has at least £600 in the savings account, the Government will lend another £600. This is interest-free for the first five years. After that time, the house-buyer can pay it back or begin to pay the interest on it. A proviso adds that if the house is sold to someone else during these first five years, the £600 must be returned immediately.

Bank loans

It should be noted that a trend in recent years has been for banks to offer more loans for house purchase. By the end of 1984, this trend had changed:

Year	£ million	% of all loans for house purchase
1980	500	6.8
1981	2265	23.8
1982	5078	35.8
1983	3639	25.2
1984	2314	13.9

Source: *Building Societies' Association Bulletin*, July 1985.

As the figures show, the amount of money banks make available for house purchase is likely to vary.

CHECK THIS OUT

Write out the following sentences, filling in the missing words:

1 Building societies need to be registered with the Registrar of _____ _____.

2 The largest lump sum you will pay when taking out a mortgage is the _____.

3 The usual maximum amount you can borrow from a building society or bank for a mortgage is two and a half times your _____ _____ _____.

4 Regular monthly payments to pay off the loan and interest are made under a _____ mortgage.

5 Premium payments are made to an _____ company under an endowment mortgage.

6 A recent trend was for _____ to offer loans for house purchase.

Saving with a building society

Building societies must obtain funds in order to lend money for house purchase. They do this by borrowing from the many small savers who are willing to invest with them in return for interest on their savings. Savings accounts can be divided broadly into deposit and share accounts. Deposit accounts are slightly more secure because they are repaid first if a society gets into difficulties, but share accounts offer highest interest and the right to vote in elections for directors and on other matters. There are a variety of share accounts, for example:

- *Ordinary shares* allow in-payments and withdrawals whenever desired and without notice;
- *Notice accounts* offer higher interest than ordinary but notice of withdrawal has to be given, for example seven days or 90 days;
- *Saver shares* require regular monthly amounts to be paid in and offer a good interest rate;

- *Monthly income shares* allow interest to be paid out monthly instead of quarterly or half-yearly;
- *Term shares* require a firm investment for one year or more in return for a higher interest rate.

Over 20 million people now have various building society accounts.

The interest paid on any building society account is tax free unless you pay more than the basic rate of tax on your other income, because the societies pay a special 'composite' rate of tax directly to the Inland Revenue. Until recently, the amount which any one person could invest in building societies was limited, but the maximum is now £250 000.

Automatically Abbey

Other building society services

Building societies have in recent years been developing a wide range of other services. Some now offer 'cashcard' savings accounts which allow the withdrawal of cash by using a personal card in machines located in the outer wall of their premises. In-payments can be made and a balance or statement obtained immediately on the machine's display. Standing order payments are also possible from these accounts.

Cheque accounts are now available with some societies. Interest is paid (at a lower rate) on these in the same way as on other savings accounts, but a cheque book is issued as well. Cheques can then be used to make payments to other persons.

Most building societies as yet do not provide many of the services available from banks. However, the 1986 Building Societies Act, which started to operate in 1987, greatly extends the range of financial services in which building societies *may* become involved. For example, they may provide:

- a full range of money transmission services, including standing orders and direct debits;
- personal loans for other purposes as well as house purchase;
- estate agency services;
- foreign exchange facilities;
- cheque guarantee cards;
- insurance broking services;
- agency or managing services for unit trusts.

From 1988, they can also change their legal status to public companies (see Chapter 5) and will be able to operate abroad. A few of the larger societies are now introducing some of these services, such as cheque guarantee cards for cheque accounts or personal loans, but many smaller societies are likely to change very little, at least for some years.

SHORT QUESTIONS

1 What is a mortgage loan?

2 Name *two* institutions, apart from building societies, which lend money for house purchase.

3 Where and when did the first building society start?

4 What is the basic difference between *terminating* and *permanent* building societies?

5 How much deposit will a first-time buyer usually need to pay?

6 Identify *two* charges which a house buyer will usually need to pay when buying a house, apart from the cost of the property itself.

7 Give *two* pieces of information which a building society, or a bank, will need to have before making a loan for house purchase.

8 Name the scheme by which the Government helps people to buy their own house.

9 Name any type of building society savings account.

10 Name *two* financial services which building societies may provide under the 1986 Building Societies Act.

MULTIPLE CHOICE QUESTIONS

There are four possible answers to each of the following questions. Study the introductory sentence, and then decide which of the alternatives correctly answers the question or completes the sentence. Write down the question number and follow it with (A) (B) (C) or (D), according to your choice.

1 When buying a house, the purchaser does NOT need to know
   (A) what the general rates payable are
   (B) what the water rates are likely to be
   (C) how to do a survey on the property
   (D) if there is any redevelopment planned in the area.

2 Shareholders in a building society receive
   (A) fluctuating profits according to the year's business
   (B) untaxed dividends
   (C) an agreed rate of interest
   (D) shares in a firm of house builders.

3 An advantage of an endowment mortgage is that
   (A) the interest which has to be paid falls rapidly
   (B) if the borrower dies, the loan is paid off automatically
   (C) the loan is repaid by standing order through the bank
   (D) the loan is repaid by repaying the interest only.

4 Which of the following costs normally need NOT be taken into account when buying a house?
   (A) Solicitor's fees
   (B) The vendor's fee to the estate agent
   (C) Removal expenses
   (D) Life insurance for the person taking out the mortgage loan.

5 Building societies often favour people who save the house deposit
   (A) through the National Savings Bank
   (B) through a commercial bank
   (C) with an insurance company
   (D) with the building society from which they wish to obtain a mortgage loan.

6 The MIRAS scheme provides
   (A) a loan of £40 000 or more for first-time buyers
   (B) tax relief so that interest is paid net of income tax
   (C) a mortgage which runs for 30 years instead of for 25 years
   (D) tax relief direct from the Inland Revenue.

7 When buying a house, the purchaser needs to
   (A) pay the price which the vendor asks
   (B) make an offer which is considered fair
   (C) ask the building society to send a valuer to the property
   (D) pay stamp duty on any house costing over £30 000.

8 If a person finds circumstances have changed and has temporary difficulty in keeping up the mortgage repayments, he/she should first
(A) sell the house
(B) contact the building society to see if help can be offered
(C) let arrears build up and hope to pay them off eventually
(D) contact a solicitor.

9 It is an advantage to be a first-time buyer because
(A) you have saved a high deposit
(B) you will get a mortgage easily
(C) you have no home to sell first
(D) it does not matter where the house is situated.

10 Which of the following items of information is NOT required when arranging a mortgage?
(A) How much you have saved
(B) How much you earn
(C) How much you want to borrow
(D) How you are going to get to work.

There are four possible answers to each of the following questions.

If you think (1) only is correct, write down A.
If you think (1) and (2) only are correct, write down B.
If you think (3) and (4) only are correct, write down C.
If you think (2), (3) and (4) only are correct, write down D.

11 Building societies use their investors' money
(1) to lend to people for house purchase
(2) to hold in small quantities to meet cash withdrawals
(3) to buy company shares
(4) to buy low-risk securities.

12 Building societies may find a fall in the number of investors when
(1) there is an increase in the availability of labour for house building
(2) there is an increase in the price of housing
(3) there is a fall in the interest rates they offer
(4) other institutions are offering higher interest rates.

13 Building society mortgage loans DO NOT usually depend on
(1) a large percentage deposit being paid
(2) a bank reference for the purchasers
(3) the joint earnings of a couple
(4) the purchasers having an income.

14 Which of the following accounts is offered by a building society?
(1) National Savings account
(2) Saver Share account
(3) Ordinary share account
(4) Term share account

STIMULUS RESPONSE QUESTIONS

1 Look at the illustrated story on the opposite page and answer the questions which follow.

(a) How could Jane's investment of £5 in a premium bond earn her £10 000? *(1 mark)*
(b) What is the main problem with Peter's form of saving? *(2 marks)*
(c) (i) How is Mary saving her money? *(1 mark)*
    (ii) Why does Mary prefer her way of saving to Peter's? *(1 mark)*
(d) What does Ian mean when he says that his Building Society Share Account gives 7.25% after tax? *(3 marks)*
(e) In what way is Peter wrong in his statement about bank deposit accounts? *(3 marks)*
(f) Explain whether you think all four of these people are saving in a sensible way. *(8 marks)*

(g) Another friend, Micky, has been listening to the four and says, 'I think you are all stupid to save. I want things now. I'd get the car on credit.'
Do you think he is right? *(8 marks)*

(Specimen question from the GCSE Commerce paper reproduced by permission of the Northern Examining Association.)

2 Read the following information carefully and then answer the questions about it.

Banks, building societies and insurance companies are all willing to lend money for mortgages at the moment, and the cost of borrowing is down from last year.

What Jane, Ian, Mary & Peter think ...

Jane, Ian, Mary and Peter were all at school together and now meet regularly on Friday nights at the local pub. Mary is a trainee computer operator, Peter works at the local hairdressing salon, Ian is training to be a car mechanic and Jane is unemployed.

Peter has just informed them of his long-term plan to buy a car.

I've just been to the local Post Office to buy a £5 premium bond. I've now got five of them. Just wait until I win £10,000 – I'll have no problem affording a car.

You're daft, Jane. It's like keeping money in an old sock. All you are doing is making sure nobody can pinch it. But you're not going to win are you? You don't even go into the draw for three months. So what's the point? I'm putting my money in a Save As You Earn scheme and will get a lot of interest.

That's O.K., Peter, but what if you want the money quickly? Can you withdraw it?

You don't understand. The point is that I get a lot of extra money back and I don't have to pay tax on it.

Yes but the interest is only 'peanuts' – 5½% – and you have to pay tax on it. If prices go up you will take that much longer to save for the car. I will get more interest so it won't take me so long.

And when can you get it out? You don't want to admit it's five years, do you? And another two years if you want the full benefit. Now if you put your money in a bank deposit account you can get it out at any time, it only takes one week.

My Building Society share account gives 7.25% after tax and I can withdraw money at any time.

So can I, all I have to do is write in for them.

The Building Society opens all morning on Saturdays, not like most banks. I don't even have to wait two weeks for administration like Premium Bonds.

Many banks and building societies now let their borrowers inspect a copy of the valuation, house-buyer's report or survey which the borrower has to pay for and which tells the financial institution if the house or property is worth the amount which is being asked for it, as there must be security for the mortgage loan.

House-buyers can save money by shopping around and getting several quotations for estimates of legal charges, removal expenses and the fees charged by estate agents.

(a) Which institutions will lend money for mortgages? *(3 marks)*

(b) Is this a good time to borrow money for house purchase, compared to last year? Give a reason for your answer. *(3 marks)*

(c) Make a list of the institutions mentioned in the first line which lend money for house purchase, with the institution lending the largest amount first, and the one lending the smallest amount last. *(3 marks)*

(d) Why do financial institutions ask for a report before they will lend money for a mortgage? *(5 marks)*

(e) Name *three* ways in which a house-buyer can cut costs. *(6 marks)*

3 Read the following information carefully and then answer the questions on it.

Although building societies can borrow money from the international money markets, they would rather get it from investors at home. The Woolwich offers 8 per cent interest on its 90-day Capital Account and those investors who keep £10 000 in their account can withdraw money without losing any interest.

Nationwide, Abbey National, Halifax and Leeds Permanent also offer instant access for the same amount. The Scarborough's Solid Gold account offers 8.05 and the Skipton's Sovereign Share offers 8.1 per cent interest on balances of £10 000 and over. The minimum sum to be invested in any of these high-rate offers is £500.

(a) From whom do building societies prefer to borrow money? *(2 marks)*

(b) How much notice would investors have to give the Woolwich if they wished to withdraw £2000 from an account of £9000 without loss of interest? *(3 marks)*

(c) What does 'instant access' mean? *(4 marks)*

(d) Which building society offers the best return on sums of £10 000 and over? *(2 marks)*

(e) Why are interest rates higher on 90-day accounts than ordinary share accounts? *(3 marks)*

(f) Name *three* other institutions which might compete for savings with the building societies. *(6 marks)*

4 Read the following information carefully and then answer the questions on it.

When new share offers come on the market, such as those for British Gas and the Trustee Savings Bank, building societies sometimes find that their net receipts slump below the income which they need to satisfy new borrowers.

The National Savings Bank offers a very competitive alternative to building society shares, and building societies may consider putting up the rate to borrowers in order to attract investors. Demand for mortgages is about three and a half billion pounds each month, and some societies give priority to borrowers who have been saving with them for some time in the past.

(a) In what circumstances do building societies find that their income does not meet the mortgage demand? *(3 marks)*

(b) What priorities are then established for borrowers? *(2 marks)*

(c) How much do building societies need each month in order to meet mortgage loan demands? *(1 mark)*

(d) Give *two* reasons why people invest in company shares rather than in building societies. *(4 marks)*

(e) Explain the phrase: 'The National Savings Bank offers a very competitive alternative to building society shares.' *(5 marks)*

ESSAY QUESTIONS

(a) Describe the steps which would be taken to arrange a house mortgage. *(10 marks)*

(b) What information would a building society or bank manager require before giving you a loan? *(6 marks)*

(c) How will the maximum loan be decided? *(4 marks)*

2 (a) Explain the term 'mortgage loan'. *(5 marks)*

(b) Describe *two* main types of mortgage available to a prospective house purchaser. *(15 marks)*

3 (a) Explain *three* main types of building society accounts which are available. *(10 marks)*

(b) Give one reason why each type of account might be preferred. *(10 marks)*

NOW TRY THIS

Choose the correct word and re-write the following sentences, filling in the blanks:

considered earns mortgage endowment building deposit vote

1 Under a house _____ loan, the lender holds the deeds of the property and can sell it in order to retrieve the loan, if the borrower fails to meet the repayments.

2 Many houses in the United Kingdom are bought with a loan provided by a _____ society.

3 House owners in years gone by had an important position in society because they were the ones who were allowed to _____.

4 First-time buyers may need to find a _____ of about 5–10 per cent of the house price.

5 A building society manager might ask a would-be purchaser how much has been saved and how much he or she _____.

6 In a case of 'joint ownership', the spouse's earnings are also _____.

7 The two main kinds of mortgage are: repayment and _____.

LEARN IT YOURSELF

1 Choose a building society (for example, the Halifax Building Society) and write to them, or visit them, asking for any information they may be able to let you have about the development of their society.

Contrast the growth of societies in their early days with that of the last two decades and suggest reasons for any differences you may find.

2 Imagine that a young couple, both of whom are in employment, decide to buy a house.

Collect information from building societies and, giving an indication of the time-span you are using, make a report of the steps they will need to follow from their initial decision to completing the purchase.

You may also find information from banks and estate agents useful in this project.

3 The 1986 Building Societies Act changed the status of building societies. Gather information from the branch offices of building societies about activities, other than mortgage loans, which are available (or about to be made available) to clients of the societies, and make a display of them.

4 Collect information about the various schemes for investors operated by building societies and draw up a report about them.

In your report suggest which schemes might be the most attractive to different categories of people: for example, a person liable for a high rate of income tax, someone saving the deposit for a house which they hope to buy in two years' time, people saving for retirement in ten years' time, and so on.

5 Collect information on methods of personal saving from:

Unit trusts (through the clearing banks)
National Savings Bank
Building societies
Life assurance companies

Compare the methods of saving money offered b these institutions and draw up a report, including any recommendations you feel able to make.

ASSIGNMENT – THE HOUSING MARKET

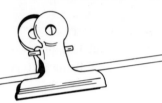

The term 'housing market' refers to the buying and selling of houses, and those factors which influence the supply and demand.

Make a survey of the housing market in your area, using a map to define the locality covered.

Find out local prices for different kinds of housing, including:

- detached houses
- semi-detached houses
- detached bungalows
- town houses
- terraced houses
- purpose-built flats
- converted flats.

Look at the factors which affect the choice of housing, such as the demand for accommodation in the area, the jobs which people do (which in turn affect the price they can afford to pay) and the availability of building land.

Mention the factors which affect the level of bulding society funds and the availability of mortgage loans, such as rates of interest and alternative forms of saving and investment.

Look out for newspaper articles or advertisements which might have a bearing on this subject, and include them in your project.

You may find photographs or illustrations useful.

Include a table showing each type of housing, and the top price and the bottom price which each type costs. Work out the average price asked for each type of housing and include that in your table.

Introduction

Until the end of the nineteenth century there was no legal protection for the consumer unless he or she could afford to bring a case against a seller in the courts. This was very expensive and had no guarantee of success. Consumers needed to be very careful when buying goods, particularly those which were expensive. This rule was known as *caveat emptor*, which means 'let the buyer beware'.

Since then, however, a large number of laws have been passed by Parliament in order to give consumers some protection, and the major ones are discussed in this chapter. Some of these laws give consumers special legal rights in civil cases which they may wish to bring against sellers (or the other way round), but others make certain actions criminal offences, so that the State can bring a case against sellers who may be fined or even, in extreme circumstances, imprisoned.

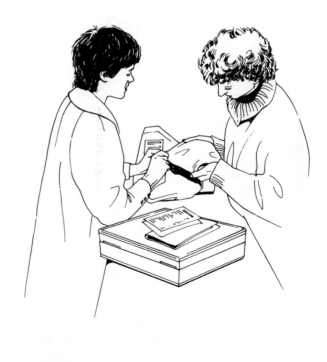

It is still sensible to be careful before buying goods, in spite of al this legal protection, because mistakes can be made which are no the seller's fault and legal action can mean much trouble, time and expense. Consumers should be particularly careful when buying expensive goods and spend time comparing different makes and suppliers who may offer different deals. Any available literature should be read and careful consideration given to what precisely i expected from a particular product. If you decide to buy a new product, or a less well-known one at a lower price, then you position may be less secure than when buying a proven produc under a well-established brand name. You should also see whether there have been any independent tests of the products and wha recommendations were made (see later).

Reasons for consumer protection

The consumer is always at a disadvantage in 'cash' sales, as opposed to buying on credit, because the obligation is on him or her to recover the money if dissatisfied with the product. Buyers are often individuals who have limited understanding of their legal rights and smaller financial resources compared with the businesses doing the selling. One individual customer is not important to a large business In addition, individual consumers can have a very limited knowledge about products, particularly mechanical or technical products such as cars, video recorders and washing machines. This all means that the consumer is in a relatively weak position and it is widely accepted now that a certain degree of specific legal and other protection is needed.

Consumers need to be protected from a range of possible dangers such as:

- advertisements and other publicity material giving false or misleading information;
- goods which are dangerous;
- articles which may be described incorrectly on packaging;
- goods being sold in incorrect weights and sizes;
- goods which are not suitable for the purpose shown;
- failure to deliver goods after they have been paid for;
- the quality of the goods being so poor as to make them unusable;
- prices being manipulated to give a false idea of a 'bargain';
- firms getting together to keep prices artificially high;
- credit terms being offered which may not give a true picture of the extra cost;
- persuasive door-to-door salesmen making a contract with the customer to buy something which is regretted later.

The remainder of the chapter shows how consumers are protected from these hazards by laws and by various organisations.

Consumer laws

Sale of Goods Act 1979

The first Act to protect consumers was the Sale of Goods Act 1893. This was later combined with the Supply of Goods (Implied Terms) Act 1973 to form the Sale of Goods Act 1979. This sets out the following conditions under which goods can be bought and sold:

- goods must be legally owned by the seller;
- goods must suit the purpose for which they are sold;
- goods sold by description must fit the description;
- goods sold by sample must correspond with the sample;
- goods must be of merchantable quality, that is, they must be usable.

According to the breach of law involved, the buyer has the right to return the goods and have the charge refunded, or to claim compensation.

Goods must be legally owned . . .

Here are some examples:

- if interior decorating paint is sold for external use, then it is not fit for the purpose intended;
- if a box of glasses indicates that they are 'half-pint' but they turn out to be 50 cl, they do not match the description;
- Wellington boots which let in water are not of merchantable quality (nor are they fit for the purpose intended).

The importance of the 'Implied Terms' section is that businesses cannot offer consumers a guarantee with the goods which takes away their rights under the Sale of Goods Act, as was possible before 1973. If you look on the packaging of many products, you will see that firms state that any special guarantee given does not affect your statutory legal rights. These rights must apply in any case and a special guarantee given does not affect this fact.

In 1982 the Sale of Goods laws were extended by the Supply of Goods and Services Act to include services in addition to goods.

Goods must suit the purpose for which they are sold . . .

Weights and Measures Acts 1963 to 1979

These Acts make it a criminal offence to give (even by accident), or intend to give, short weight or measure, for example when selling litres of petrol or pounds of potatoes. Local authorities employ trading standards officers to enforce these Acts and, as a part of their work, they regularly visit shops and other premises to check the accuracy of the scales and the other measuring devices used. Only the measuring equipment checked and approved by the officers can be used and most prepackaged goods must have the quantity clearly marked on the outside of the container. At one time, every single pack had to contain not less than the precise quantity shown, but now under EEC rules, the *average* quantity for batches supplied is accepted, so that some packs may be slightly under and some over.

Prices Act 1974

Under this separate law, some prepackaged goods such as certain foodstuffs, such as cheese and bacon, must also show the price *per unit* according to weight or volume, so that consumers can compare different packs and makes more easily. This Act also requires that prepacked foodstuffs are date-marked so that consumers know when goods are stale, or by which date they must be eaten. Licensed premises must also show a list of drinks and their prices.

Food and Drugs Acts 1955 and 1976

These Acts aim to ensure that any food sold for human consumption is fit to eat. Food has to be of the nature, substance or quality expected by the purchaser and there are a large number of regulations defining the minimum content of many types of foodstuff. An instance of this is the minimum amount of meat to be put in sausages. It is a criminal offence to give any false or misleading descriptions of food (for example, in the ingredients) and most prepacked foods must have a label showing the ingredients.

These Acts also cover the conditions under which food is prepared and sold. Environmental health officers, employed by local authorities, visit factories and shops to check on hygiene; you may have read stories in newspapers about the unhygienic conditions which are sometimes found. Fines can be imposed, and premises can be forced to close down if minimum standards are not reached

Food must be suitable for human consumption . . .

Trade Descriptions Acts 1968 and 1972

Under the 1968 Act it is a criminal offence to describe goods or services for sale in a false or misleading way. If a handbag made of plastic is described as leather, then an offence has been committed. This applies to verbal as well as written descriptions, and suppliers must take care that their advertisements do not contain wrong information about goods for sale.

At one time, consumers could be deceived into buying goods in a sale which had one price crossed out and another price substituted. They did not realise that the goods had never been offered at the crossed-out price before the sale. Cheap goods could be bought ready for the sale, and the public misled into thinking that they had been genuinely reduced in price. These practices are also forbidden by the 1968 Act and a clear indication must be given as to whether the same goods have recently been on sale at the higher price. Under the 1972 Act, imported goods which are sold under a British trade mark must also show the country of origin, so that people are not misled.

Unsolicited Goods and Services Act 1971

This Act protects people when goods are sent to them which have not been requested. Rather than consumers having to pay for such goods, or to return them at their own expense, they can ask the supplier to collect them, and if this is not done within 30 days, they are entitled to keep them. Alternatively, consumers need do nothing, in which case the goods become their property after six months have passed.

Consumer Credit Act 1974

This is a very important and wide-ranging Act which covers most of the forms of credit, including leasing and rentals, that are granted to consumers for the purchase of goods and services. The main provisions are:

It is a criminal offence to describe goods in a misleading way

- all dealers in consumer credit, such as banks, finance houses, television rental firms and retailers, and all those indirectly involved (for example credit reference agencies and estate agents), must be licensed by the Office of Fair Trading;

- the providers of credit, as well as the sellers of goods, can be liable for faulty goods sold;

- *true* annual percentage rates (APR) of interest must be quoted in credit deals as well as the *flat* percentage rate. For example, 10 per cent flat on the full amount borrowed over two years and repaid monthly is, as a true rate, nearly 20 per cent APR;

- the cash price and the total amount payable on credit terms must both be stated, together with the value and number of repayment instalments;

- where a deal is agreed and signed off trade premises, for instance at home, then the buyer can change his or her mind within a few days and cancel the agreement. This is called the 'cooling off' period;

- where credit is repaid early, then a rebate of interest must be given according to a formula laid down;

- in the case of hire purchase (see Chapter 3), the seller or credit-provider cannot reclaim the goods without a court order where one-third or more of the price (including interest) has been paid;

- in the case of hire purchase, where the buyer has paid at least half the price (including interest), the goods can be returned in good condition without further liability.

These rules do not (at present) cover transactions under £50 and over £15 000 in value, building society mortgages and credit given to corporate bodies (see Chapter 6) as opposed to individuals.

Fair Trading Act 1973

This Act set up an Office of Fair Trading under a Director-General of Fair Trading. It has very wide responsibilities concerning unfair trading practices which affect consumers directly or indirectly (see later). It is the responsibility of the Office of Fair Trading to ensure that trade is carried out according to the law.

Don't worry, it isn't as frightening as you think

If not, you may be advised to go to court

Consumer adviser may sort things out with the shopkeeper

An extract from an Office of Fair Trading leaflet

Consumer protection organisations

The British Standards Institution (BSI)

The British Standards Institution is an independent body, supported by grants from the Government, whose main aim is to draw up standard specifications and test products against them. If a product has been tested and approved by the Institution, it is entitled to bear the *Kitemark*. This marks shows that the product reaches the minimum standards set by the Institution, and BSI inspectors will subsequently carry out spot-checks on the producer's factory and test samples of the product. Items covered by the *Kitemark* include car seat-belts and pressure cookers.

The Standard laid down by the BSI often includes quality and safety, but standard units of measurement may also be required, for example in clothing and shoes, and certain terms/symbols may have to be used. The BSI also gives a Safety Mark for some goods, covering only the safety aspect.

BS 857

The British Electrotechnical Approvals Board (BEAB)

This body is concerned chiefly with the safety of electrical appliances used in the home, for example electric blankets and televisions. Producers can apply to have their products tested, and are allowed to use the 'BEAB' mark if they are passed as safe.

BEAB-Mark of Safety

Consumers' Association

The Consumers' Association is a non-profit making body to which anyone who pays the subscription can belong. It checks the standard of quality and performance of various products, publishing the results in a monthly magazine called *Which?*. Products bought in the ordinary way are carefully tested and then arranged in order of the 'best buy'. Consumers can consult the magazine to find out the Consumers' Association recommended best buy, and goods which are termed 'not recommended' may force their manufacturers to raise their standards. There are also special versions of *Which?* covering motoring and money affairs.

Citizen's Advice Bureau

The Citizens' Advice Bureau has offices (or bureaux) located in most districts, and the address of the nearest one can be found in the telephone directory. It publishes booklets and pamphlets on a wide range of consumer and other problems and provides a free no-appointment service for anyone needing help. The service is completely confidential and aims to help people to find the answers to their problems and worries.

Consumer Advice Centres

These are different from the Citizens' Advice Bureaux in that they are operated by local authorities and provide advice only on consumer affairs. They are not found in all areas and many have been closed down as part of cost-cutting exercises.

Mail order protection schemes

There are several different schemes operating, including those run by the Newspaper Publishers' Association (NPA) and the Independent Broadcasting Authority (IBA). The NPA, for example, checks out all advertisers beforehand and each has to pay into a compensation fund. If the mail order firm fails to deliver the goods and the money paid is not refunded, then the consumer can claim compensation through the newspaper which carried the advertisement. Not all goods, however, are covered by these arrangements, in particular from those firms which advertise goods sent on approval.

In addition, there is a Mail Order Traders' Association and an Association of Mail Order Publishers, which have certain rules by which their members should operate. If you are not satisfied with your dealings with a member, you can complain to the particular association.

Office of Fair Trading

This Government organisation was established through the Fair Trading Act 1973 but does not deal with the individual complaints of consumers, although it is interested to hear of problems which may be of general importance to consumers. Its main responsibilities are:

* recommending to the Government where changes in the law or new laws are needed to protect consumers;
* publishing information for consumers about their rights, for example in leaflets and press advertisements;
* researching firms where monopoly practices are suspected, for example charging excessively high prices (under the 1980 Competition Act);
* referring firms to the Monopolies and Mergers Commission for full investigation where a monopoly exists;
* holding a register of restrictive agreements between firms, which may be causing prices to be higher than necessary;
* referring such agreements to the Restrictive Practices Court to decide whether or not they are in the public interest;
* responsibility for enforcing the law on credit sales under the 1974 Consumer Credit Act, in particular the giving and cancelling of licences which allow dealers in credit to operate;
* persuading and helping groups of businesses in various trades to set voluntary codes of practice for dealing with consumer problems.

National Consumer Council

This body, although set up and funded by the Government, operates independently and makes published recommendations to the Government about changes in consumer law and practices which it considers necessary.

Consultative councils

Each of the nationalised industries, such as coal or electricity, has its own consultative (or consumer) council which acts as an independent voice in protecting the interests of consumers dealing with the particular industry. Consumers can complain directly to these councils, for example the Post Office Users' National Council (POUNC).

Trade associations

These are formed by groups of businesses in particular trades for various reasons, but many have set up their own codes of practice and sometimes compensation funds for dealing with consumer complaints and losses. Well-known examples are the Association of British Travel Agents (ABTA) and the Motor Agents Association (MAA).

This chapter has covered the major Acts of Parliament and the work of many organisations protecting the consumer, but there are many others which it is worthwhile researching. For example, how do the Consumer Safety Act 1978 and the Resale Prices Act 1976 help consumers? What is the work of the Industrial Design Council, the National House Building Council and the Automobile Association in protecting consumer interests? You should also refer to Chapter 7, which gives more detail about consumer protection in respect of advertising.

CHECK THIS OUT

Write out the following sentences, filling in the missing words:

1 It is sensible to be _____ before buying goods.

2 The Sale of Goods Act 1979 states that goods must suit the _____ for which they are being sold.

3 The Weights and Measures Act 1963 states that it is an offence for a trader to give _____ measure.

4 The Prices Act 1974 requires shops to mark the price per _____ of certain prepacked goods.

5 The Food and Drugs Acts 1955 to 1976 aim to ensure that food is pure and fit for _____ consumption.

6 The Trade Descriptions Act 1968 forbids describing goods for sale in a _____ way.

7 Under the Unsolicited Goods and Services Act (1971), unsolicited goods become the property of the receiver if not reclaimed within _____ _____.

8 The Consumer Credit Act 1974 aims to regulate most forms of _____ arrangement when consumer goods are being sold.

9 The Fair Trading Act 1973 appointed a _____ _____ of Fair Trading to monitor practices and recommend changes.

10 The British _____ _____ aims to draw up standard _____ and test products against them.

11 The Citizens' Advice _____ helps people with a wide range of problems.

12 The Office of Fair Trading issues _____ giving information to consumers about their rights.

Putting things right

Suppose a shopper has made a purchase which is faulty, and the fault was not pointed out at the time (the goods were not bought as 'seconds' in a sale). What can be done about it?

All receipts should be kept somewhere safe so that shoppers have proof of purchase. Faulty goods should not be used, but taken back as soon as possible and an explanation of what is wrong given to the retailer. Most retailers are happy to replace faulty goods, but if there is not a replacement available they may offer the shopper a credit note. The shopper does not have to accept a credit note and can ask for the money to be returned.

Teenagers often find that it is better to go back with an adult if they want to change faulty goods, but shoppers who do not get satisfaction can always get help from the Citizens' Advice Bureau.

If shoppers have damaged the goods themselves, they are not entitled to ask for them to be replaced – nor are they entitled to take back items which they have decided are the wrong colour or where they have changed their minds for other reasons. However, it is worth asking shopkeepers if they will exchange goods, because many of them will do so as a favour to shoppers in order to keep their goodwill.

If a purchaser is buying second-hand goods (a motorbike for example), it is a good idea to take someone along to act as a witness to anything said about it. Special care must be taken when buying anything second-hand.

Although there are many Acts, government and voluntary organisations to help the consumer, consumers can help themselves by looking for a Kitemark as a test of quality, reading labels, consulting *Which?* to find out the recommended 'best buy' and generally reading about major purchases beforehand. If shoppers know their rights, then manufacturers have an incentive to produce goods of a high standard which consumers will want to buy. By researching on important purchases beforehand, they can get the most possible out of the money they spend.

SHORT QUESTIONS

1 What is the British Standards Institution?

2 Suggest *one* thing which the Prices Act 1974 requires shops to do.

3 What must credit agreements state about rates of interest?

4 Give *one* way in which the Office of Fair Trading helps to protect consumers.

5 Explain the term *caveat emptor*.

6 What does the Weights and Measures Act 1963 specify as an offence?

7 What is *one* of the aims of the Food and Drugs Acts 1955 and 1976?

8 What is the Consumers' Association's main source of income?

9 In broad terms, what is the purpose of the Citizens' Advice Bureau?

10 Suggest *one* way in which a Mail Order Protection Scheme helps consumers.

MULTIPLE CHOICE QUESTIONS

There are four possible answers to each of the following questions. Study the introductory sentence, and then decide which of the alternatives correctly answers the question or completes the sentence. Write down the question number and follow it with (A) (B) (C) or (D), according to your choice.

1 Until legal protection was given at the end of the nineteenth century, the golden rule for a consumer was
  (A) a verbal agreement is binding
  (B) mistakes must be put right
  (C) let the buyer beware
  (D) do not buy from a travelling pedlar.

2 Which of the following is NOT a possible hazard for a consumer?
  (A) Goods not suitable for the purpose intended
  (B) Prices manipulated to give a false idea of a 'bargain'
  (C) Items incorrectly described on the package
  (D) Leaflets accompanying goods describing how to use them.

3 The Sale of Goods Act 1979 does NOT state that goods must
  (A) be sold by sample
  (B) suit the purpose for which they are sold
  (C) be usable
  (D) fit the description by which they are sold.

4 The requirement to have a sell-by date on some prepacked goods comes under the
(A) Weights and Measures Acts
(B) Sale of Goods Act
(C) Food and Drugs Acts
(D) Prices Act.

5 The Food and Drugs Acts aim to ensure that
(A) licensed premises must show a list of drinks and their prices
(B) items must match their description
(C) food sold for human consumption is fit for that purpose
(D) prepackaged goods must show the price per unit.

6 Which of the following is NOT part of the Trade Descriptions Acts?
(A) Goods sold by sample must correspond with the sample
(B) Goods for sale must not be described in a false or misleading way
(C) Cheap goods may not be bought for a sale and marked to suggest a price reduction
(D) Imported goods must show the country of origin.

7 The Citizens' Advice Bureau provides
(A) advice only on consumer affairs
(B) a free no-appointment service
(C) a magazine called *Which?* giving best buys
(D) a safety mark for good products.

8 Which of the following is NOT a dealer in consumer credit?
(A) Bank
(B) Trade Association
(C) Finance house
(D) Retailer.

9 Which statement is NOT true of the British Standards Institution?
(A) It is a Government body
(B) It gives the Kitemark to tested and approved goods
(C) The standard tested includes quality of goods
(D) Some goods are given a Safety Mark.

10 Which of the following statements is NOT true?
(A) 'BEAB' on products means that they have been passed as safe
(B) All mail order goods are covered by the Mail Order Protection Scheme
(C) Advertisers in newspapers are checked out by the Newspaper Publishers' Association
(D) Consumers can complain to the Mail Order Traders' Association about its members.

11 Which of the following is NOT the responsibility of the Office of Fair Trading?
(A) Recommending changes in the law to protect consumers
(B) Acting as an independent voice to protect consumers
(C) Publishing information for consumers about their rights
(D) Enforcing the law on credit sales for consumers.

12 A purchaser who wishes to complain about faulty goods should first
(A) be prepared to accept a credit note
(B) be prepared to tell the shop assistant off
(C) go back to the seller and explain what is wrong
(D) complain at once to the Citizens' Advice Bureau.

There are four possible answers to each of the following questions.

If you think (1) only is correct, write down A.
If you think (1) and (2) only are correct, write down B.
If you think (3) and (4) only are correct, write down C.
If you think (2), (3) and (4) only are correct, write down D.

13 Shops must exchange goods if the
(1) goods have a fault but were supposed to be perfect
(2) shopper prefers another colour after the goods have been paid for
(3) goods are damaged just after they have been paid for
(4) shopper has changed his/her mind after goods have been paid for.

14 Consumers can help themselves by
(1) researching on important purchases before they set out to buy
(2) looking for labels which show goods have passed a test of quality
(3) comparing prices only
(4) complaining only to their friends.

15 Goods bought on hire purchase cannot be reclaimed without a court order if
(1) more than one third of the price has been paid
(2) the deal has been signed off the firm's premises
(3) the goods prove to be faulty
(4) the retailer has failed to give proper instructions.

16 The Unsolicited Goods and Services Act states that
   (1) goods not requested must be returned at the receiver's expense
   (2) the receiver must ask the supplier to remove unwanted goods
   (3) goods left with the receiver for six months then become his/her property
   (4) consumers need not pay for any goods which were delivered but not requested.

17 Which of the following is NOT a provision of the Consumer Credit Act 1974?
   (1) All dealers in consumer credit must be licensed by the Office of Fair Trading
   (2) The true rate of interest for goods sold on credit must be disclosed
   (3) Goods sold on hire purchase can be automatically reclaimed if a customer cannot pay an instalment
   (4) A hire purchase deal signed at home and witnessed by two people must stand

STIMULUS RESPONSE QUESTIONS

1 Read the following information and answer the questions on it.

Leroy Watson wants to buy a television set which has a cash price of £300. If bought through hire purchase, it would require a 10 per cent deposit followed by 24 monthly instalments of £20.

   (a) Calculate, showing workings, the *extra* cost of buying the television set on hire purchase. *(4 marks)*
   (b) State *two advantages* and *two disadvantages* to Leroy of buying through hire purchase. *(4 marks)*
   (c) Apart from hire purchase, state *two* other methods of credit which Leroy might have used to buy the television set. *(2 marks)*
   (d) Leroy decides to buy the television set at one particular shop even though its cash price is lower elsewhere. Suggest reasons for his decision. *(4 marks)*
   (e) In what ways might Leroy benefit from government legislation on credit? *(6 marks)*

(Specimen question from the GCSE Commerce paper reproduced by permission of the Southern Regional Examinations Board.)

2 The following advertisement in the window of Hughview, a High Street TV and electrical goods retailer, attracted the attention of Chris Segrow.

> ## STARLIGHT VIDEO RECORDERS
> Bring more pleasure to your leisure
> DON'T miss your favourite programmes
> ### *A REAL BARGAIN!!*
>
> Manufacturer's   Our
> Price   **£420**   Price **£350**
> ### *SAVE £70*
>
> **Specification:** Stereo sound, automatic record, remote control, video camera input.
> **Terms:** Deposit 10% 24 monthly payments of £16.70 or 18 monthly payments of £19.60
> APR 32.5% (VAT included)

   (a) Write out the following abbreviations in full. Explain briefly the meaning of each.
       (i) APR *(3 marks)*
       (ii) VAT *(3 marks)*
   (b) (i) What is meant by the 'Manufacturer's Price £420'? *(2 marks)*
       (ii) Why is the shop's price lower than the manufacturer's price? *(4 marks)*
   (c) How much does the video recorder cost if it is paid for immediately? *(1 mark)*
   (d) Calculate the HP price over:
       (i) 24 months; *(2 marks)*
       (ii) 18 months. *(2 marks)*
   (e) What is the brand name of the video recorder? *(1 mark)*
   (f) Why do you think the manufacturers of the video recorder have given it a brand name? *(3 marks)*
   (g) 'Hughview' want to find another way of advertising their video recorders. They are not happy with just using the window display.
       (i) Suggest to Hughview ONE suitable way of advertising their video recorders. *(1 mark)*
       (ii) Explain why you made this suggestion rather than any other. *(6 marks)*
   (h) Advertising can give consumers information and also persuade them to buy goods. How persuasive is this advertisement? *(6 marks)*

(Specimen question from the GCSE Commerce paper reproduced by permission of the Northern Examining Association.)

ESSAY QUESTIONS

1 Explain how the following Acts protect consumers:
   (a) Weights and Measures Acts; *(6 marks)*
   (b) Trade Descriptions Acts; *(7 marks)*
   (c) The Fair Trading Act 1973. *(7 marks)*

2 (a) Why do consumers need protection? *(6 marks)*
   (b) Describe the work of *two* of the following voluntary organisations in providing safeguards for the consumer:
      (i) Consumers' Association;
      (ii) The Newspaper Publishers' Association Mail Order Protection Scheme;
      (iii) The British Standards Institution. *(14 marks)*

3 (a) Describe *four* ways in which consumers are protected by legislation. *(8 marks)*
   (b) Give details of the ways in which a consumer can make complaints or get help if he or she is not satisfied with products or services. *(6 marks)*

   (c) Name *three* organisations which will provide help and information. *(6 marks)*

4 With reference to the different legislation which relates to each section, explain how consumers are protected when buying:
   (a) goods on credit; *(6 marks)*
   (b) prepackaged goods; *(6 marks)*
   (c) food and drink. *(8 marks)*

5 (a) In what ways does the Sale of Goods Act 1979 help to protect consumers? *(12 marks)*
   (b) How, and for what purpose, was the coverage of this Act extended in 1982? *(8 marks)*

6 Choose *two* Acts of Parliament and *two* voluntary organisations and explain how each protects the interests of the consumer. *(20 marks)*

LEARN IT YOURSELF

1 Make contact with a retailer who offers hire purchase, and request a visit for a small group when the shop is quiet. Ask if a member of their staff will simulate a sale using hire purchase forms for one or two of the group. The students will role-play a member of the public who has a job, so prepare beforehand by choosing a job which you would like to do and find out what the average salary is. You can then supply details necessary for hire purchase. Mark the forms which you use 'simulation' and make copies for other members of the group. Use these copies to illustrate a brief report about what items can be obtained from that retailer under hire purchase terms. Do not forget to follow up this exercise with a 'thank you' letter to the retailer.

2 Write a joint letter from your group or class to your local Citizens' Advice Bureau (the telephone number and address is in the Phone Book) and ask them to visit you to give a talk on the work they do.

3 Working in a group, make a list of consumer durables which have been purchased by parents, relatives and friends and which carry the Kitemark. Make a separate list of other items, with brand names, which do not carry the Kitemark. Include the cost. Find out what percentage of goods with and without a Kitemark have been bought by your research group. Draw conclusions from your research.

4 Working in a group, allocate each member a shop or shops which you know offer unwrapped foods for sale. The group member should notice and write down the precautions taken by shop staff to avoid contamination (for example, cooked meat handled by tongs, dogs forbidden to come into the shop). Compare your shops and make a joint report. Recommend a list of five hygiene rules which you think all food shops should obey.

5 Design a leaflet or pamphlet showing the places in your area to which a consumer could go for help, if necessary, with a complaint about a purchase.

ASSIGNMENT – CONSUMER PROTECTION

This is a useful assignment for a group who do not want to write at length.

The group will work together.

They are going to make up a picture story about a consumer complaint using photographs with captions underneath the pictures.

The complaint could be about: faulty goods, services such as catering, general repairs, etc. Material from the Office of Fair Trading, 310c Field House, Bream's Buildings, London EC4A 1PR might be used for information.

Plan each picture in order to tell the story, and decide what caption to put underneath it.

Choose members of the group, helped by staff if you think this is necessary, to play the roles. It gives life to the photographs if the group role-plays the story while photographs are being taken.

When all the photographs have been taken and developed, choose the ones which are best to show the story.

Type out the captions, or write them very neatly in black ink or biro, and cut them out to paste underneath the photographs.

Arrange your page of photographs with writing underneath until you have the complete story.

Make a title page.

Photocopy your story and make it up into a leaflet, pamphlet or magazine.

Each member of the group should keep a photocopy of the whole effort.

You may like to include a list of rules for shoppers which will help them to avoid making a bad purchase.

CHAPTER

15

FOREIGN TRADE

Exports and imports

All the countries in the world have to trade with other countries in order to meet their needs. The money which a country earns by selling goods and services abroad (*exports*) is used to pay for the goods which have to be brought in (*imports*). Foreign or overseas trade gives us a wide choice of goods – often at a price lower than the one we would have to pay if we had tried to produce everything ourselves. This fact has meant that countries have become specialists in the production of certain goods and services (for example, Brazil for coffee and Ghana for cocoa).

Visible and invisible

Imports and exports are not confined to goods, but also cover services like tourism and consultants' fees. For example, if the United Kingdom exports farm machinery, this is an example of 'visible' export. On the other hand, if we have to bring in (import) rubber, this is known as a 'visible' import. Many British insurance companies receive income in return for giving insurance cover to overseas firms. This results in money coming into the country in return for a service going out, so we would class this as an *invisible* export. An example of an invisible import into the United Kingdom would be tourism: a British tourist staying in a foreign hotel and paying money for a service received outside this country. In short: visibles are anything we can see, for example wheat, machinery or coal; invisibles are things we cannot see, such as the use of a hotel room or advice from an engineering consultant. In addition, there are also transfers of money between countries, and not only those concerned with payments for the goods and services mentioned in the last paragraph. Large amounts of money are moved internationally for investment purposes for example, to buy a villa in Spain or to purchase shares in an American company. Such transfers are also regarded as part of foreign trade and are known as *capital* items.

Reasons for foreign trade

Foreign trade has developed because of the differences which exist between the different parts of the world. If everything was available everywhere, there would be no need for such trade. These differences can be listed as:

variations in the type and quantity of natural resources which
are found within countries, for example mineral deposits such as
iron ore, natural fuels like oil, and the climate and geographical
position;

skills which have been developed by the people over the years,
enabling them to produce goods and services which others
cannot;

capital resources which have been built up over the years, for
example factories, mines, machinery and roads, without which
goods and services cannot be produced elsewhere;

greater efficiency in producing goods and services, using the
skills and capital accumulated, compared with other countries
which may also have developed these.

These differences mean that there are benefits to be obtained from
foreign trade, although these must be set against the difficulties (and
therefore extra costs) which are discussed later in the chapter. These
benefits can be listed as:

- a greater variety of goods and services, for example tropical
fruits, fresh vegetables out of season and holidays abroad in the
sun;

- the ability to make goods by using imported raw materials not
available in the worker's own country, thus widening choice;

- greater output by being able to specialise in producing the goods
and services in which a country is more efficient;

- greater output because specialisation allows large-scale
production, which is more efficient;

- greater employment opportunities through expanding export
markets and therefore greater earnings;

- generally higher living standards because of the greater variety,
greater efficiency and higher income.

The balance of payments

It has always been important for countries to keep track of their
imports and exports so that they can adjust policies for maximum
benefit. By taking away the total value of all imports from the total
value of all exports, it is possible to calculate a country's *balance of
payments*. If the balance shows that a country is paying out more
than it is earning, the country is said to have an *adverse* balance of
payments. A *favourable* balance occurs when more is earned than is
paid out. It is obviously much better to have a favourable balance.
This indicates that a country can cover its expenditure on visible
imports and can bring in additional goods and services. All the
foreign trade of a country is recorded in terms of the types of goods
and services imported and of their value. The balance of payments
summarises all this trade, showing the payments made to other
countries and the payments received.

These payments are divided into the three main types:

- visible items;
- invisible items;
- capital items.

The visible items refer to the foreign trade in goods. When, in a given period (usually a year), the value of visibles exported by a country is compared with the value of visibles imported by that country, the result is called the *visible balance* or *balance of trade*.

For example:

1986	£ millions
Value of goods exported	1900
Value of goods imported	2000
Visible balance of trade	−100

These figures show that the visible balance is *adverse* because the cost of goods imported is higher than those exported. This loss is called a *deficit*. The United Kingdom often has an adverse balance of trade.

The invisible items refer to foreign trade in services – that is invisible exports (services sold to foreign countries which bring money into the country) and invisible imports (services bought from foreign countries which result in money leaving the country). When the value of invisible exports by a country is compared with the value of invisible imports in the same period the result is called the invisible balance.

For example:

1986	£ millions
Value of goods exported	1000
Value of goods imported	800
Invisible balance	+200

The figures above show that more has been earned than paid out. The invisible balance is therefore said to be *favourable*. This is known as a *surplus*. The United Kingdom normally has a surplus on its invisible balance.

When the visible balance is compared with the invisible balance for a country in a given period, this is called the *current balance* or *balance of payments on current account*.

Using the previous figures:

1986	£ millions
Visible balance	−100
Invisible balance	+200
Current balance	+100

This produces a favourable current balance of £100 million, which is a surplus.

The third group of payments, the *capital items*, shows the amounts of money which have been lent abroad in a given period and the amounts which have been borrowed from abroad in the same period. For example, British businesses invest abroad, and foreign businesses invest in the United Kingdom, by setting up factories, buying shares in companies or depositing money in banks. The interest, profits and dividends which result from these investments appear in the invisible balance (see above).

When money is lent abroad, the capital sum is a transfer of money out of the country and is regarded as an import, in the same way as payment for imported goods. When money is brought into the country, it is regarded as an export in the same way as payment received for exported goods. It must be remembered that some time in the future, whether it is weeks or years, money lent or borrowed will have to be repaid.

When these capital items are considered and set against the current balance, then the *total currency flow* for the year can be calculated. Suppose that capital items produce a deficit (that is, a loss) of £300 million in the year concerned, which means that more has been lent than borrowed. Using the previous figures, we find:

1986	£ millions
Current balance	+100
Capital items	−300
Total currency flow (net)	−200

This means that the country has paid out to other countries £200 million more than it has received in the year concerned. How is this loss going to be paid for?

Balancing the books

The central bank in the United Kingdom is called the Bank of England. A country's central bank holds the State's reserves of gold and foreign currencies. The loss of £200 million could be paid out of these reserves but, if they are not sufficient, the Bank of England for example, could temporarily borrow funds from the central banks of other countries, such as the Federal Reserve Bank of the USA, or from the International Monetary Fund (IMF) which was specially set up to help in this way. If the total currency flow had been positive, then the central bank could build up its reserves of foreign currency in order to pay any future deficits, or it could repay funds previously borrowed from other central banks or from the IMF. In this way, a country balances its books in its dealings with other countries.

CHECK THIS OUT

Write out the following sentences, filling in the missing words:

1 All the countries in the world have to trade with each other because of differences in weather and _____ _____.

2 Imports and exports are not confined to goods, but also cover services such as insurance, banking and _____.

3 Visible exports are anything we can _____ such as _____ and invisible exports are things we _____ _____ see such as _____.

4 An example of differences between countries leading to foreign trade is _____.

5 A benefit of foreign trade is _____.

6 An *adverse* balance of payments is made when a country is _____.

7 A *favourable* balance of payments is when a country is _____.

8 The balance of payments of a country is a _____ of all the trade showing _____ made to other countries and the _____ received.

9 The value of *invisible* exports by a country compared to the *invisible* imports of that country is called the _____ _____.

10 When money is borrowed from abroad, money is brought into the country and is regarded as an _____.

Pattern of UK visible foreign trade

A country's pattern of visible foreign trade can be looked at in two broad ways:

(i) types of exports and imports
(ii) countries being traded with.

The block graphs below show the types of goods being exported and imported by the United Kingdom in 1985 and their relative importance.

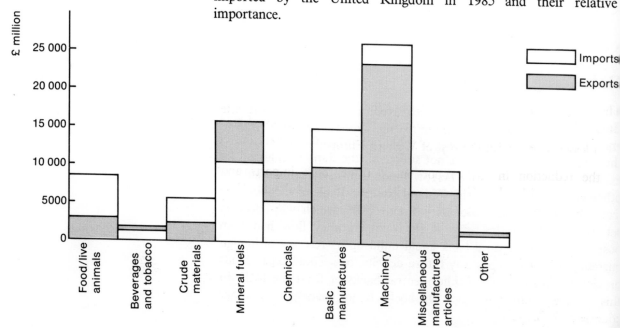

A country's pattern of trade can change greatly as the years pass, and in recent years the most important changes for the United Kingdom have been:

the reduced reliance on oil imports and the growth of oil exports, as a result of North Sea oil production;

the rapid growth in the value of imports of manufactured goods, such as cars and electrical goods, and a decline in exported manufactured goods.

The block graphs below show the main areas of the world with which the United Kingdom traded in 1985 and their relative importance:

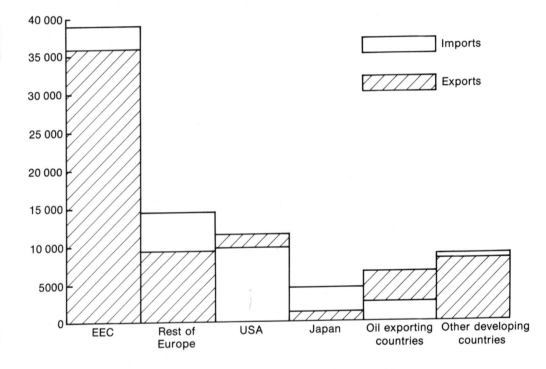

A country's pattern of trade in terms of different areas of the world can also change greatly over the years, and in recent years the most important changes for the United Kingdom have been:

- the rapid growth in trade, both exports and imports, with the European Economic Community (the Common Market) and to a lesser degree with the rest of Western Europe;

- the reduction in the proportion of trade, both imports and exports, with the Commonwealth countries, such as New Zealand, which paid special low import duties before the United Kingdom joined the EEC;

- the rapid growth in exports to the oil exporting countries, mainly in the Middle East;

- the rapid growth of manufactured goods imported from the Far East, especially Japan.

Dealers and agents in foreign trade

Foreign trade is very complex, so there are businesses involved in making the necessary arrangements and helping to overcome any problems. These firms have specialised knowledge and offer expert help to both large and small export businesses. The following section explains the terms used for firms dealing with the *transfer* of goods and other forms of assistance are covered later in the chapter. In foreign trade, there is great variety in different types of dealer and agent and there are no rigid rules about the use of names. This is a summary of the main forms.

Export and import wholesale merchants

These firms buy and sell on their own behalf, and receive profits from any deals which they make. They do not work for another business on a commission, or other fee, basis. Export merchants find their own customers abroad, while import merchants find customers within the receiving country. They usually specialise in particular trades.

Export and import agents

These firms work on behalf of another business and receive commission as a percentage of the sales or purchases which they handle. Export agents make arrangements for exporting the goods. They arrange transport, obtain insurance cover and see that all the documents are complete and in order. Import agents make all the arrangements to receive goods for importing firms.

A special type of agent is the *del credere*. These firms accept responsibility for any bad debts which might arise from the failure of their clients to pay for goods provided. The business which is exporting goods is protected, but has to pay extra to the agent for this service.

Export and import houses

The word 'house' means 'firm'. These businesses may act as both merchants and agents, and they carry out work similar to the agents and merchants you have just read about.

Export commission houses

This term usually refers to businesses which work for foreign buyers. They locate goods needed for import and then arrange their transfer.

Confirming houses

These are a special form of commission firm. They take their name from the work which they do, of confirming with manufacturers that they can deliver on time the goods which have been ordered.

Forwarding agents

Another name for this type of firm is *freight forwarders*. They make arrangements for the transfer of exported goods. This work includes preparing documents, booking transport and obtaining insurance cover.

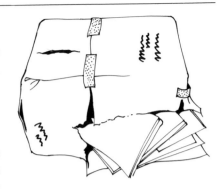

Shipping brokers

These firms specialise in arranging shipping space for goods to be exported.

Packing agents

These firms make sure that exported goods have the best possible packaging and the correct protection for their journey. Goods packed properly are less likely to be damaged in transit.

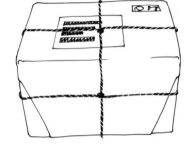

CHECK THIS OUT

Write out the following sentences, filling in the missing words:

1 Firms involved in helping other businesses to import and export goods have _____ knowledge and offer _____ help to both large and small businesses.

2 Firms which buy and sell on their own behalf and receive profits from any deals which they make are known as _____ and _____ wholesale merchants.

3 Firms which work on behalf of another business and receive commission on sales of purchases which they handle are known as _____ and _____ agents.

4 Businesses which act as both merchants and agents are called export and _____ _____.

5 Export commission houses work for _____ buyers by locating goods needed for export and arranging their _____.

6 Confirming houses confirm with _____ that they can deliver on time any _____ which have been ordered.

7 Forwarding agents make arrangements for the _____ of exported goods.

8 Shipping brokers arrange _____ _____ for goods to be exported.

9 Exported goods are correctly packed for export by _____ agents.

Foreign trade problems

Buying and selling abroad is generally more difficult than trading at home for a variety of reasons, such as:

Documentation

More documents are needed for foreign trade than for trade within a country, and more information has to be included on the documents. As well as the normal commercial documents such as insurance cover, others concerned with special payment methods and Customs and control arrangements are needed. The SITPRO aligned documents have helped to simplify the system. You should try to find out more about these.

Foreign languages

When dealing with non-English speaking countries, documents, advertising material, information leaflets and labels may need to be in a foreign language. Businessmen selling abroad should be able to use the language of their customers.

Foreign currencies

Transactions abroad have to be converted from and into the currencies of other countries. However, currency values can vary between the date that a deal is agreed and the payment made. Importers and exporters may gain or lose as a result. Ways of overcoming the danger of loss are dealt with in the later section on foreign payments. Some countries also operate 'exchange control' regulations which may make it difficult to obtain foreign currency to pay for imports.

Measurements

The methods used for measuring such things as distance, length and weight vary between different countries. Although there has been an increase in the use of metric measurements in the United Kingdom, miles and feet, tons and pounds are still widely used. Other items such a brick sizes and the weight of foodstuffs, use metric measurements.

Debt collection

When exporters fail to receive payment for goods which have been delivered abroad, it is more difficult to recover bad debts than it is within their own country. The language and the legal system are different, and communication over long distance is both difficult and expensive.

Distance and transportation

Distance can also be a problem, as businessmen may have to travel long distances in order to sell the goods, which then have to be transported to the buyer. Arranging transport takes time and money and extra packaging is needed to protect the goods on the long journey.

Legal and cultural differences

Foreign laws about advertising and selling may be different from those in the United Kingdom. There may also be special rules and regulations applying to particular goods (for instance, the United States has rules about the emission of exhaust gas from cars). People's ways and standards of living vary. For example, there is not a large market for frogs' legs in the United Kingdom, and it is no use trying to sell diamonds to the people of a poor country.

Import duties and restrictions

Most countries charge a tax called import duty on goods coming into the country, which makes it difficult for the imports to compete with home-produced goods. Sometimes, the import of certain goods may be completely banned, or a limit (called quota) is placed on the quantity allowed in per year.

NOW TRY THIS

Choose one of the following (A) (B) or (C) to complete the following sentences. Write out the sentence with the correct ending which you have chosen.

1 Documentation for foreign trade will include

 (A) advertising literature in a foreign language
 (B) Customs arrangements
 (C) a United Kingdom driving licence.

2 When selling abroad, the language of the country where the goods are being bought should be used for

 (A) a United Kingdom buyer for a villa in Spain
 (B) directions to the manufacturers in this country
 (C) advertising documents, information leaflets and labels.

3 When buying and selling abroad

 (A) currency values must never change
 (B) payment may be made in foreign currency

 (C) foreign currency can only be accepted for imports.

4 It might be difficult to collect payment for goods sold abroad because

 (A) the language and the legal system are different
 (B) there are no banks which could make the transaction into English currency
 (C) there may be import duties on goods coming into the country.

5 Foreign laws about advertising and selling goods

 (A) may be difficult to find out
 (B) may insist on United Kingdom firms arranging transport
 (C) may be different from those in the United Kingdom.

Customs and Excise Department

This is a United Kingdom Government department which deals with the collection of various indirect taxes, such as customs duty, excise duty and value added tax. The Department also has responsibility for collecting the statistical information on imports and exports, which is used in compiling the visible balance (see page 236).

Customs duties are levied on certain goods being imported into the United Kingdom, depending on their type and/or the country of

origin. These duties are collected at the various seaports, airports and other inland centres. Excise duties are levied on goods such as cigarettes and beer which are produced *within* the country, while value-added tax is levied on the *sale of most goods and services* in this country. Cars, electrical goods and meals at a restaurant are examples of items which carry VAT (value added tax) but food, books and newspapers are items which are not subject to this tax at the moment.

These indirect taxes may be *ad valorem* or *specific*. *Ad valorem* means that the tax is levied as a percentage of the *price* at which the goods are sold. At present, VAT is levied at the rate of 15 per cent and is an example of *ad valorem*. If your meal costs £10.00 and VAT is 15 per cent, another £1.50 is added to the bill. Excise duty is a specific tax which is charged according to quantity. An example would be 5p added to every litre of petrol.

Some goods are imported into the United Kingdom and then re-exported in the same or a very similar form, and such trade is called *entrepôt*. The goods may normally be liable for tax, but no duty is payable if they are not used in the United Kingdom. In order to ensure that they are in fact re-exported, they are held in bond, usually in *bonded warehouses*. These warehouses are owned by private owners who have given their agreement – their bond – not to release goods without customs duty being paid on them, unless the goods are re-exported. Goods can be held there without payment of duty until the time they are re-sold by the importer. Sometimes the goods can be processed in various ways while still in bond: for example, wine imported in barrels can be bottled. Goods produced within the United Kingdom and liable for excise duty are also sometimes held in bond. An example of this is whisky, which can be held whilst it is maturing.

A recent development in the United Kingdom connected with this is that of *freeports* which the Government has powers to set up. Various port areas, including inland ports, can be approved as 'free', which means that goods can be imported to, and then re-exported from, such areas, without Customs duty having to be paid. This enables goods to be held there and processed if required, and 'freeports' are really an extension of the bonded warehouse idea. Examples of freeports are Liverpool, Southampton and Birmingham.

CHECK THIS OUT

Write out the following sentences, filling in the missing words:

1 The United Kingdom Government department which deals with the collection of customs duty, excise duty and value added tax is called the _____ and _____ Department.

2 Customs duties are collected at _____, _____ and other inland centres.

3 Excise duties are levied on goods such as _____ produced within the country.

4 An example of *ad valorem* indirect taxation is _____ _____ _____.

5 Excise duty is a _____ tax which is charged according to quantity.

6 When goods are imported into the United Kingdom and then re-exported in the same or very similar form, it is known as _____ trade.

7 Bonded warehouses are used to store goods until _____ duty is paid on them, or until they are re-exported.

8 A freeport is a port area where goods can be imported to, and exported from, without having to pay any _____ _____.

9 The bill of lading is used when sending goods by _____ and gives the holder legal _____ of the goods.

10 A certificate of origin states the country from which the _____ first came.

International trade documents

The problems of trading abroad are even greater than the problems of trading at home. The three main problems are:

- the large distances involved;
- using foreign currency;
- different languages.

There are, of course, many other problems – for instance, certain goods may have to be altered to comply with different safety regulations in another country, or the different climate. Other problems are the lack of efficient advertising and distribution of goods in a foreign country. The Government through the Department of Trade and Industry tries to help exporters to overcome these problems.

The main documents which exporters need to use are explained in the next pages, including the section on payment methods.

The bill of lading

This is used when sending goods by sea. Goods sent by air are accompanied by a similar document called an airway bill. The bill of lading gives the holder of the original bill legal ownership of the goods mentioned on it. Several copies are made: one is given to the ship's captain, one to the consignee (the person sending the goods) and one to the consignor (the person receiving the goods). The bill of lading gives a full description of the goods and says where they have to go. To take possession of the goods, the consignor must show his or her copy of the bill to the captain of the vessel or his representative.

If the goods are damaged in transit, a note has to be made on the bill. This is sometimes called *endorsing the bill*. If the goods are not damaged, the bill is said to be *clean*, but if an endorsement has been made, it is a *fouled* or a *claused* bill.

The export invoice

This is prepared in the same way as an invoice for internal use, with the addition of the marks and numbers of the packages and also the name of the ship which is transporting them. One copy of this

A bill of lading is necessary to claim ownership of goods

invoice is attached to the bill of lading. Copies of other invoices which may have been received from various suppliers of the goods are attached to the export invoice, which saves having to enter details.

Certificate of origin

Countries may charge a levy or tariff on goods which they import, unless the country from which the goods are being imported belongs to a cartel like the EEC or GATT, in order to force up their price and thus make home-produced goods more attractive to the buyer. Customs authorities need to know from which country the goods have originated. In order to know this, the Customs and Excise require a certificate of origin which states the country from which the goods first came.

Consular invoice

As well as charging import duties, countries often restrict the numbers of certain types of goods coming in so that their home products are protected. These *quotas*, as they are called, are sometimes made compulsory by the countries receiving the goods. Alternatively the importing and exporting countries may come to voluntary agreements about the amount of imports which come into a country. The advantage of voluntary agreements is that countries are not as inclined to respond with harsher quotas. The consular invoice authorises the imports to take place. The invoice contains a declaration, sworn before the consul of the importing country, that the particulars in the invoice are correct. The consul then certifies the invoice and charges a fee for doing so.

Customs specification

Everything imported into or exported out of the United Kingdom must, by law, be declared to the Customs and Excise Department. This information is used by the Department of Trade in preparing statistical information on imports and exports. When goods are exported, a *specification* on the prescribed customs form giving particulars about the goods exported is given by the exporter.

Making payments overseas

There are two problems to contend with when making payments to foreign countries. One is that countries have their own currencies and money has to be converted, and the other is that of avoiding bad debts: that is, not receiving money for goods which have been forwarded, or not receiving goods which have been paid for. Various payment methods in foreign trade have been devised to help to overcome these problems.

Bills of exchange

When a sale of goods has been agreed, the seller draws up and signs a bill of exchange, which is then passed to the buyer for acceptance by signing across it. This means that the buyer has agreed to pay the sum involved by the date (which is some time in the future) shown on the bill. The most common date is three months' time. This is legally binding, provided that the goods are delivered. The goods should arrive at their overseas destination before the bill *matures* (that is, becomes due for payment.) The buyer has the goods and the seller gets paid, so that both are satisfied.

There is still a problem if the seller wishes to receive his money earlier. One way is for the seller to *endorse* the bill, by signing on the reverse, and then to use it to pay another business for goods bought from them. The seller has then received goods to the value of the bill, and the second business waits until the bill matures and receives money, or perhaps passes it on in payment for goods from a third business.

Another way is to *discount* the bill with a bank or discount house. This means that the bill is sold for an amount slightly less than its face value. The bank holds the bill until it is mature, and claims the full value. The difference between the amount the bank paid for the bill and the amount received when it matures is the reward for waiting for payment and for taking the risk of non-payment. Bills may be discounted several times before they mature, for instance moving from one bank or discount house to another.

There is still a risk, with such bills, that the debtor may fail to *honour* the bill (that is, to pay when it falls due). A way round this is to have the bill *accepted* by an acceptance house, for example a merchant bank, which agrees – for a small charge – to take responsibility if the debtor fails to pay. This makes the bill *first-class*, and it can be discounted easily at a favourable rate.

Another risk is that of foreign currency becoming worth less to the exporter or the bank in terms of home currency, during the period until the bill matures. One solution is to have the bill payable only in sterling (for a United Kingdom exporter), while another is to have an agreed exchange rate on the bill. A third possibility is for the expected foreign currency to be sold 'forward' on the foreign exchange market. This means that the current agreed price will be paid when the bill matures. These methods help the person receiving payment to know precisely how much of his *own* currency he will receive on the agreed date.

Documentary bills

These are also bills of exchange, but there are various foreign trade documents 'attached'. These documents vary according to the requirements of the importing country, but include the bill of lading, export invoice and insurance certificate. The most important is the bill of lading (see page 245) which proves ownership. When the importer has paid or 'accepted' the related bill of exchange, he can receive the bill of lading and present it to claim the imported goods. The procedure is usually handled between the banks of the exporter and the importer.

While this arrangement makes sure that the bill is accepted before the goods are handed over, there is still the risk that the bill could be 'dishonoured' – that is, not paid in due course by the importer. For this reason, a more secure method of payment, called a letter of credit, may be used.

Letters of credit

These are sometimes also referred to as documentary credits or bankers' commercial credits. The importer requests his own bank to send a letter of credit to an *advising* or *corresponding* bank in the exporter's country. When the exporter provides the necessary documents, including the bill of lading and other shipping documents, showing that the goods have been sent, he is paid direct by the bank. The documents are then sent to the importer's bank, which hands them to the importer when payment is made, so that the goods can then be claimed. Where a period of credit is required, this can still be arranged through the use of a first-class 'accepted' bill of exchange (see above).

By this method, the importer's bank is accepting responsibility for payment, but to be safe, the letter of credit should be made *irrevocable*, so that the bank still has responsibility even if anything goes wrong. As a further safeguard, the advising bank can also be asked to give a *confirmed* credit, which means that in the case of default by the importer's bank, the advising bank will not claim against the exporter but only against the importer's bank.

Direct payments

- *Bank drafts*   These are cheques which are drawn on banks rather than on customers' own accounts. The bank has already received the money from the customer and so the creditor has more confidence in receiving payment against the draft, which is guaranteed by the bank. Bank drafts are also used in home trade where large sums are involved, for example in purchasing a house or a car.

- *Cable transfers*   These involve the transfer of funds electronically between banks. No money is physically transferred, so that there must be complete trust between the banks concerned, or they may be branches of the same international bank or a subsidiary. Settlement between the banks occurs later when a number of such payments are 'set off' against each other, when these payments occur in both directions. This method is extremely quick and is especially useful where urgent payments need to be made.

CHECK THIS OUT

Write out the following sentences, filling in the missing words:

1 The two problems which occur when making payments to foreign countries are _____ and _____.

2 A bill of exchange states that the buyer has agreed to pay the sum involved by the future _____ shown on the bill.

3 If a seller wishes to receive money earlier than the date shown on the bill of exchange, he/she may _____ the bill by _____ on the _____ and then use it to pay another business for goods bought from them.

4 A bill of exchange can be discounted with a _____ or a _____ _____ which means that it is sold for less than its face _____.

5 A solution to the risk of foreign currency becoming worth less to the exporter of goods between the time a price is agreed and payment made is to have a bill of exchange payable only in _____.

6 Bills of exchange with various foreign trade documents attached are called _____ bills.

7 When an importer's bank sends a letter of credit to an exporter's advising bank, the exporter provides the necessary _____ showing that the goods have been sent and is _____ direct by the bank.

8 Bank drafts are cheques drawn on banks rather than on customers' own accounts and the payment is guaranteed because the bank has already received the _____.

9 Cable transfers involve transfer of funds _____ between banks and no money is physically _____.

Help with foreign trade

The British Overseas Trade Board

This was set up in 1971 as the British Export Board and gives help in such matters as finding overseas agents, guidance on trade problems in particular countries, giving information on tariffs and import regulations abroad and market research, promotion and publicity for products.

The Export Credits Guarantee Department

This is controlled by the Department of Trade and Industry and provides an insurance service for firms trading overseas against the possible non-payment of debts by customers. The same department also offers advice and information for firms trading abroad.

The Department of Trade and Industry

The Fairs and Promotion Branch advises exporters in the United Kingdom who want to exhibit at trade fairs held in other parts of the world. The Export Services Division provides expert help and information about overseas markets and keeps up to date with import regulations and changes in tariffs.

Commercial and merchant banks

Many firms specialise in a particular market or a particular range of products and undertake the work of exporting goods. They pay the producers at once and often extend credit to the buyer from abroad. Some firms work on commission and many buy goods on their own account. They help the manufacturer by assuming the technical and financial worries of selling goods abroad.

Trade and employers' associations

Some trades establish a subsidiary company overseas in order to overcome some of the problems of trading in a foreign country. This company may receive orders and pass them on to the main company, it may sell from stocks or assemble or pack goods which have been exported to its branch.

Foreign trade quotation terms

In both home and foreign trade, it is important to know the precise terms on which goods are being bought – that is what charges there may be in addition to the price of the goods, for example customs duty, transport and insurance costs. Because of the longer distances involved between buyer and seller and the greater difficulties in foreign trade in general, these extra charges may form a very substantial part of the total cost of foreign goods, when compared with home trade.

The existence of these additional charges, if any, will be noted in quotations provided, and the amounts will then appear on the invoices if orders are placed. The following abbreviated terms are some of those used in foreign trade quotations, and each one shows the charges which *are* included in the price and therefore those which are not.

- Ex-works – includes only the basic cost of the goods, as collected from the seller.
- FAS (Free Alongside) – includes all charges for bringing the goods to the dockside in the country of origin.
- FOB (Free on Board) – includes all FAS charges plus loading charges onto the ship (or other transport).
- CIF (Cost, Insurance, Freight) – includes all transport charges to port of destination and insurance cover, as well as the cost of the goods.
- CIFE (CIF and Exchange) – includes all CIF charges plus cover for any exchange rate risks between order and payment.
- Franco – includes all charges right up to delivery at the buyer's premises.

There are other examples not given above. Try to find out what they are.

International trading organisations

As nations have developed, some have found it to be in their best interests to form groups with others so that they can enjoy special treatment in trading and develop closer economic and political links. There is 'free trade' between the member countries. This does not mean that goods and services traded are not paid for, but that there should be no barriers to trade. Four of the main associations, or 'cartels' as they are called, are:

1   The European Economic Community (EEC)

This group is often referred to as the Common Market, because it tries to provide a market for member countries to sell their goods in. The main founder members are Italy, France, Belgium, West Germany, The Netherlands and Luxembourg who formed themselves by the Treaty of Rome in 1957 into the European Economic Community (the EEC). The Treaty had the following objectives:

- to form a customs union and gradually adopt a common protective tariff against non-members;

- the free movement of capital and labour within the Community;

- the establishment of a common agricultural policy;

- the formation of institutions aiming at some sort of political unity.

There are now 12 members, including Denmark, Ireland, Greece, Spain and Portugal. The United Kingdom joined in 1973.

The Assembly (the European Parliament) now has 518 members, elected by the member countries, who may suggest amendments on proposals when consulted by the Council of the Commission. Resolutions are adopted by the Assembly by a simple majority of those members who are present.

The European Court of Justice ensures that European law is observed in the interpretation and application of the Treaty and deals with alleged breaches by a member state.

There is a Common Agricultural Policy which aims to increase agricultural activity and ensure a better standard of living for the agricultural community, to stabilise prices and ensure certainty of supplies at reasonable prices to consumers.

Advantages of belonging to the Community are that British manufacturers have access to a vast 'home' market in Europe and more than half the United Kingdom's exports now go to EEC countries. Labour is also able to move freely to other parts of the Community. Disadvantages are that the Community food prices are higher than could be obtained in the world market because of the Community's agricultural policy and Britain pays more into the Community funds than do some of the other countries.

2   The European Free Trade Association (EFTA)

This Association is made up of countries which chose not to join the EEC and it tends to concentrate on matters affecting trade and the standard of living in member countries. There are links between EFTA and the EEC, but EFTA does not aim at the eventual integration of member countries, as the Common Market does. Two important members of EFTA are Switzerland and Finland.

3   The General Agreement on Tariffs and Trade (GATT)

While the EEC has only a dozen members, GATT covers over 60 countries. Many of these countries were at one time controlled by the United Kingdom, but are now independent. Nevertheless, relations are generally good between the United Kingdom and GATT members.

4   The Organisation of Petroleum Exporting Countries (OPEC)

The Organisation of Petroleum Exporting Countries (OPEC) is a cartel which is slightly different from the other cartels mentioned so far. The other organisations we have mentioned all control goods and services entering member countries, as well as seeking to give preferential trade arrangements to other members, OPEC has no joint arrangements for the import of goods to member countries but tries to establish agreement among its members for the price and levels of output of petroleum. By having agreed price and output levels member countries can be sure of satisfactory levels of income for their produce. It is important for these countries to have an agreement as many of them have very little else to export which is of such value. OPEC is an important organisation as its members produce a large quantity of the world's petroleum products. Most other non-member countries, such as the United Kingdom, fix the price of their petroleum at around the same level as OPEC. One leading OPEC member is Saudi Arabia.

NOW TRY THIS

The following questions must be answered verbally but without using the words 'YES' or 'NO'. The teacher may ask the questions round the class or groups may ask each other in turn.

Each person keeps a score of their own answers, provided that they have been made correctly without using the words 'YES' or 'NO'. At the end of a round of questions, the scores are totted up to find the winner(s). The players MUST USE FULL SENTENCES.

An example of a question might be:
'Is excise duty levied as a percentage of the price the goods are sold at?'

An example of a correct answer would be:
'Excise duty is not levied as a percentage of the price the goods are sold at.'

A wrong answer would be:
'No, it's not' or 'Yes, it is'
as these use the forbidden words.

If two teams are formed, a time limit can be put on the questions and answers to see which group manages to answer correctly the most questions in a given time.

1 Is the money which a country earns by its exports used to pay for its imports?

2 Is Brazil a specialist producer of dairy foods?

3 Are tourism and consultant's fees counted as exports?

4 Is insurance a visible export?

5 If a country pays out for imports more than it earns for exports, is this an adverse balance of payments?

6 If more goods have been imported than exported, does this mean that a country has a favourable balance of trade?

7 Is nearly half the United Kingdom's trade done with the EEC?

8 Is another name for the EEC the Common Market?

9 Does the United Kingdom follow the OPEC oil and petrol prices?

10 Would you say that different currencies produce problems when firms export to foreign countries?

11 Is a bill of lading used when sending goods by sea?

12 Is it true that goods need not be protected by insurance as long as they are in transit?

13 Is a bill of exchange restricted to foreign trade only?

14 Is a bonded warehouse used for goods on which duty is payable?

15 Does *free on board* mean that there is no charge to either buyer or seller when transporting goods by sea?

MULTIPLE CHOICE QUESTIONS

There are four possible answers to each of the following questions. Study the introductory sentence, and then decide which of the alternatives correctly answers the question or completes the sentence. Write down the question number and follow it with (A) (B) (C) or (D), according to your choice.

1 An example of an invisible export is
(A) vegetable oil
(B) coal
(C) an engineering consultant's fee
(D) freight sent by air.

2 The balance of trade is the difference between
(A) the value of all visible imports and all visible exports
(B) the value of all invisible imports and all invisible exports
(C) the total value of ALL exports from ALL imports
(D) the total value of ALL imports from ALL exports.

3 An ADVERSE balance of trade is where
(A) a country brings in less goods and services than it exports
(B) a country brings in more goods and services than it exports
(C) a country does not keep track of its imports and exports
(D) a country earns more for INVISIBLE exports than it pays out for INVISIBLE imports.

4 Most of the United Kingdom's exports go to
(A) North America
(B) OPEC countries
(C) The European Economic Community (the Common Market)
(D) none of these.

5 We DO NOT depend on OPEC members for
(A) close political links with the United Kingdom
(B) supplying oil and petrol to the rest of the world
(C) keeping the price of petroleum low
(D) producing all the petroleum in the world.

6 A special BONDED WAREHOUSE is NOT needed to store
(A) rubber
(B) whisky
(C) tobacco
(D) wine.

7 A bill of lading is used when goods are sent by
(A) air
(B) Datapost
(C) juggernaut lorry
(D) sea tranport.

8 A certificate of origin states
(A) the country in which goods were packaged for sale
(B) the country in which the goods started out
(C) all the countries through which the goods passed before they reached the retailer
(D) the amount of customs and excise duty payable to the country of origin.

9 The most reliable method of payment is for the buyers to get
(A) documentary proof that the goods have been sent off
(B) a bank loan or overdraft for buyers in the currency of their country
(C) a credit account with the buyer's bank
(D) payment by advance credit.

10 Difficulties of international trade DO NOT include
(A) producing goods which are surplus to a country's needs
(B) changing rates of currency
(C) difficulties with differing standards (such as voltages) in goods
(D) import restrictions.

There are four possible answers to each of the following questions.

If you think (1) only is correct, write down A.
If you think (1) and (2) only are correct, write down B.
If you think (3) and (4) only are correct, write down C.
If you think (2), (3) and (4) only are correct, write down D.

11 Customs duties or tariffs
(1) can force up the price of goods
(2) can bring an income from customs duties to the Government
(3) can include the cost of insurance on imported goods
(4) must be paid on everything which is brought into the United Kingdom.

12 An invisible export can be
(1) a British tourist on holiday in Italy
(2) the sale of a British-made aircraft to America
(3) an Australian tourist on holiday in the United Kingdom
(4) payment to a British insurance company for insuring a dam in Africa.

13 United Kingdom membership of the European Economic Community has meant that
(1) trade with Greece and Spain has expanded
(2) members can move to EEC countries to work
(3) trade with the Commonwealth countries has expanded rapidly
(4) Britain no longer needs to export manufactured goods.

14 A bill of exchange is
(1) a bill which is only issued by a merchant bank to the buyer
(2) a promise written by the person who signs the bill, to pay a certain amount at a fixed time in the future
(3) a bill exchanged for foreign goods which can be cashed in this country
(4) a certificate which can be legally exchanged for imported goods.

15 The Government offers help to exporters through
(1) issuing a documentary credit
(2) voluntary agreements about import and export quotas
(3) information from the Department of Trade and Industry
(4) an insurance service from the Export Credits Guarantee Department.

STIMULUS RESPONSE QUESTIONS

The following questions carry a mark of 20. Each section of a question shows the marks for the correct response.

1 Look at the following table and answer the following questions.

Visible trade	Exports (%)	Imports (%)
Food, etc.	7.0	12.5
Raw materials	5.0	9.5
Fuels	13.6	13.8
Semi-manufactured goods	25.0	23.0
Manufactured goods	40.0	30.0
Others	9.4	11.2
	100.0	100.0

(a) What proportion of semi-manufactured and manufactured goods is imported? (*3 marks*)

(b) Which part of the export trade showed the highest percentage of exports? (*3 marks*)

(c) Which items show a deficit of exports over imports? (*4 marks*)

(d) Why do we import more raw materials than we export? (*4 marks*)

(e) What does this table suggest about agriculture and farming? (*6 marks*)

2 Look at the figures below and then answer the questions.

Value of exports as a percentage of all goods produced	UK	France	West Germany	Italy
	22.3	19.0	27.9	21.1

(a) Which of these countries relies most on its export earnings? (*2 marks*)

(b) Name an international trading organisation to which these four countries belong and say how membership benefits them. (*4 marks*)

(c) (i) If each country's currency weakened by 10 per cent which country would stand to gain most and why? (*6 marks*)

(ii) What is the average value of exports as a percentage of these countries' production? (*6 marks*)

(iii) Name one factor which might cause a currency to strengthen and one which might cause it to weaken (*2 marks*)

ESSAY QUESTIONS

1 Exporters may find difficulties when they engage in foreign trade.

(a) Give details of difficulties which firms may experience when they take part in foreign trade in:
(i) delivering the goods:
(ii) import restrictions;
(iii) language. (*12 marks*)

(b) What other difficulties could firms encounter? (*4 marks*)

(c) In what ways does the United Kingdom Government help firms who export goods? (*4 marks*)

2 (a) (i) Explain the meaning of the term 'invisible exports'. (*4 marks*)

(ii) How do 'invisible exports' help to maintain the balance of trade? (*4 marks*)

(b) Why is export trade essential to the economy of the United Kingdom? (*6 marks*)

(c) How does the United Kingdom Government restrict international trade? (*6 marks*)

3 (a) What are the factors affecting the prices of imports? (*4 marks*)

(b) How do bonded warehouses differ from other types of warehouse? (*6 marks*)

(c) Describe the type of work which may be carried out on goods while they are stored in a bonded warehouse. (*6 marks*)

(d) Why do countries have customs duties? (*4 marks*)

4 (a) What is the difference between the balance of payments and the balance of trade? (*6 marks*)
  (b) What do you understand by
    (i) an adverse balance of trade;
    (ii) a favourable balance of trade. (*6 marks*)
  (c) Explain the following statement:
    'Deficits in the balance of trade account may be offset by a surplus on invisible exports.' (*6 marks*)
  (d) Give two example of invisible exports. (*2 marks*)

5 (a) Why are terms relating to the price of goods important? (*4 marks*)
  (b) Imagine that your firm received three identical quotations from foreign exporters but with the following different conditions of price:
    (i) CIF (ii) Franco (iii) FOB.
    Explain the meanings of these abbreviations. (*6 marks*)
  (c) State, giving rasons, the quotation which you would advise your firm to accept. (*6 marks*)
  (d) What other factors affect the price of foreign goods being imported into the United Kingdom? (*4 marks*)

6 Explain the following documents:
  (a) bill of lading; (*5 marks*)
  (b) certificate of origin; (*5 marks*)
  (c) consular invoice; (*5 marks*)
  (d) certificate of insurance. (*5 marks*)

7 (a) Explain why countries find it necessary to trade with each other. (*10 marks*)
  (b) What difficulties might a firm encounter in obtaining information through market research in another country? (*4 marks*)
  (c) With which countries does the United Kingdom do the most trade? (*6 marks*)

LEARN IT YOURSELF

Look in a national newspaper or local bank and see if you can find the following exchange rates:

Pound against the Dollar
Pound against the Franc
Pound against the Dinar
Pound against the Punt
Pound against the Mark.

Note them down with the date. Check the same currencies one week later. Note how they have changed. Can you suggest any reasons for some of the largest changes? In the case of each example, say if you think traders in the United Kingdom seeking to export goods would be pleased with the changes. Would those seeking to import goods feel the same?

Understanding Data

With thanks to Martin Grady of North Manchester College.)

n commerce information will very often be presented in a way which ses numbers, symbols and diagrams. Imports, exports, interest rates nd sales figures are some of the material that might be presented in this way. In order to understand such things fully information about the most common techniques used in presenting and understanding data is provided below.

Graphs

There are *five* simple rules to remember about presenting information in he form of a graph:

1 Be eye-catching. Use different colour pens or pencils for each part or section.

2 *Always* give a title. The title should explain what your graph shows.

3 Clearly label each part of your graph.

4 Show what units of measurement you are using, e.g. '£m' means 'expressed in millions of pounds', '000' means 'expressed in thousands'.

5 Show the amount of time the measurements were taken over, e.g. 'per year', 'per month', 'per week'.

Probably the most simple graph to draw or understand is the *pictogram*. n a pictogram simplified pictures are used to represent a stated quantity of what you are measuring.

Could mean 1000 people or

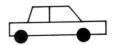

could mean 10 motor cars. The following pictogram shows the number of cars using Callaghan's petrol station per hour.

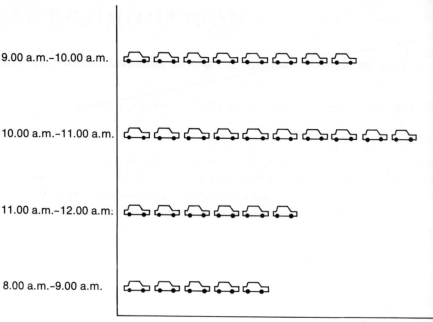

BAR CHART   This is another simple way we can show data. Each bar represents a different set of readings and a glance at the length of the bars helps to make comparisons. The bars can be drawn bottom to top or left to right. It is important to make sure how long each bar will be and what scale you will use before you begin otherwise you may waste much time and effort. The five rules mentioned above also apply here.

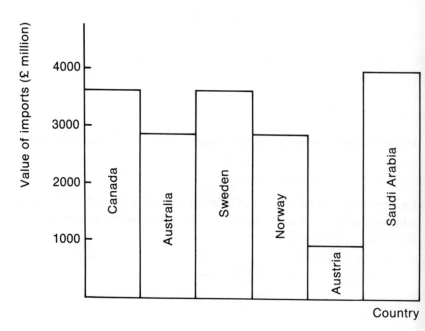

Example of a bar chart.

PIE CHARTS   These are used to show the size of each part of a total amount compared to the other parts. Each item is like a slice of the whole pie. To draw a pie chart each separate part of the total figure should be turned into a percentage of the total figure. (If you are not sure how to do this look at the section below on percentages.) Then, when you have found the percentage figure, find out the same percentage of 360° (the number of degrees in circle) and that is how big the slice will be. Check your calculations by making sure that the number of degrees you intend to use adds up to 360 – you have made a mistake if the figure is different.

So, if Eltonia gets 25 per cent of its imports from Britain, 25 per cent from France, 40 per cent from Sweden and 10 per cent from Zimbabwe then Britain and France would get 90° each (25 per cent of 360 being 90). Sweden would get 144° and Zimbabwe 36°. Together this gives a total of 360°.

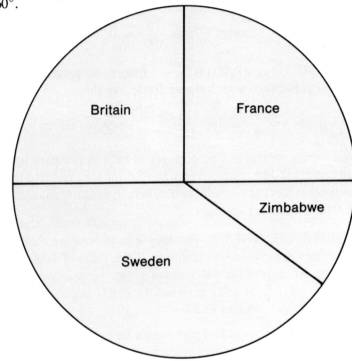

Percentages

We can use percentages to compare data which at first glance might be difficult to compare. One of the most common uses of percentages in commerce is to calculate tax rates.

If we know that £30 of Michelle Callaghan's weekly wage of £120 is paid in tax we can find out what percentage this is by putting the number we wish to express as a percentage over the number it is a percentage of and multiplying by 100, so if we want to express *one number as a percentage of another* as in the case of Michelle's tax

$$\frac{£\,30}{£\,120} \times \frac{100}{1} = \frac{3}{12} \times \frac{100}{1} = \frac{1}{4} \times \frac{100}{1} = \frac{100}{4} = \frac{25}{1} = 25\%$$

Even if the numbers we wish to measure are fractions or decimals it is easy to convert them by following these steps:

FRACTION TO PERCENTAGE   Multiply the fraction by $\frac{100}{1}$.

Using this method $\frac{1}{2}$ becomes 50 per cent as:

$$\frac{1}{2} \times \frac{100}{1} = \frac{1}{1} \times \frac{50}{1} = 50\%$$

DECIMAL TO PERCENTAGE   Multiply the decimal by 100 and add the per cent sign.

Using this method 0.987 becomes 98.7% as:

$$0.987 \times 100 = 98.7$$

or 98.7% when the per cent sign is added on.

PERCENTAGE TO A DECIMAL   Divide the percentage by 100.

76% becomes 0.76 as $\frac{76}{100} = 0.76$

PERCENTAGE TO A FRACTION   Ignore the percentage sign and write the percentage over 100 and divide like this.

75% as a fraction is $\frac{3}{4}$ because $\frac{75}{100} = \frac{3}{4}$ when we cancel by 25

As we said earlier we can use percentages to help us compare figures which are expressed differently. Even when figures are expressed in the same way percentages can be useful as they help us measure changes and compare them with other changes.

PERCENTAGE CHANGES   We may wish to compare changes in figures that are not very easy to compare. If the value of sales of two shops change we may wish to compare them. Grogan's Ltd have increased their sales from £895 per week to £1100. Salim's Ltd have grown from £990 per week to £1300.

Simple subtraction of the old and new figures for each shop would give us an idea of the bigger and smaller of the two but not an idea of how big the change was compared to previous sales. To find that we must use percentages in the following way.

$$\text{Grogan's Ltd} = \frac{205 \text{ (actual change)}}{895 \text{ (original figure)}} \times \frac{100}{1}$$

$$= \frac{41}{175} \times \frac{100}{1} = \frac{41}{35} \times \frac{20}{1} = \frac{41}{7} \times \frac{4}{1} = \frac{164}{7}$$

$$= \underline{23.4\%}$$

$$\text{Salim's Ltd} = \frac{310}{990} \times \frac{100}{1} = \frac{31}{99} \times \frac{100}{1} = \frac{3100}{99}$$

$$= \underline{31.3\%}$$

From this, we can see that Salim's Ltd have achieved the greater overall growth in sales.

Averages

The most common measure of an average is to find 'the mean'. To arrive at this average you should add up all the readings you are measuring and divide this answer by the number of readings you started with. If there are five shops selling make-up bags in one road and you wish to find the mean, or average, price you would first find the various prices each of the five shops were charging:

Shop 1: £3.50
Shop 2: £2.75
Shop 3: £7.20
Shop 4: £5.50
Shop 5: £2.90

Total £21.85

This figure of £21.85 should now be divided by FIVE (the total number of shops).

$$\frac{£21.85}{5} = £4.37$$

The answer, £4.37, is the mean or average price of make-up bags. The mean helps to find the centre point of all the prices and gives us a very general idea about prices of make-up bags on this road. If three shops on the next road were selling make-up bags and we wished to find the mean we would add up their prices and divide by three. By comparing the answers from both roads we would know which of the two sets of shops tended to sell make-up bags cheapest. The average, or mean, helps us to decide on the centre of a set of figures. By finding the centre of several groups comparisons of different groups or sets of figures are made easier.

Index

Acknowledgement 47
Actuaries 161
Ad valorem Tax 244
Advertising
    agencies 95
    arguments against 95
    benefits 94
    generic 93
    media 89
    rules and regulations 96
    techniques 91
Advice note 47
Agents in foreign trade 240
Aids to trade 4
American Express 114
Articles of Association 61
Assurance (see Life Assurance)
Automatic vending machines 14
Averages – how to work out 261

Balance of payments 235
Bank account (opening) 115
Bank drafts 114, 248
Bank of England 106, 237
Bank Giro Credits 112
Banks
    clearing 105
    clearing system 120
    loans 211
    merchant 106
    opening an account 115
    overdrafts 108
    savings 104
    services 107
    statements 108
Banker's order 109
Baltic Exchange 35
Barter 7
Bears 68
'Big Bang' 80
Bill of Lading 245
Bills of Exchange 247
Body Corporate 57
Bonded warehouses 244
Branded goods 93
British Electrotechnical Approvals
    Board 225
British Overseas Trade Board 249
British Standards Institution 225
British Telecom services 193
Broker/Dealer 80
Brokers 79
Budget accounts 109
Building societies
    Act 1986 212
    growth of 207
    operation of 207
    savings 211
    services 213
Bulls 68
Bureaufax 195
Business documents 43

Business loans 112
Business reply service 178

Cable television 201
Cable transfers 248
Capitalist system 56
Cargo ships 136
Cash-and-carry wholesalers 34
Cash discount 49
Cash dispensers 110
Cash flow 112
Cash on delivery 180
Cargo liners 35
Caveat emptor 219
Certificate of incorporation 62
Certificate of origin 246
Certificate of posting 179
Chain of distribution 13, 32
Channels of distribution 32
Charge cards 114
Chartering agents 35
Charters – types of 136
Cheques
    advantages 118
    disadvantages 118
    filling in 118
    referred 119
Cheque guarantee cards 107
Citizens' Advice Bureau 225
Civil Law 219
Clearing Banks 105
Coastal vessels 137
Commerce 3
Commercial and merchant banks 250
Commercial bank services 107
Commercial services 5, 7
Commodity markets 35
Computers in retailing 24
Computers in the Stock Exchange 82
Confirming houses 241
Consular invoice 246
Consultative councils 227
Consumer 7
Consumers' Association 225
Consumer Credit Act 223
Consumer durables 19
Consumer laws 221–4
Consumer Protection (putting things
    right) 228
Consumer Protection (reasons for) 220
Containerisation 142
Co-operatives 21, 22, 70
Credit cards (banks) 114
Credit cards (mail order) 23
Credit note 50, 51
Creditworthiness 47
Crossed cheque 117
Criminal Law 219
Current accounts 107
Customs and Excise Department 243
Customs specification 246

Data (Understanding it) 257

Datapost 181
Datel 197
Dealers (Foreign trade) 240
Dealers (Stock Exchange) 80
Debentures 68
Debit note 51
Del credere agent 26
Department of Trade and Industry 249
Department of Transport 129
Department stores 20
Deposit accounts 109
Desk research 98
Direct debits 110
Direct payments 248
Direct services 3
Discount 49
Discount stores 19
Dividend 21
Division of labour 5, 6
Documentary bills 247

Electronic post 182
Endowment mortgage 113
Enquiry 43
Enquiry forms 44
Entrepôt trade 244
European Economic Community 239,
    251
European Free Trade Association 252
Exchange 6
Excise duties 244
Executors (banking) 111
Export and import agents 240
Export and import houses 240
Export and import wholesale
    merchants 240
Export commission houses 240
Export Credits Guarantee
    Department 249
Export invoice 245
Exports 234
Extractive Industry
    (see Primary production)

Factoring 112
Facsimile Transmission (see Fax)
Fair Trading Act 224
Fax machines 195
Federal Reserve Bank (USA) 237
Financial Services Act 83, 84
First-class post 177
Food and Drugs Acts 223
Foreign languages 242
Foreign trade
    currencies 242
    debt collection 242
    distance and transportation 242
    documentation 242
    import duties and restrictions 242
    legal and cultural differences 243
    measurements 242
    problems 241

quotation terms   250
reasons for   234
UK patterns of   238, 240
Forwarding agents   241
Franchise   20
Franking machines   181
Freephone   199
Free ports   244
Freepost   178
Futures contracts   35

General Agreement on Tariffs and Trade
(GATT)   246, 252
General Post Office   176
Gilt-edged stock   79
Government departments   72
Graphs   257, 258

Home-loan scheme   210
Household delivery service   178
House purchase   206
Hypermarkets   19

Imports   234
Independent shops   15
Information services   199
Insurance
annuity assurance   155
assessor   166
business interruption   156
calculating risks   161
cash in transit   157
claims   166
contributions   166
employer's liability   157
fidelity guarantee   158
fire   156
goods in transit   157
holiday   160
household (buildings and
contents)   159
indemnity   166
insurable interest   163
life assurance   154
life endowment   154
marine insurance
cargo   158
floating policy   158
freight   159
hull   159
liability   159
open policy   158
motor insurance
excess   163
fully comprehensive   162
no claims bonus   162
third party   159
third party, fire and theft   160
plate glass   157
pool   152
pooling of risks   151
premiums   161, 162
public liability   158
subrogation   155
term   154
theft   158
uninsurable risks   163
whole life   154
with-profits   154
without-profits   155
Intelpost   182
Intelstat   195
Intermediary   23
International datapost   182
International Monetary Fund (IMF)   237

International trade documents   245
International trading organisations   250
Interstream   198
Interest   104
Invisible imports/exports   153, 234,
240
Investments (banking)   111
Invoice   47
Invoice form   48
Itinerant traders   15

Jobbers   79
Jonathan's Coffee House   78

Kilostream   198

Leasing   112
Letters of credit   248
Liners   136
Life Assurance   154, 155
Limited liability   57
Lloyd's   151, 167, 168
Lloyd's Register   137
Local authority enterprise   72
London Commodity Exchange   35
London Metal Exchange   36
Loss leader   17
Lutine Bell   168

MACE   16
Mail order   22
Mail order protection schemes   226
Manufacturing (see Secondary production)
Market makers (Stock Exchange)   80
Market stalls   15
Market research   96, 97
Media (advertising)   89
Megastream   198
Memorandum of Association   61
Merchant Banks   106
Middleman   33
MIRAS   208
Mixed economy   56
Mobile shops   15
Mortgages
arranging   208
banks   113
endowment   209
repayment   209
types   208
Multiple shops   19

National Consumer Council   227
National Savings Bank   184
National Savings Bonds   185
National Savings Certificates   185
National Girobank   183
Needs and wants   1
Nightrider   179
Night safes   113
Night Star Parcels   134

Office of Fair Trading   224, 226
Oftel   192
Open cheque   116
Opening a bank account   115
Order   45
Order form   46
Organisation of Petroleum Exporting
Countries   252
Overseas mail   181
Overseas payments   246

Packet Switch Stream   198
Packing agents   241

Parcel post   178
Partnership   58, 59
Passenger Transport Executive   129
Payment   50
Percentages (how to do them)   259
Personal loans   111
Phonecards   199
Pie charts   259
Postal order services   185
Postal services   177
Poste restante   180
Premium Savings Bonds   185
Premium (Insurance)   151
Prestel   196
Price list   45
Prices Act   222
Primary production   2
Private boxes   180
Private companies   59
Private enterprise   58
Private sector   58
Private treaty   35
Privatisation   56, 57, 192
Production   1
Promotion (see Sales promotion)
Prospectus   67
Public company   60
Public corporation   70, 71
Public sector   58, 70

Quotation   45

Radio communication   206
Radio paging   196
Radiophones   196
Railway letters   179
Receipt   50
Recognised Investment Exchange
(RIE)   83
Recorded delivery   179
Red Star Parcels   134
References (status enquiries)   111
Registered letters and packets   179
Repayment mortgage   113
Retailer   13

Safe deposits   111
Sales promotions   98
Satellites   194
Satellite television   201
Satstream   198
Savings Banks   104
SEAQ (Stock Exchange Automated
Quotes)   81
Secondary production   2
Second class post   177
Selectapost   181
Securities and Investments Board   81, 82,
83, 84
Securities Association   83
Self Regulatory Organisations (SRD)   83
Shares
Alpha group   81
Beta group   81
deferred   65
Delta group   81
example of   64
issuing   63, 66
origins   78
ordinary   65
preference   65
rights issue   66
transactions   78
Self sufficient   5, 6
Shipping brokers   241

Shipping conferences 136
Socialist systems 56
Sole owner 58
SPAR 16
Special delivery 179
Specialisation 5, 234
Speculators 67
Spot contracts 35
Stags 67
Standing orders 109
Status enquiries 111
Stock Exchange 78, 79, 80, 81, 82
Stock Exchange Council 79
Store cards 114
Street vendors 14
Subscriber Trunk Dialling 194
Supermarket chains 17
Swiftair 181

Talisman (Stock Exchange) 83
Telecom Gold 196
Teleconferencing 197
Telemessages 197
Telephone services 193
Television 200
Telex 199
Tenders (for shares) 67

Tertiary production 3
Test marketing 97
TOPIC (Teletext output of Information by Computer) 82
Trade and employers' associations 250
Trade Associations 227
Trade Descriptions Acts 223
Trade discount 49
Tramp ships 35, 136
Transport
    air 138
        advantages of 139
        disadvantages of 140
    benefits 128
    containers 142
    inland waterways 141
        advantages of 141
        disadvantages of 141
    methods 129
    own fleets 132
    pipeline 142
    rail 133
        advantages of 134
        disadvantages of 133
    road 129
        advantages of 132
        disadvantages of 133

    sea 135
        advantages of 138
        disadvantages of 138
Travellers' cheques 111
Turnover 17

Unsolicited Goods and Services Act 223
Underwriters 168

Variety chain stores 20
VAT 224
Visible imports and exports 234, 238
Vendors, street 14
Voicemail 196

Waiters 78
Wants (see Needs)
Weights and Measures Acts 222
Which? 225, 229
Wholesale markets 34
Wholesaler 32
Wholesale transactions 36
Writing a cheque 116

X-stream services 197